Essays by

Eric Berne

William Carse

George A. De Vos

Joseph C. Finney

Rena Gazaway

Herbert W. Hargreaves

John J. Honigman

Charles C. Hughes

Oscar Lewis

Thomas W. Maretzki

Raymond Prince

Hart Ransdell

Tressa Roche

culture change, mental health, and poverty

Joseph C. Finney, *editor*

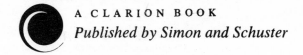

A CLARION BOOK
Published by Simon and Schuster

A Clarion Book
Published by Simon and Schuster
Rockefeller Center, 630 Fifth Avenue
New York, New York 10020

FIRST PAPERBACK PRINTING, 1970

SBN 671-20548-X
Manufactured in the United States of America

To President John W. Oswald and

Vice President A. D. Albright,

whose timely support made

this symposium possible.

preface

1965 was the University of Kentucky's centennial year. In celebration, a number of conferences were held at the university at which distinguished guests spoke. Among the events was a conference on ethnopsychology and cross-cultural psychiatry, the areas of common concern to psychiatrists, psychologists, and cultural anthropologists. The editor organized the conference, invited the participants, and served as chairman. Twelve distinguished scholars and scientists from throughout the United States and Canada accepted the invitation and took part. Five were psychiatrists by professional training (including two psychoanalysts), five were anthropologists, and two, psychologists.

As the correspondence went on, leading up to the meeting, it became clear that the guests had more than a theoretical, scientific interest in the problems that they studied. They were also genuinely concerned, as human beings, with the plight of people in suffering. Interest seemed to focus on the kindred psychosocial problems of culture change, mental health, and poverty.

This concern, practical as well as theoretical, fitted well into the University of Kentucky. Sparked by the leadership of a faculty group that had held seminars for several years, the university had decided to create a Center for Developmental Change. There was strong interest in projects dealing with underdeveloped parts of the world, as well as with the poverty-stricken Southern Appalachian Mountain region of Eastern Kentucky. Many of the University of Kentucky faculty attended the conference and took part in the discussions.

Each of the distinguished visiting scholars and scientists had thought deeply about the psychosocial problems, and from his own experience and study had formulated conceptions of how the malfunctionings work, and how they can be repaired. It should not be surprising that there was less than full agreement. This book unfolds the story of how the scientists met and how they interacted with each other in working at their task together.

contents

CONTENTS

introduction

In this book, the result of a conference held at the University of Kentucky, psychiatrists, psychologists, anthropologists, and economists discuss the interplay of culture change, mental health, and poverty.

Vivid descriptions of the ways of life of troubled people in Eastern Kentucky, Puerto Rico, Nigeria, and the outcaste group in Japan led to an attempt to clarify cause and effect. As the discussion progressed, it became clear that the problems of culture change, mental health, motivation, and poverty are so closely related that no one of the problems could be understood without the others. The kinds of psychotic and psychoneurotic problems of individuals, and the ways of alleviating them, were found to depend on the kind of society and the personality or cultural values. There was general agreement on a cybernetic framework of circular causation in which stable patterns are repeated while changes are introduced, and in which human problems arise from a malfunctioning of the control system.

As human beings with concern for other people, the scientists considered what can be done to relieve self-defeating ways of life with its accompanying suffering and apathy, and to promote self-fulfillment and satisfaction. Sharp disagreements developed on specific issues, though within a common frame of reference. It may be helpful to review the common principles and common ground, and to point to the sources of difference.

All the participants follow a basic model of cybernetics and systems analysis in which every human being is a system, with homeostatic feedback processes working to maintain a steady state, gain satisfactions, and relieve distresses. Societies are also systems at another level, with their own homeostatic regulating mechanisms. Both individuals and societies, as working systems, are liable to breakdowns, sicknesses, and malfunctionings, which are not always self-correcting. Since malfunctioning societies usually have many malfunctioning members, many serious problems are psychosocial and need attention at both levels. Among these are problems that have been studied under such varied names as delinquency, mental illness, culture of poverty, culture conflict, and the disintegration of civilizations. Charles Hughes's paper described this concept in detail.

THE CULTURE OF POVERTY

A consideration of the culture of poverty was one of the main concerns of the conference. Oscar Lewis, who invented the term, pointed out that it has been used too loosely by certain contemporary writers, who apply the term to all the poor. In Dr. Lewis's more precise use, there are many people who are poor by economic standards but who do not live in a culture of poverty.

Dr. Lewis defines the culture of poverty by 62 traits. The central point is psychological: "a feeling of not belonging . . . that the institutions of the larger society are not there to serve their interests." It is a feeling of alienation, of cynicism, of purposelessness, of rootlessness, of anomie (Durkheim), of not-belonging. George De Vos calls it a loss of role. These are much the same qualities that Karl Marx used to define the proletariat—a psychological concept based on a sense of alienation. Arnold Toynbee, with his cyclic theory of the rhythmic rise and fall of civilizations, believes that western civilizaton, like the Roman civilization of two thousand years ago, is disintegrating through the formation of alienated groups, the external and internal proletariats—the culture of poverty. The line between Hollingshead's Class IV and Class V may correspond roughly with the bounds of the culture of poverty as Oscar Lewis draws it. Or perhaps not: the question has not been studied.

A poor man in a traditional village of India, no matter how desperately poor he may be by any economic measure, does not live in a culture of poverty. He is comforted by the belief that by bearing his hardships nobly and doing his duties he will be reincarnated with a higher standing. In the traditional peasant societies of Europe, Christian beliefs in an afterlife may give a meaning to life's hardships and prevent the growth of cynicism. In traditional Japan, too, the peasant, no matter how poor, was part of a political and religious system that through its myths, rituals, and symbols gave meaning to his life.[1] In the Soviet Union, likewise, the people's hardships are lightened by their sense of belonging to a great political and religious movement, Marxism, in which each man's daily sufferings are thought to be sacrifices that contribute to national progress, eventual worldwide victory, and the building of a Utopia. Each of these systems, through its ideology, mythology, and assignment of duties and roles to everyone within a master plan, gives each person an identification and a sense of purpose and belonging. It is only when these belief systems fade, and people become cynical about them, that a culture of poverty grows. A major concern of this conference is that in the United States and in other parts of the world,[2] the traditional cultures or ways of life with their belief systems are breaking down, and societies with the culture of poverty, known as slums, are spreading in both cities and rural areas.

George De Vos describes it among certain groups in Japan. Oscar Lewis and Marvin Opler describe it among the Puerto Ricans. Rena Gazaway describes it in a rural hamlet in Eastern

[1] The Japanese peasant's compulsive thrift brought him no great reward in Japan, but paid off when he migrated to the opener society of the United States. Beginning as sugar-cane plantation laborers working for their room and board and three dollars a month, the Japanese saved money and rose to join the middle class in Hawaii.

[2] Russian cities have slums with delinquency and a culture of poverty. The official line is to explain them away as vestiges of capitalism, or as results of the corrupting influence of American jazz.

Kentucky. Some of these culture-areas have religious institutions (mostly Catholic in Puerto Rico and fundamentalist Protestant in Eastern Kentucky), but the religions, including the Kentucky snake-handling sects, produce only sporadic magical gestures of relief and fail to provide a sense of the meaning of life and the continuous ethical guidance in everyday dealings with people that results from participation in a whole society.

Behavioral scientists are trained to skip over the subjective and to talk about what is outwardly measurable and verifiable. Still, it may not be amiss to examine the phenomenology, the subjective side, the inner feelings of the impoverished way of life. A member of the culture of poverty feels neglected, deprived, unloved, unwanted. He feels useless: that nothing he does is important to anyone, is appreciated, or is needed. He cannot but feel worthless: his self-esteem is as low as it can be. He is haunted by the feeling, "I'm unloved because I am unlovable; people give me nothing because I deserve nothing." At the same time he feels bitter and resentful toward the world: angry at people because they have treated him badly. He feels cheated. And he feels justified in cheating the world in return. At this point he does not distinguish people clearly. He cares little that he does an unjust act, that the one he cheats or steals from is not one who has cheated him. His bitterness toward people is generalized, and any stranger can symbolize the world that has neglected him and failed to give him his share. So he alternates between blaming himself and blaming other people, and settles into an apathetic, cynical, unproductive passive hostility that cheats him—while it cheats the world of the contribution that he might have made.

It is small wonder that this way of life results in crime, delinquency, psychosis, hospitalized schizophrenia, and mental illness.[3]

The question arose whether the ordinary man in the culture of poverty, one who is not a hospitalized psychotic or disabled by physical symptoms, should be considered as ill. Ari Kiev

[3] An exception to this point of view is the position of Dr. Margetts, who believes that both the incidence and the prevalence of schizophrenia, despite the figures, are the same in all peoples throughout the world, and are not related to culture, social class, or poverty.

pointed out that people living in Gazaway's Branch do not in general have symptoms that would justify a label of psychosis or psychoneurosis. Some participants felt, however, that people in such a culture have a sickness of spirit that can be diagnosed as a personality trait disorder or personality pattern disorder, if not as a sociopathic (perhaps dyssocial) disorder. The bounds to which the diagnosis of personality and character disorders should extend, however, are so unclear as to pose a serious problem for epidemiology in mental health. By some standards, whole villages can be considered psychologically sick.[4]

THE CULTURE OF CONVERSION REACTION OR HYSTERIA

Another great culture pattern found in many parts of the world is associated with the psychoneurosis known as hysteria or conversion reaction. The diagnostic term *hysteria*, as used by a psychiatrist, does not mean what the layman means by the word. Hysteria or conversion reaction is a kind of bodily symptom of psychological source. It should not be confused with such psychosomatic (or psychophysiological) reactions as asthma, peptic ulcer, migraine, or high blood pressure. Hysteria or conversion reaction consists of sensory symptoms (aches, pains, smothering, anesthetic areas of the skin) or of motor symptoms (paralysis, weakness, convulsions, vomiting).

Symptoms are not merely signs of sickness or distressing conditions that need to be treated and alleviated. They represent urges or strivings of the individual. This is most strikingly true of conversion reaction, whose symptoms consist of changes in

[4] People's willingness to accept this view depends on how it is worded. If we say, "These people, as a result of unfortunate things that happened to them early in life, are disspirited and confused, and have a sickness of spirit," it is acceptable. If we say, "These people are chronic psychotics and have character disorders," it is unacceptable. The two statements have the same denotative meaning, but the emotional tone sounds sympathetic in one, and harsh in the other. This striking example shows that in the social and behavioral sciences a proposition is often accepted or rejected less by its factual content than by the emotional tone implied by its utterer, or inferred (truly or falsely) by its audience.

perception and in the control of the skeletal muscles. These are
changes in the functioning of the highest levels of control in the
nervous system, a level closely related to consciousness and
verbalization; and to control of a person's interaction with the
outside world, especially with other people.

Like other outward actions (and, in general, all actions using
the skeletal muscles) a symptom is rewarded, reinforced, and
perpetuated by satisfying (i.e., reducing) certain drives or urges.
These satisfactions may be considered the purposes of the
symptom. Some satisfactions can only be observed inwardly:
these include such simple biological drives as hunger, as well as
complex fantasies. One purely inward purpose of a symptom is
to reconcile a person's ideals with his selfish urges and to give
symbolic expression to both. Other satisfactions of the symptom
produce more outward evidence, since they require the patient
to induce other people to respond in a certain way—such as by
caretaking and by rejection. In such cases, the most obvious
characteristic of a symptom is that it is a message, a form of
communication. Freud stressed the inward satisfactions, while
Sullivan stressed the outward communication, the interpersonal
relationships. These viewpoints are by no means opposed, as is
sometimes thought. Symptoms are "overdetermined" (Freud's
phrase); that is, a given symptom is chosen and perpetuated,
among many possible symptoms, because it simultaneously satis-
fies several purposes.

The purposes of a symptom, like the purposes of any other
action, may be classified in several ways; primary and secondary
are common labels. The distinction between primary and secondary has varied somewhat with the psychologist or psychiatrist.
Clark Hull distinguished primary (inborn) and secondary (learned)
drives, and in a different way distinguished primary and secondary
reinforcement. In this book, "secondary gain" means the financial
reward (or other tangible, outwardly measurable reward) of a
symptom, while "primary gain" means the emotional satisfaction,
albeit biological (relief of hunger, anger, or fear) or social
(dependency, sympathy), inborn or learned.

Conversion reaction or hysteria characterizes many peoples in far parts of the world. Hart Ransdell and Tressa Roche call it the Eastern Kentucky syndrome. Edwin Weinstein calls it the Western Virginia syndrome. Marvin Opler calls it the Puerto Rican syndrome, and also the syndrome of the ancient Hebrews of the Bible. Raymond Prince alludes to its prevalence in Nigeria.

Conversion reaction affects only a few persons at a time, and never a whole population. Why, then, do we characterize whole peoples, whole cultures, by this syndrome? The reason is that the whole population has built its way of living on a certain way of communicating, a certain way in which a person interacts with others, sends his messages to others. Those who have conversion reaction are only using in extreme form the communication methods that are the way of life of the whole society.

These people have commonly been called nonverbal. Raymond Prince calls them motoric. He points out, however, that they talk freely *as* themselves, expressing their feelings without self-consciousness. What they cannot do is talk *about* themselves; they become tonguetied when asked to describe their feelings in words. They cannot become aware of (or put into words) their interactions with others. They may play games (in Eric Berne's sense) and manipulate other people, using their conversion reactions and other ploys to do so, but they cannot admit in words, even to themselves, that they do so. Typically, they repress anger when it is aroused but erupt into sudden violence under culturally defined conditions. They may hold mutually incompatible beliefs by dissociation, keeping at least one of the pair out of awareness at any given time. People of this sort feel that life is a series of unpredictable events that happen to them, not something that they can plan or make for themselves. They seek relief from their conversion symptoms and other troubles through mystic ritual performed by a magician, in which they themselves play only a passive, submissive role. Raymond Prince calls this system a "cone of authority."

This way of life has no generally accepted name. Because of its association with hysteria or conversion reaction, it has been called hysterical personality, hysterical culture, or hysterical way of life. The drawback is that the common meaning of the word *hysterical* in English differs from its technical psychological use. The same objection applies to the term *conversion,* which would be mistaken for a reference to religious conversion. *Motoric way of life* and *dissociating way of life* have advantages, but are not well known.

The culture of poverty and the motoric-converting-dissociating way of life have fused in some peoples and not in others. The Puerto Ricans, as described by Oscar Lewis and Marvin Opler, have a way of life that fits both descriptions; so do the people of the Southern Appalachians, as described by Hart Ransdell, Tressa Roche, and Rena Gazaway. On the other hand, a number of intact cultures, both primitive and modern, belong to the motoric-converting-dissociating group and not to the culture of poverty, while Japan's outcaste, as described by George De Vos, is a culture of poverty that is not motoric-converting-dissociating.

In the Southern Appalachian culture of poverty, a lingering work ethic is recognized. A man who does not work is expected to have sickness as a justification. One of the rewards of conversion reaction, which fosters and perpetuates it, is that it is regarded as a sickness and so gives a man a position of dignity and respect when he is not working.

THE ETHICS OF INTERVENTION

One of the key questions that troubled the participants of the conference was this: under what circumstances do we have a right, or a duty, to change another people's way of life? This question was raised by John Honigmann in the opening speech, and continued to haunt the discussion.

All the participants live in the United States and Canada and all adhere to a basically western middle-class ethic. This ethic was never put into words by the conference, but clearly consists of two commandments: 1) Do good, not harm, to people. 2) Do not be ethnocentric; that is, have tolerance for the way of life of other people. Do not try to change people into something more like us; all value systems are products of a particular culture; other people's ethical and moral value systems may be as good as our own, or better.

Though the two principles seem simple, they contain two paradoxes that kept cropping up and were never identified. These paradoxes were the unrecognized source of disagreements in concrete detail among experts who seemed to agree in abstract principle.

One paradox arises from the inclusion in an ethical system of a principle that the system itself need not always be regarded as right, and should be prepared to yield (in unspecified circumstances) to other, different systems. A corollary of this principle is the duty of tolerance: not to be ethnocentric, we should allow and encourage other societies to maintain their own cultures and ethical systems. But, as Redfield has pointed out, most other societies do not share this antiethnocentric value: they do not follow our standards of tolerance either within their society or externally, toward us or toward some third society. One possible interpretation of our obligations under our principles is to turn the other cheek: this was Redfield's conclusion, that we should be tolerant of other societies that are not tolerant of us. This line of thought, however, shows hidden problems. What shall we do about a society that, in our judgment, is intolerant or unfair toward some of its own members (or toward neighboring outsiders)? We may make this judgment about the traditional white-dominated society of Alabama, or about the Black Muslims in Detroit, or about the caste society of Yap Island in Micronesia. If we try by our standards to enforce tolerance of individuals within the society, we are being ethnocentric and intolerant toward the society and have abandoned our principles of cultural relativism. But if we tolerate the society, we allow intolerance within it. The dilemma is logically insoluble; we cannot be tolerant at both levels at the same time: a choice must be made.

A similar paradox stems from the lack of full consistency

between the principle of benevolence and the principle of toler-ance. Suppose our judgment is that a given society, with its culture and value system, is bad for its members. (Many of the experts felt that way about the culture of poverty in general, and about Gazaway's Branch in particular.) The benevolence principle tells us, "Do what is good for these people. If they don't realize how unfortunate they are, help them to become aware of it, and make them aware of what they can do to change it. Don't leave them in ignorance. Expand their horizons. Educate them to change their cultural value systems. Offer them help, and per-suade them to desire to change." On the other hand, the tolerance principle cautions, "It is only our narrow parochial ethnocentric middle-class values that make us think that our way of life is better than theirs. To assimilate them would be cultural canni-balism. Our duty is to leave them alone, not to try to change them."

No member of the conference advocated one of these principles to the exclusion of the other. Some stressed benevolence and others stressed tolerance, but everyone recognized both principles and tried to make some compromise between their conflicting demands. It was the different resolutions of this conflict that led to disagreements in detail over what should be done about the psychosocial problems of Gazaway's Branch and of other peoples.

In the judgment of some of the participants, the culture of poverty is not an unmixed evil. Rena Gazaway, John Honigmann, and Oscar Lewis each pointed out that within the immediate group a member of a poverty culture may find more sense of belonging and less alienation than a middle-class person who may lead a lonely life in a city. Still, the consensus of the conference was that the culture of poverty is a sad condition; that it is a subsociety whose members are, in some sense, psycho-logically sick, disabled in spirit; and that it represents a malfunc-tioning or disintegration of the larger society of which it is a part. There was a general consensus that social and behavioral scientists can legitimately undertake the task of social or behavioral engineering—using their scientific skills as a technology to change the culture of poverty into a better way of life.

PROBLEMS OF CULTURE CHANGE

An agent promoting change must begin with the people where they are, encouraging them to take the initiative and to work toward the goals that they themselves feel are important; change should spring from within the group to meet its own needs, and not be imposed by the wishes of an outside group. Most of the participants felt that it is wise to encourage a group to change only what is essential, to resolve a malfunction, and to keep its reservoir of traditional cultural values intact. The group should build on the existing culture instead of trying to change the whole structure. Not all agreed, however.

There was also some feeling that a sick subsociety, such as Appalachia and the other rural and urban groups with a subculture of poverty in the United States, cannot be treated without overhauling the larger society, which may continually produce and reject the impoverished elements as an excretion.

It is also difficult to promote change in a society composed of two or more groups with partially conflicting interests, in which a majority or powerful minority may succeed in blocking changes that might upset its vested interests. Rena Gazaway described how that happens in Appalachia. A group that feels threatened may block changes even though in the long run it stands to benefit from the changes. This statement applies both to the elite "power structure" and to the poor.

Hart Ransdell and Tressa Roche described a method of treating people with conversion reactions and other disabilities by a combination of sympathy and firmness.

Raymond Prince pointed out that many people in many parts of the world, including the blue-collar classes in North America as well as certain nonliterate peoples in Africa, have a motoric-converting-dissociating way of life. Conventional psychotherapy aimed at insight does not fit their ways of communication. Instead of trying to change their ways of communication—a monumental task of culture change—Dr. Prince suggested letting their mental-health or personal problems, including conversion reactions, be treated by fundamentalist religious leaders, using mystical and magical rituals. There was some opposition. Victor Sanua objected to encouragement of Christian sects, and Edward Margetts objected to encouragement of African tribal practices, on grounds that such methods are irrational, superstitious, and ineffective, and hinder people from getting modern scientific help.

Using the outcaste group of Japan as an example, George De Vos pointed out that a mistreated group develops psychological features to protect its self-esteem that perpetuate a sense of mistreatment (and perhaps the mistreatment itself). These psychological features become part of the subculture and, like other cultural features, are perpetuated from generation to generation through child rearing. In Japan, long after legal discrimination has disappeared and informal segregation has lessened, the persecuted mentality persists among the former outcaste group and retards its absorption into the larger society. Dr. De Vos gives the name "psychological lag" to this process.

In a vigorous democratic society it can be hoped that an element with the culture of poverty can be reabsorbed into the main group and inspired with its ideals, its identity, and its sense of purpose. If the larger society is disintegrating, however, or has lost its ability to inspire confidence, or leaves some caste unabsorbed, purposeless, and neglected, the alienated group is ripe for conversion to a new political and religious movement that gives it a purpose and fights the larger society. Under skillful leadership, the people of an alienated group can be roused from their apathy and led to turn their bitterness outward in violent action.[5] At times, as in the Watts riot, the violence is poorly directed, destroys without building, and even destroys the goods

[5] The self-punishment does not disappear. Works by Erich Fromm and Eric Hoffer describe the masochistic satisfaction in belonging to a crusading totalitarian movement.

of its perpetrators. Although the irrational destruction is deplorable, nonetheless, as Marvin Opler points out, a violent group such as the Watts rioters shows better mental health than an apathetic one such as Rena Gazaway's hamlet in the Kentucky mountains. A violent group pulls itself out of the culture of poverty by acquiring a sense of group identity and of purpose, even though a destructive one. George De Vos feels that among the outcastes of Japan the radical political movement is one of the healthier signs. When a group is at its lowest ebb, hopelessness and apathy prevail. When conditions improve a group raises its sights, becomes aggressive, and lashes out in violence because its growing expectations are not being met swiftly enough. The outcome of the clash depends on the strength and response of the larger society.

When a disaffected element, guided by a new political and religious movement, seeks to overthrow an established order, economic motives become least effective. A weakness of U. S. policy has been too exclusive reliance on economic development to solve psychosocial problems at home and abroad. A government may offer a program of great economic benefit to a troubled group only to meet with rejection because of the group's hatred of the established government and because of its psychological identification with an insurgent movement. The most urgent concern of those who would solve psychosocial problems must be the building of identification and sense of purpose.

middle class values
and cross-cultural
understanding

John J. Honigmann

Contemporary social psychiatry, most notably in the work of
August B. Hollingshead, Alexander Leighton, Leo Srole, and
Thomas Langner, impresses me as much as any development in
midcentury social science. Its methods, leading to significant
empirical findings, have rapidly expanded our knowledge concerning the social and cultural conditions antecedent to personality disorder. At almost every step in its history, its findings
have promptly generated fresh problems on higher theoretical
and methodological levels, problems that promptly became the
bases from which new research took off. Almost every new piece
of research built on the shoulders of its predecessors, not only
attacking the unfinished problems but constantly improving on
earlier designs and methods. Such a clear—almost ideal—picture
of cumulative growth is not to be found in all contemporary
fields of social science; hence I take special pains to acknowledge
it in this one.

Since the standards of social psychiatry are particularly rigorous,
the critical questions I propose to ask seem to be especially
warranted and pertinent. I have indicated that some aspects of
the recent work and thought puzzle me. It is my intention in this
critical, somewhat skeptical, paper to air those perplexities in

order to stimulate discussion. Some years ago psychiatrists and social scientists were debating whether psychotherapy should aim primarily to strengthen a person to survive in the world as it was, or should try to make the world better suited for human beings. Although, as far as I know, neither side ever succeeded in answering all the questions put to it, psychiatry nevertheless bent its efforts in one direction rather than the other. I have no intention of resuscitating this dead issue. Some seemingly momentous problems simply expire without ever being clearly resolved. The questions I have to ask about social psychiatry may also never be finally answered, but to talk them out may influence the direction social psychiatry takes.

I am aware of the dangers of overstatement, but I am equally aware of the fruitlessness of qualifying everything that one says, and so effectively losing the point. I hope I can avoid sounding too extreme. I am sure that any overstatements as well as any mistakes I make will be corrected in the course of this conference.

I speak as an anthropologist, though without implying that all anthropologists share my view of the culture of poverty, the culture of psychiatry, and the interaction between them. If that interaction is not quite the same as the contact between European colonialism and nonwestern people, I fear that it comes close to committing some of the same errors and distortions with which the colonial epoch made us familiar. To give an example of what I mean, here are a few sentences written by an anthropologist which took me aback when I first read them in the second volume of the Stirling County study (Hughes, 1960b, 245-46).

> Here one sees through scattered clearings the sweep of be-draggled houses, some as small as play houses, a few large but ghostly with a sense of desertion. . . . Here is the face of a rejected community, built on pride of exactly the opposite values of the surrounding communities. . . .
>
> Are they unhappy in their poverty? One does not gain the impression that they are, so chained do they appear to their environment, as if the limitations of their horizon shielded them from caring. Young children can be beautiful on the road. . . . But as these children grow older they will press

> against the ceiling laid down upon them and lose themselves in the aimless and amoral world of their fathers and mothers.
>
> It is a challenge to enter a home here. It is not they who rise to meet you; it is you who must brace yourself to meet them. No concessions are asked or given by these bedraggled people. You must like them or reject them on their own grounds. It is you who must sacrifice a part of your values to reach equality with them—and if you can do this, they will be your friends.

That question "Are they unhappy in their poverty?" and other manifest signs of cultural shock in the quotation, might be the response of any middle-class investigator confronting a culture many of whose norms, activity patterns, and artifacts run directly against his own cultural values and sensibilities. The question reminds me of Abram Kardiner's evaluation of Alorese basic personality. He too asks whether they are unhappy and concludes that certainly "they are not aware of their wretchedness" (Kardiner, 1945, p. 253).

Several thoughts occur to me as I read that culturally different people are more wretched than they know. I realize that the observer's attitude is very different from that with which many of the classic ethnographies were written. Anthropologists have traditionally understood even people heavily threatened by weather, hunger, aggression, and disease without so persistently sounding the tocsin of distress. Few ethnographically known people have lived as precariously, and under such harsh conditions, as the Central and Eastern Arctic Eskimo, but until the Eskimo came under the influence of Canadian culture few professional anthropologists found their harsh existence a cause for pity. Rather they extolled the Eskimo's resourcefulness and praised their specialized cultural adaptation to an Arctic setting. This positive evaluation of the Eskimo is consistent with the appreciation that anthropologists have traditionally displayed for most of the people they have studied, except possibly the Dobuans. This attitude changed soon after anthropologists who called themselves functionalists began to work with peasants and other cultures that were neither isolated nor relatively independent. It also changed as anthropologists became psychologically, or, better, psychiatrically, sophisticated, that is, as they became more concerned with difficult rather than with successful adaptation and lost interest in what Murray and Kluckhohn (1953, p. 13) call relatively directionless, mainly nonfunctional "modal activity," activity engaged in for its own sake. Western society impinging on such part-societies demanded that they adapt to its terms, and penalized cultural withdrawal. The psychological sciences emphasized stress and hearkened to the ever-constant danger of maladaptation. In response to those cues, anthropology learned a new orientation. The trend did not occur in anthropology alone, but in the other social sciences as well, and it constitutes, quite naturally, the dominant orientation of social psychiatry, with which I am most directly concerned.

These observations lead to my first question. I wonder if anthropology and the other social sciences, including social psychiatry, have not become one-sided in their predominantly negative approach to a great range of behavior. Social psychiatry recognizes that in some communities and social strata benign cultural conditions outweigh noxious elements, but it puts emphasis on communities and classes in which it believes that noxious elements predominate. As Margaret Mead (1952) has said, social scientists listen for distortion with both ears, paying almost no heed to cultural patterns and social arrangements that might compensate for undeniably harsh phases of existence. Oscar Lewis believes that concern with what people suffer from is pragmatically more justified than investigating enjoyment because it produces more insight into the human condition and provides a lever for constructive social change (1960, pp. 179-80). This implies that the major aim of social science should be change. But might it not also benefit the human condition to maintain the current effective patterns of adapation and of expression as far as possible, assuming that they could be identified through research?

The aim of change is implicit or explicit in much that social psychiatrists and other helping professions do. But the limited course they follow to implement this aim puzzles me. If the object of social science is indeed to alter cultural arrangements in communities where noxious elements have a predominant influence, how can this best be done, recognizing that those communities are, in fact, part-societies, like peasant villages and like all communities of the modern world?

Being liberal rather than radical men, social scientists recommend rather small changes in ways of life. They hope, by altering circumscribed areas of troublesome cultures, to eradicate conditions that their research tells them underlie personality disorder and other forms of deviance. For example, social psychiatrists visualize that more people will join community associations; they hope to reduce the harshness of parental discipline and other painful circumstances of early life and to increase the effectiveness of communication between psychotherapists and people of every social class. Such goals also appeal to me. I too sympathize with greater schemes for reconstituting slums, disintegrated communities, and pockets of poverty, and watch current attempts to do so with more than academic interest. But I often watch with more exasperated pessimism than optimism and wonder why social scientists don't visualize, even if only as an ideal, such communities as part-societies, products of a larger social system that may also need some degree of overhauling if the parts are to be altered significantly for the better. It is not that I see any inherent value in revolutionary cultural change, but theory and evidence lead me to suspect that piecemeal social action which is not preceded by an inquiry into larger social arrangements is not always sufficient, despite the good it does. Is this not a proper lesson to draw from Dorothea Leighton's final report on Stirling County (1963, p. 350), which demonstrates that a more advantaged occupational position and more years of schooling make little difference in the mental health of people living in the county's depressed areas? The total community itself is at fault, she implies, and, I suspect, so is the larger society that contributes to the disadvantaged social status of those people. *Girls at Vocational High* (Meyer, 1965), which reports on an experiment in Manhattan, shows that no matter how helpful counseling and social-work intervention are in particular cases, more is needed to insure a high degree of wholesome personality change in troubled girls. The girls who were developing into problems received intensive social-work services, as a result of which three-fifths changed " 'a little' or less, and more than one third . . . 'hardly at all.' " A major object of the program was to prevent them from dropping out of school. An identical proportion of the experimental and control groups had graduated from high school by the end of the project, and no consistent or significant differences characterized the attendance records of experimental and control cases. The program had results, but they were small and disappointed the investigators. You may also have seen the *New Yorker* article (Rice, 1965) that reported on how attempts to rehabilitate youthful drug-takers failed as soon as the youths returned to their Manhattan slum neighborhood.

The conclusion I draw is that the whole social system, and not only its actors and other subsystems, warrants attention if new forms of behavior are to be elicited successfully. This is what sociologists have long been claiming, for example, in pointing out that broken homes do not automatically trigger delinquency. Along with other essentially neutral factors, broken homes are likely to trigger delinquency in disorganized parts of the city, which are, in turn, products of larger social systems. Recently anthropologists have come to consider that the most effective way of implementing constructive change, so that it occurs with a minimum of internal contradiction, is to involve people in a quick and revolutionary transformation of almost the whole system of their behavior (Mead, 1956).

Note the view that people themselves must create change in their way of life, or, as community developers say, change must emerge out of felt needs. Self-directed change can be defended on pragmatic grounds as well as on the basis of democratic values.

However, as the current poverty program illustrates, considerable difficulties oppose the shift of power necessary if self-planning is to be effective.

I wish I knew just what systemwide transformations might deal more effectively with the problems to which social psychiatry gives attention. Few Americans have dared give much thought to broad questions of social reconstruction during the last thirty years of military emergencies, growing affluence (that did not, however, redistribute shares of the national income), and creeping conservatism. I have raised the topic not because I have a solution to offer but because I think it needs to be discussed.

I have implied that we social scientists (like almost everybody else) may be too eager to remake somebody else's way of life without considering whether doing so does not simultaneously require that we change our own. I have also referred to a cultural gap between the experts and the people whose unsatisfactory, suffering lives those experts presume to evaluate. From now on I will confine myself mostly to that discontinuity.

A social psychiatrist who designates behavior as disordered and identifies its antecedent cultural conditions as stressful or disintegrated necessarily offers value judgments. However considered and technically couched his opinions may be, he judges some behavior and its attendant circumstances to be less desirable than others.

In dealing with a personality disorder, a diagnostician may ask himself in which readymade disease category the symptoms fit; or (I now have in mind the existential psychiatrist) he can attempt to understand the disorder phenomenologically—from the inner world to which the patient is oriented, the situation he confronts, and the goals toward which he strives. Whichever of these two diagnostic modes of approach dominates, the psychiatrist has reason to feel that there is something undesirable about the goals the patient pursues, the means he uses in striving, the inordinately great or minuscule amount of energy he expends in adaptation, his emotionally inappropriate tone of behavior, or the character of his relationship with other people. In one or more of these dimensions, the psychiatrist sees the patient as deviating from some ideal pattern which the psychiatrist leaves unvoiced. I don't now question the value of psychiatric judgments arrived at professionally. I am concerned with their source and character as value judgments and with the consequences that follow.

Psychiatric judgments are value judgments made by some members of a class-divided society about other members. The ability to make such judgments authoritatively—to make them stick—occurs by virtue of the psychiatrist's professional status, which confers on him power over the person to whom he refers. Note one consequence. The psychiatrist has power to implement certain values and standards (namely his own) over other competing values and standards that he regards as dangerous to the patient or to society.

Anyone who makes expert judgments—social worker, economist, or TV repairman—always occupies a particular position in a structure of unequal knowledge and values. The expert has a vested interest in a given set of norms, or in a special way of life. Equally so, a psychiatrist. He speaks from a special vantage point when he appraises as undesirable such behavior as homosexuality, alienation, denial as a defense mechanism, extramarital or premarital sexual intercourse, or drug-taking, on grounds that they endanger health, symptomatize a breakdown in personal equilibrium, or indicate social disequilibrium. Now, the question that troubles me is this: Don't the psychiatrist's values and diagnostic judgments sometimes represent behavior norms that stem from his social class position? If, as to me seems likely, they do embody class-bound behavioral values—call the middle-class values for brevity's sake—then is he not like social workers, teachers, and judges, acting to alter another way of life by trying ethnocentrically to convert it to fit his own? The psychiatrist inevitably oversteps his therapeutic functions when he aids and abets the current aim of our society, which is to promote the spread of middle-class standards and values with respect to such things as knowledge, skills, language, education, property, and other ideals. Values and behaviors at variance with such middle-class ideals may remain in force only to the degree that they do not contradict the dominant values on which national stability, economic development, and happiness are seen to depend. This is a long way from increasing the range of cultural tolerance, as anthropologists have traditionally sought to do, in order to accommodate in society the greatest possible number of temperaments, eccentricities, and unusual types.

My concern grows partly out of findings reported in the second volume of the Midtown Study (Langner, 1963, pp. 87-88, and chaps. 15 and 16). Langner and Michael report that mental health varies, much more than might be expected, among three socioeconomic levels—high, middle, and low. To put it in operation terms, persons of low socioeconomic status are likely to come through a psychiatric screening with worse mental health ratings than persons of middle or high status who have earned the same numerical score for amount of lifetime stress reported. Stress scores do climb from high socioeconomic status to low, but mental health risk increases still faster. Why do respondents of low socioeconomic status come through psychiatric screening with worse mental health ratings than those of higher status? Langner and Michael point out that people of relatively high status react to stress in predominantly neurotic fashion, becoming nervous, restless, obsessionally worried, and so on. They become mentally ill in ways that are tightly controlled and therefore consistent with their middle- and upper-class values. People of low socioeconomic status, on the other hand, respond to stress in ways compatible with their isolation, passivity, dependence, mistrust, and social inadequacy. Their symptoms exaggerate, or at least use, the class-bound behavior patterns that they also show in normal situations.

Why are lower-class ways of getting sick worse than middle-class ways of getting sick? We have only the middle-class-bound psychiatrists to tell us how this happens. Undoubtedly, by the standards of their profession they felt fully justified in evaluating the lower classes as worse off. They acted cautiously and honestly and proceeded rigorously. But I am asking if those standards are not ethnocentrically contaminated by the evaluator's own class-bound values to such a degree that those values block him from getting a fuller, truer view of the people whom he is judging. When psychiatrists include their class-bound values in evaluating personality disorder, people who show strain by acting out or falling to pieces emotionally and cognitively, as lower-class people predominantly do, are judged as worse off than people who feel unworthy or who constantly visit the doctor with difficult stomachs.

Despite my use of the declarative mood, I am asking questions more than making pronouncements concerning a field about which I know too little. Is there not something dubious and unsatisfactory about a powerful, authoritative system that finds it better to get sick in upper- or middle-class fashion than in lower-class fashion?

Not only does the psychiatrist's judgment of personal mental illness constitute a value judgment, but in all likelihood so do standards of positive mental health. They favor the self-accepting person, who can live with his potentialities and limitations; who continues sustainedly to actualize himself through growth and moves progressively closer to his own goals, as much as his potentialities permit. The mentally healthy person is able to relax. His various aspects of personality work together in an integrative manner, with the result that he experiences himself as a coherent whole. He is resilient, able to bend under stress without lasting distortion. He treasures his autonomy and can make discriminations independently. Able to relate to others, he trusts them. He loves and is loved. He meets situational requirements dependably and efficiently, and he plays his social roles synergically, satisfying personal needs while fulfilling social obligations and meeting others' definition of the situation.

Despite my admiration for many of these qualities, I am afraid that some of them assume standards of behavior that are class-bound and suited only to a special way of life. Some of these criteria of positive mental health imply that the person who possesses them occupies an economically secure, socially authoritative position that allows him a comfortably wide area in which to initiate action and permits him to choose behavior more often than he is forced or merely given the opportunity of saying yes or no. They imply strong mutual commitment between an accepting society and a person who is not being asked to conform to others' values.

I don't in the least object to augmenting everyone's power and social acceptability, at least to the extent that his pursuit of such ends is self-directed. Currently, however, these well-intentioned criteria of positive mental health penalize the poor as well as all other people who may be culturally patterned in a direction other than that which middle-class Americans idealize.

We may also be premature in defining positive mental health without more documentation about what it takes to play social roles adequately, according to the standards of cultures other than our own. If we aren't cautious about extolling our ideals, we will—like some nineteenth-century social scientists talking about western culture—make our culture-bound ideals the acme of all development.

To the value judgments that a clinical psychiatrist makes when he designates a person's behavior as disordered, sick, or—as Mowrer might have it—sinful, the social psychiatrist adds professionally informed value judgments that concern the patient's social setting.

The stress concept, or some analogous notion such as that of blocked strivings which result in seriously upset personal equilibrium, provides the bridge that connects personality disorder to etiologically significant, antecedent cultural conditions. When used in a psychological sense, stress and its counterpart, strain, are applied figuratively or analogically to the meaning they hold in engineering. Poverty, broken homes, a person's failure to achieve vital goals, cognitive dissonance, and many more experiences are figuratively conceived as acting like physical forces that wear down physical materials.

Stress is certainly ubiquitous in human life, but social scientists believe that it inheres much more heavily in some sectors of social space—especially in some levels of a stratified community—than in others. The Midtown Study's recent attempt to test this hypothesis by measuring stress objectively led to interesting results (Langner, 1963). The study inquired about, and quantitatively rated, such deductively formulated stressors as poor physical health in childhood, broken homes, economic deprivation in childhood, current worry about work or about socioeconomic status, and marital worries. The designers of this research assumed not only that stress can be identified objectively but also that it can be quantified. There is a good reason why social scientists proceed in this objective fashion: it allows them to cover large samples of people efficiently and systematically in collecting relatively specific facts that can be used statistically to explain other facts, like personality disorder. Some 1,600 carefully selected Midtown adults each received a stress score based on factors in his life like those I have mentioned, including his current physical health; whether he was worried about work, overwork, getting ahead, and the cost of living; and whether he enjoyed only few or no social affiliations with neighbors, close friends, or comembers in organizations. The Midtown investigators were surprised to learn that stress scores varied little between high, middle, and low social strata. People of low socioeconomic status scored an average of 5.7; people of middle strata scored a 5.3 average; and people of higher levels scored a 4.7 average. By the social psychiatrists' own admission, they had probably overestimated exposure to stress in lower socioeconomic levels. Social science is generally eager to find evidence of heavy stress. Anthropologists have perceived it, for example, in migrants and especially in situations of rapid, heavy culture change, such as that which accompanies the impact of western culture on small-scale social systems of the nonwestern world. In doing so anthropologists have often overestimated the stressful components of such situations, sometimes misreading the normal tension that accompanies growth and becoming, for the abnormal tension of stymied adaptation (Mead, 1956; Ritchie, 1956, pp. 162-65; Mangin, 1964).

Alexander Leighton prefers to identify the etiologically significant background of personality disorder by the concept of social disintegration, which also implies stress (1959, pp. 157-60, and chap. 6). In a disintegrated community noxious (i.e., stressful) factors outweigh benign ones. A disintegrated community may be recognized through such objective markers as a high frequency of broken homes; few and weak associations; few and weak leaders; a high frequency of hostility, crime, and delinquency; and weak, fragmented networks of communication. Environments of this sort can sometimes also be predicted; for example, from a recent history of disaster, extensive poverty, widespread ill health, and widespread culutral confusion.

Stressors also arise primarily from within a person as he moves through his environment, but in that I am not much interested. I am mainly concerned with the significance of the view that in disintegrated social environments and in lower socioeconomic status neighborhoods—that is, in cultures of poverty—people encounter especially heavy stress.

Stress in the psychological sense is figuratively compared to physical stress. For this reason one cannot safely assume that it can be identified objectively. Does the nature of psychological stress not make it much more likely that a knowledge of it requires understanding the situation the distressed person confronts, how he interprets the situation, and what compensation he receives? When the social psychiatrist deals with a culture in many ways different from his own, it seems especially important to hold firm to a phenomenological point of view in identifying psychological stress.

My professional training as an anthropologist makes me wary about approaching an unfamiliar culture mainly deductively, in terms of previously formulated traits whose presence or absence the observer simply checks off or which, if present, he rates quantitatively. I am aware that contemporary anthropology has reduced its devotion to relativism, but I don't think that a culturally relative orientation can ever be totally abandoned. I am also aware of another trend in present-day anthropology, one replacing the crude search for functions. We have become alert to discovering meaning in cultural data. In order to do so it has become more necessary than ever to know a culture thoroughly from within, so that its peculiar logic can be learned and applied to circumstances that otherwise remain puzzling. This new trend is distinctly unfavorable to a prematurely objective, nonrelativistic approach, like the one found in social psychiatry when it ranges cross-culturally.

Anthropologists do not in principle oppose quantitative evaluation. Experience, however, has taught us to be suspicious of yardsticks or scales that are culture-bound because of their integral connection either with western culture or with a middle-class way of life.

What is life like in a disintegrated community? By what logic do the people make their decisions? I suspect that such a setting possesses features significantly different from those Leighton selects for his purpose, and that these features are also likely to be relevant to the problems that Leighton and other social psychiarists pose. Of course, abstraction is necessary in science, as it is in every other walk of life. But it perturbs me that social scientists may be seriously distorting the many-faceted culture of poverty by abstracting only its misery. We may be describing a stereotype. If I cannot speak more positively about the contours of that culture, it is because I sense the same honorably intentioned but class-bound bias in practically all the ethnographic work to which I turn for information. I should, however, note one exception, *The Urban Villagers* by Herbert J. Gans (1962), a book that deals with working-class Americans of Italian descent in Boston.[1]

[1] This is also a suitable point to acknowledge what the sociologist S. M. Miller has pointed out typologically (1964), and what I have so far neglected—that the poor make up a heterogeneous lot and that they are not all equally strained by their conditions of life.

While I recognize the advantages that objectivity on a high level of abstraction confers in social science research, if at present I had to choose I would bypass those advantages in order to say free to uncover the unique dimensions of relatively unknown experience in another culture. I think such information is greatly needed if we are to understand better the culture of poverty in our midst. But, of course, we don't have to choose. Both approaches are possible, provided that neither one is prematurely closed off, and provided we alert our students to the promise in, and necessity of, both.

Social psychiatry and much of social science, not to speak of the crash program recently launched against poverty in this country, seriously overlook possibilities for new learning. By emphasizing only one side of the culture of poverty, they block off unexpected discoveries of new facts. Of course, I may be exceedingly naive in assuming that more is to be learned. But for the time being that is the assumption I will operate with. New facts and more insights are also needed to achieve a truly transcultural psychiatry.

My questions have been predicated on the assumption that American social classes or socioeconomic strata are in some ways culturally as incommensurable as societies that have traditionally been studied by ethnographers, like the Trobriand Islanders, Hopi Indians, and Samoans. In our highly diversified social system, social psychiatrists are primarily rooted in one cultural segment, which I have taken the liberty of calling middle class (or middle-class culture), from which they confront the lower-ranking culture of poverty. More specifically, the social psychiatrist represents a professionally oriented variant of our American middle-class culture. This is not to say that the social classes possess relatively self-contained, total cultures. They may be termed subcultures; or, to put it more precisely, they are distinguished by cultural specialties and alternatives. These, taken together with our cultural universals, make up the United States, culturally speaking.

The principal questions that I have asked are two. First, I

asked whether the standards that social psychiatry uses to evaluate personality disorder and its antecedent factors are not culture-bound. Second, I asked whether the standards and methods of social psychiatry do not inordinately reduce the possibility of obtaining better knowledge than we have, bearing on the human condition in the culture of poverty. If, as I suspect, my doubts are warranted, then a more open-ended, relativistic position is called for in transcultural psychiatric research.

That a concept or method yields theoretically significant, reproducible data indicates one kind of utility and objectivity. I must grant that such data have been extremely valuable. But what if the data objectively yielded are sifted by the presuppositions and values of a single culture? What if they omit important concepts bound up with the intentions and experiences of the people being studied, omit a cultural frame of reference different from that of the social scientists? Then what seems to be objective turns out to be culturally highly subjective, and serious, unintended consequences follow.

One cannot quarrel with the social psychiatrist's findings when he correlates personality disorder or deviance with specific social conditions. One can only demur at the limited view of the conditions involved. The facts may not mean the same thing to the actors and to the person doing the study. The variables an investigator selects, such as little communication in the home, mutual misunderstanding, and a lack of togetherness, betray his middle-class values.

Alexander Leighton objectively regards extramarital sexuality as a short-lived, unwholesome form of recreation that constitutes evidence of social disintegration. Judged from the ideals of middle-class, professional Americans, extramarital sexuality no doubt possesses this and other characteristics, but a similar meaning need not follow in every culture; for example, among the Vunta Kutchin (Balikci, 1963), where extramarital sex relations are institutionalized and call for presentations to the woman's husband.[2] Leighton, in fact, began to perceive the culture-bound

[2] Also Powdermaker (1933), where a lover gives a gift to his partner's husband.

nature of his criteria of social disintegration among the Yoruba (1963) but he still vastly underrates the significance of this problem.

In the same way that some colonial administrators formerly assumed that they were preparing culturally exotic people for western education, political forms, and religion, so social psychiatrists, teachers, social workers, and city planners appear to assume that the people whom they regard as underprivileged not only want dignity, material amenities, health, and other advantages glorified by our society but also are prepared to accept the manners, style of life, emotional restraints, and what Marie Nyswander (1965) calls the compromises, half-truths, and withheld statements favored by successful, middle-class Americans. In fact, we are not tolerantly prepared—personally or culturally— to see the poor adapt in any other fashion. I call to mind what studies of people, as, for example, the Eskimo, report. Although the Eskimo are rapidly assimilating our job skills and recreational forms, they are not, at anything like the same rate, becoming carbon copies of ourselves (Chance, 1965). Hence, I doubt that a single national culture pattern, a single national character, or even all the serviceable middle-class habits that we would like to see adopted, will become equally manifest in all classes of our society as poverty and slums increasingly disappear and other desires of the underclasses become fulfilled. Would it not save agony and frustration if we allowed for the emergence of something new rather than planning only in terms of what we know in our own limited cultural experience? From this viewpoint, too, it becomes important for change and planning to be self-directed in order that such change and planning may be wise as well as democratic. However, self-direction also demands that *we* change, for it requires that the middle and upper classes give up more of their power than they now seem ready to do.

Much that I have to say reiterates the view, closely adhered to in history and criticism, that in order to avoid unfair and misleading interpretations, men and their work ought to be understood in the perspective of the time when they lived. Similar misconstructions and distortions seem likely to occur when social psychiatrists operate exclusively from the narrow cultural perspective of the social class to which they belong.

I call for more relativism. Complete relativism is impossible in cultural anthropology as well as in social psychiatry. Nobody reared in one way of life can transport himself wholly into the assumptions, values, rules, and language of another culture in order to study it from within. Nor do I believe that we should let a person who has grown up in a culture and lives in it write its ethnography. The result would also be highly biased. An observer always imposes his frame of reference in some degree when he observes social or psychological reality and interprets that reality according to current concepts. Historians have said this in many ways; Aron has stated it most refreshingly (1961, p. 47) when he claims that imagination helps to determine the nature of truth.

My experience as an ethnographer also convinces me that an ethnography can never be a faithful reflection of external reality. It should not be regarded as a direct translation of one realm of experience into another. Social psychiatrists' view of the culture of poverty, like any ethnographic formulation or like a formulation of individual personality or of history, will inevitably represent a dialectic resolution of a state of tension that has been generated between the observer and the material he seeks to understand. A completed ethnography is a tentative synthesis of that tension, a temporary resolution of a prolonged state of dialectic opposition. The tension may return as soon as others disagree with the formulation, either because new facts have come to light or because fresh concepts have been coined which render the account unsatisfactory.

The problem we confront as anthropologists and social psychiatrists is to learn to understand another way of life without imposing too much of ourselves or our culture on the culture we seek to know. The task is to make greatest use of the structure that is, as Sapir puts it, inherent in the data being observed

(Preston, 1964). Instead of letting an inhabitant of the culture of poverty write his own account, I call for incorporating his experience and the pattern of his life as fully and as fairly as this can be done through constantly improving our methods of cross-cultural understanding. We will never thereby discover a fixed, immutable truth, for truth in social science is only a relatively stable equilibrium that has been established between the scientist and his critics after he has resolved the tension that existed between himself and the subject matter he sought to understand.

psychotherapy and the chronically poor

Raymond Prince

The past year saw the publication of two important books, *The Mental Health of the Poor*, edited by Frank Riessman (1964), and *Magic, Faith and Healing*, edited by Ari Kiev (1965). These represent two important emerging interests in western psychiatry; moreover, they are complementary. On the one hand, there is a growing awareness that psychotherapeutic practices aimed at independence and insight are not appropriate for a large and important segment of our western population, the chronically poor; on the other hand, it is becoming clear that the vast majority of the emotionally disturbed of the nonwestern world can be successfully treated (and are being successfully treated) by techniques that foster dependency and unreasoned belief. I will try to show here that the psychotherapeutic needs of the chronically poor (as described in the Riessman volume) could be met by many of the techniques employed by native healers in primitive cultures (as outlined in the Kiev volume).[1]

PSYCHOTHERAPY AND CLASS

One of the few undisputed findings of social psychiatric research over the past decade relates treatment to social class. If a psychiatric patient is well educated or has a good income, he will likely receive some form of insight psychotherapy; if he is poor, he will probably not see a psychiatrist at all, but if he does, his treatment will probably be short-term supportive psychotherapy or some form of physical treatment (Hollingshead, 1958; Schaffer, 1954; Kahn, 1957). Furthermore, lower-class patients discontinue treatment much sooner than middle-class patients (Overall, 1963; Winkelman, 1965; Levinger, 1960).

Why is this so? The most obvious reasons are economic: insight therapies are expensive and time-consuming. Several studies have shown, however, that even in free clinics, patients of lower socioeconomic status (SES) are less likely to be accepted for treatment; if they are accepted, they will be treated by less experienced staff members and will discontinue treatment sooner (Schaffer, 1954; Winkelman, 1965; Brill, 1960). Do they become discouraged because they are treated by inexperienced staff? A study by Imber and others (1955) showed that even when all patients were treated by similarly trained staff (at the senior resident level) the lower-class group still showed the same significantly higher dropout rate.

There are two possible explanations: therapist prejudice; and personality factors in the lower SES group which preclude insight therapy. Does the problem lie within the personality of the therapist or the personality of the patient?

Some authors have suggested that the lower SES patient discontinues psychotherapy because the therapist rejects him. The argument usually runs as follows: most therapists come from middle-class backgrounds (or at least have espoused middle-class values). The middle-class world view clashes with that of the lower-class patient so that, although the lower-class patient is perfectly capable of insight therapy, he is unwittingly rejected in one way or another by the therapist. Other authors have accused therapists of more conscious reasons for rejection of

[1] I am grateful to Prof. Alex Leighton for permission to use case material collected during my work with the Cornell Program in Social Psychiatry. Case histories have been altered to prevent identification. My work with the indigenous Yoruba healers was supported by the Human Ecology Fund, New York.

lower SES patients. Schofield (1964) describes the therapist "Yavis syndrome," the tendency to select only patients who are young, attractive, verbal, intelligent, and successful. No doubt such prejudices do exist, and their force should not be underestimated. Few studies with this focus are available, however.

In an oblique approach to this problem, McDermott and others (1965) showed that children of unskilled blue-collar workers received more malignant diagnoses than the children of skilled blue-collar workers. The two groups of children were shown to be similar in several respects; e.g., behavior in the home, divorced or separated parents, and eating and sleeping problems. These authors argued that differences in diagnosis (and the therapeutic management implied in the diagnosis) were more a function of the diagnostician than of the patients. Their argument is not fully convincing because they did not show that the behavior of the two groups of children was the same in other important respects. A study by Haase (1964) carries more weight: psychologists were asked to diagnose Rorschach protocols of two groups of patients that were matched in psychogram and content but derived from groups of lower and higher SES. The SES information was available to the diagnosticians. There was a significant tendency for the psychologists to diagnose more pathological illnesses for the lower SES group.

PERSONALITY AND PSYCHOTHERAPY

Although it cannot be denied that economics and prejudice play some role in preventing the poor from receiving insight therapy, there is increasing evidence that the factor of critical importance is the patient's personality. In general the poor are not capable of engaging in insight therapy.

What are the personality factors that preclude insight? Although I shall try to separate these factors into categories, they are all closely linked and emerge in a coherent way from the patterns of the "culture of poverty" described by Oscar Lewis (1961) and others.

Time Concepts and the Need for Immediate Gratification   Insight therapy is a long, slow process, stretching over months or years, and therapeutic results are often slow to appear. Insight here means insight into the fact that present anxieties, hostilities, and disappointments are disproportionate because of childhood experience. In attaining insight, then, one must be preoccupied with the past so that it will yield up its secrets.

Lower ses patients are unable or unwilling to wait for such results; nor are they interested in the past.

> The family seeks immediate results in terms of symptomatic treatment. This is not solely due to lack of explanation of what therapy entails, but rather seems to be due in some cases, to a failure of internalization and development of the ego's capacity for delaying gratification; viewed from a family perspective, the middle-class values of verbalization and perseverence for longer range goals seem to be lacking. . . . The families prefer to return on several occasions scattered over time intervals if the difficulty recurs in one form or another, rather than obtain the "working through" type of treatment which the college-educated family are aware of and seek [Malmquist, 1965].

Concerning psychotherapy dropouts in Philadelphia from class IV skilled factory workers, Winkelman (1965) writes: "They were people who wanted immediate gratifications and were not willing to postpone gratifications for future rewards. They were not goal directed. . . . [There was an] inability to anticipate the future and understand the present in terms of the past." Of the poor in general, Haggstrom (1963) writes: "Caught in the present, the poor do not plan very much. They meet their troubles and make their pleasures on a moment-to-moment basis; their schemes are short term. . . . They have little sense of

the past and they go forward, but not forward to any precon-
ceived place. Their pleasures and rewards are sought in the
present; they find it difficult to delay gratification, to postpone
satisfaction."

Authoritarianism and Dependency Insight therapy requires a
detached and nondirective attitude on the part of the therapist.
Advice-giving or direction is regarded as an improper infringe-
ment on the patient's autonomy. In an atmosphere of egalitarian
acceptance, the patient is encouraged to untangle his ambivalent
dependencies and free himself from them on the basis of insight.
The desired result is a self-determining individual who can see
people and relationships as they objectively are, who, unsupported, can make his own decisions.

The poor, however, require an authoritarian attitude.[2] Of a
group of low-income patients from Lynwood, California, who
were offered psychoanalytic treatment, Hacker (1964) writes:
"The average relationship pattern of Lynwood patients more

[2] Here a logical paradox appears, of the kind that Gregory Bateson (1958)
delights in pointing out, following Whitehead and Russell. Dr. Honigmann and
Dr. Prince feel that we should avoid spreading our values to people of other
cultures or subcultures; these other people should keep or develop their own
values. But this feeling is itself a value of our western middle-class culture. The
poor, as Dr. Prince points out, do not share this value: they do not want a
psychoanalysis or a nondirective psychotherapy that requires them to make their
own decisions; they want to be told what to do. The paradox is that if we respect
their values we are *not* respecting their values. This paradox haunts much of the
discussion that follows, and it is never clearly recognized.

So far as I know, the western middle class is the only society whose cultural
values include the idea that it is wrong to spread its cultural values; there is something paradoxical in holding the value that its own values may be wrong. As
Redfield has pointed out (1953), other cultures are naïvely ethnocentric (that is,
they are not self-conscious about it and do not point it out to themselves). To
hold a set of values implies the conviction that it is the right set of values. Our
culture is the only one whose members are aware of being ethnocentric, and who
feel guilty about it. Of course, our pluralistic, relativistic, antiethnocentric, anti-
missionary value is put into action only sporadically, competing with the missionary spirit that is also part of our culture. Indeed, since the antiethnocentric
value is itself paradoxical, it cannot be put into action consistently, for following
the principle at one level of abstraction inevitably means breaking it at another
level.—Editor

often took the form of either stubborn, blind treatment rejection, or of equally blind, unquestioning submission to authority . . . the inbuilt flexibility of the therapeutic situation had to be flexibly altered into a more securely authoritative relationship (for instance, by not insisting on free association). . . . A seemingly non-authoritarian permissiveness was often so frightening to such patients that they could permit themselves nothing but the resistance maneuvers of denial and repression resulting in projective suspiciousness and treatment break-up."

Discussing their New Haven findings, Hollingshead and Redlich (1958) describe the treatment expectations of lower-income patients as follows:

> Practically all Class V neurotics drop out of treatment. The few who remain beyond the intake period are unable to understand that their troubles are not physical illnesses. They continue to hold these attitudes even when their therapist changes from insight therapy to directive-supportive therapy. These patients are disappointed in not getting sufficient practical advice about how to solve their problems and how to run their lives. They express in word and action their lack of confidence in a "talking treatment." They retain rigid attitudes towards mental illness and consider the psychiatrist a magical doctor, who can magically cure their "physical ills." They expect "pills and needles" and, also as a gratuity, sympathy and warmth, and they are disappointed at not having such demands gratified. . . . The most frequent source of difficulty between the lower-status patient in psychotherapy and the therapist is the patient's tacit or overt demand for an authoritarian attitude on the part of the psychiatrist and the psychiatrist's unwillingness to assume this role because it runs counter to certain therapeutic principles.

Of lower-class Irish Americans in Boston, Spiegal (1959) comments, "Hard work in an independent, self-responsible way for the sake of long distance goals has not been a part of his value training. . . . He is accustomed to being told what to do, right now in the present. Therefore he repeatedly asks the therapist what he is supposed to be doing, and, if he is not told, he is paralyzed. He feels that nothing is happening and he is wasting his time."

Language Insight therapy is par excellence a verbal activity. The patient is required to verbalize all the shades of his own feelings and motivations and those of his family and associates. Good candidates are generally those who enjoy introspection and love the feeling of words on the lips. The poor, by contrast, are nonverbal or at least verbal in different ways or situations from middle-class subjects. They are tonguetied when they are expected to talk about themselves or others—about motives or inner life; they can talk quite readily, however, *as* themselves, that is, in the heat of their emotions or even when acting out other assigned selves or roles. As Riessman (1964) writes: "Ask a juvenile delinquent who comes from a disadvantaged family background what he doesn't like about school or the teacher and you will get an abbreviated, inarticulate reply. But have a group of these youngsters act out a school scene in which someone plays the teacher, and you will discover a stream of verbal consciousness that is almost impossible to shut off."

One of the most stimulating papers in the Riessman volume is "Social Class, Speech Systems, and Psychotherapy," by the English sociologist Basil Bernstein (1964). Bernstein attempts to relate the peculiar linguistic style of the poor to their social system and authoritarian child-rearing practices. This paper is highly compressed and closely reasoned so that only the high points can be presented here.

Bernstein points out that the verbal IQ scores of members of the lower working class are likely to be severely depressed compared to their nonverbal IQ tests. Furthermore, studies of middle- and working-class subjects who were matched for average verbal and performance IQ indicate that the working-class group use a speech style that is markedly different from that of the middle-class group. With the former, "Speech is characterized by a reduction in qualifiers, adjectives, adverbs, particularly those which qualify feelings, the organization of the speech is comparatively simple, there is a restriction on the use of the self-referent pronoun 'I' and an increase in personal pronouns. . . . The working-class prefer much more concrete than abstract propositions."

In attempting to explain these peculiarities, Bernstein points out that when a group shares common assumptions and interests, there is no necessity for speakers to elaborate their intent. "If you know someone very, very well, an enormous amount may be taken for granted; you do not have to put into words all that you feel because the feelings are common." Such a restricted "code" is common in such communities as prisons, as well as between close friends or within a family.

Bernstein suggests that although such a restricted code is possible to any group in a society when conditions are appropriate, it may be that "a considerable section of our society, in particular, members of the lower working-class . . . are limited to this code and have no other. We have a special case, a case where children and adults can use only one speech system." He believes that this restricted code is linked with the authoritarian pattern of child rearing in lower-class groups. Discipline is commonly exercised by a simple command or threat, with no reason given or with an appeal to status; e.g., "You don't talk to your father like that." Middle-class discipline is more likely to be person-oriented: "The person-oriented appeals are very different. . . . In these appeals the conduct of the child is related to the feelings of the regulator (parent) or the significance of the act, its meaning is related explicitly to the regulated, to the child, e.g., 'Daddy will be pleased, hurt, disappointed, angry, ecstatic, if you go on doing this.' 'If you go on doing this you will be miserable when the cat has a nasty pain.' "

Bernstein feels that families who can operate only with a restricted verbal code tend to be authoritarian and use only the status-oriented or the direct-command pattern of discipline. He fails to explain why lower-class families use such a restricted form of language. Presumably it is imposed upon the child early in life so that by the time he reaches school age he is too firmly indoctrinated to adopt a more expanded, person-oriented type of verbal pattern.[3]

Acting-Out   One of the basic principles of insight therapy is that the patient must "talk out" rather than "act out." It is commonly observed, for example, that if the patient has unexpressed erotic feelings for the therapist, he may act out his fantasies in illicit sexual behavior; when such fantasies are discussed in the interview, the sexual acting-out ceases.

Low-income people eschew talk; they prefer a motoric response. The reason for this is obscure. Perhaps it is part of an inability to delay gratification. (It is the opposite to the paralyzing inability to act which is noted in some middle-class obsessionals, who have great difficulty in translating thought into action.) Such verbal inhibition may also be observed in children and some middle-class adolescents. They are unable to talk about their feelings but are able to act them out with toys in play therapy.

This motoric propensity among the poor has been noted by many observers. Riessman and Goldfarb (1964) summarize as follows:

> An outstanding characteristic of the low income persons style is its emphasis on the physical, in particular the motoric (the large muscles involved in voluntary action). It is not simply that the poor *are* physical; that their labour is characterized by working with things; that their child rearing typically utilizes physical punishment; that their religious expression very often includes physical manifestations of emotion such as hand-clapping; that when they become mentally ill they are more likely to develop motoric symptoms such as conversion hysteria and catatonia . . . ; that they are

---

[3] Bernstein's theory seems to be highly relevant to primitive cultures where groups are often small and relatively homogeneous. It would be interesting to study their linguistic patterns in the light of this hypothesis. Certainly my own experience with the Yoruba group of Nigeria indicates that insight therapy with them is virtually impossible and for much the same reasons that the western poor have difficulty (Prince, 1962).

strongly interested in sports; that they are especially respon-
sive to extra-verbal forms of communication, such as gesture.
The significant factor is that low income people work through
mental problems best when they can do things physically.
This is their habit, or style of work, and it appears when they
work on academic problems or personal problems.

To summarize, I suggest that the key reason why lower-class
patients[4] are not commonly engaged in insight therapy is that,
because of personality factors, they are unable to engage in it.
Factors involved include an inability to delay gratification, an
inveterate need for direction and authority, a limited awareness
of the inner life coupled with a verbal style unsuited to subtleties
of description, and a marked proclivity for acting-out.

SOME FEATURES OF PRIMITIVE PSYCHOTHERAPY

Magic, Faith and Healing (Kiev, 1965) contains descriptions of
the indigenous psychiatric practices of some sixteen widely
distributed cultures (including examples from the Middle East,
central India, northern Australia, West Africa, the Arctic, and the
South Pacific). It is striking that in spite of enormous cultural
differences, the therapeutic techniques are remarkably similar.
It is also striking that when one abstracts the therapeutic principles of these primitive techniques, they tally with the psychiatric needs of the western poor that I have just summarized. Let
us examine some of these principles of primitive psychotherapy.

Insight and Independence   The development of insight and the
encouragement of personality maturation and independence are
concepts that are alien to all the psychiatric systems described.

---

[4] I have used the terms *lower class, the poor,* etc., without properly defining
them. Suffice it to say that I believe there are people with the personality features
I have described and these are to be found with increasing frequency as one
descends the class scale. Not all Class V people, however, are incapable of
insight and the insight potential of some Class I and Class II individuals may be
severely limited.

Such concepts do not harmonize with their concepts of causation which in all cases focus upon magical influences (witchcraft, sorcery, curse, spirit influence) or upon heredity. Of shamanistic methods among the St. Lawrence Eskimo, Murphy (1965) writes:

> While shamanism appears to have remarkable strength to accomplish its limited aims, it is weak in encouraging independence and producing insight. One might say that the encouragement of independence is, in fact, the opposite of what shamanism purports to do. With regard to insight, shamanism involves a body of thought about the causes of disease, but does not involve a theory of personality. The insights produced through shamanistic activities have to do with cultural beliefs—discovering the patient's lost soul or his past transgressions, for example. Insight of this order is very different from what is meant, in Western psychiatry by "insight" into the patient's personality functioning.

Kaplan and Johnson (1965) say of the Navaho, "In one sense, all Navaho curing is psychotherapy. Looked at in another way, however, none of it is psychotherapy as we know it. In the sense of verbal interaction between patient and therapist, with the goal of changing behaviour through increased insight and self-awareness, psychotherapy hardly exists at all."

The patient may talk very little during healing sessions. The healer does most of the talking—indeed, in the rite of divination the patient may not even explain to the diviner the nature of his problem (Prince, 1963, 1965); it is part of the diviner's task to determine the problem by means of his magical powers. We might say that in primitive psychotherapy it is not the patient who attains insight but the doctor.[5] Divination means the discovery of the hidden; when used to diagnose disease, it provides insight into its hidden causes.

Authoritarianism and Suggestion Because of their contacts with the spirit world, primitive healers are regarded as having super-

[5] Insight of a different sort, of course, not psychological insight as I have defined it previously but insight in terms of the local beliefs.

human vision and powers. Bolstered by these sanctions, the healer takes an authoritarian attitude toward his patients. He commands them to be well. Frequently during healing ceremonies the healer commences with a demonstration, using sleight-of-hand tricks or by entering a trance state during which his appearance and voice are transformed and he is able to perform remarkable feats such as burning or cutting himself.[6] Such vivid demonstrations heighten the suggestive power of the healer's words and rituals.

Describing the Gunwinggu healers of Northern Australia, Berndt (1965) writes: "Like his counterparts in other regions, [he] is credited with ability to perform marvellous feats. He can, it is claimed, climb into the sky; render himself invisible; . . . see ghosts and spirits invisible to ordinary persons and follow them unobserved; . . . his association with the supernatural and marvellous imbues him with an aura of special privilege and knowledge. It suggests that his actions in this respect have supernatural backing, that he can draw on a resource of power that is not available to other people."

In a similar vein Murphy (1965) writes of the Eskimo:

> One shaman . . . was reputed to wrap a walrus skin rope around his neck and to direct two men standing on either side of him to pull it as hard as possible until it cut his head off. He would then wrap the head in a raincoat and have someone carry it down to the edge of the ice and throw it into the sea. When the errand was accomplished and the group reassembled, they would find his head was fastened on again. A certain shamaness was said to gnaw her hands until they were bleeding and then with her tongue, to lick them back into wholeness. . . . One shaman could make the parka of his patient rise from the ground and stand up with no one in it and nothing for support.

[6] Trickery may also be involved in these feats performed during possession. In Nigeria, Shango dancers during trance appear to thrust an ice pick through their tongues. Photographs of the proceedings demonstrated the presence of a small black slit in the tongue before the pick was inserted. Subsequent study showed that the pick was not penetrating the tongue but being pushed through a long-established fistula.

Concerning the Balahis of Central India, Fuchs (1965) writes: "The *barwas* . . . were mostly people who themselves quite sincerely believed in their own magic powers . . . a few frankly admitted however, after I had won their confidence, that their devices and cures were fraudulent and that they deceived their credulous clients. Some of them knew a few sleight-of-hand tricks, which they used to win the confidence of their patients. These tricks they had learned from their fathers or teachers, and their secrets were zealously guarded." The *barwas* also demonstrate their supernatural powers during possession: "Some of them stick knives through their cheeks or thrust them into arms or thighs. Or a *barwa* heats an iron chain in a fire, steps into the burning fire himself, and whips his bare back with the red-hot chain without apparently being hurt. It is claimed that not even a scar can be traced afterwards."

Use of Concrete Communication and Acting-Out Primitive healing ceremonies are simple, vivid, and direct. Frequently they are a dramatization of the banishment of evil—the summoning and expulsion of evil spirits, the transfer of bad luck to a scapegoat, the sucking out of a bad object, violent purgation or sweating. The drama, of course, acts out the local beliefs about causation. Communication during these ceremonies is preverbal; the participants do not talk about it, they do it.

In some of these ceremonies the patient plays a purely passive role, as among the Yemenite *mori* (Hes, 1965): "Another method . . . is to take a sheep, dove, or chicken and revolve it three times around the patient. The *mori* whispers to the spirits, 'Masters, please have mercy upon the patient and take the sheep instead.' Immediately afterwards the sheep is slaughtered." Proof that the spirit has departed from the patient is indicated by signs: a cup standing nearby breaks, or a fire lights spontaneously.

The patient may sometimes play a more active role: "A neurotic patient with somatic complaints and 'bad luck' with his wives consulted a *babalawo* and was required among other things to carry out the following ritual; he prayed to a cowrie shell that had been specially energized with medicine and incantations that his illness 'would go back from him.' He then took the cowrie into the bush and recited a prayer saying, 'I am paying the money of sickness . . . , I am paying the money of death.' He then made a ring around his head with the cowrie and flung it as far as possible into the bush" (Prince, 1965).

Perhaps the clearest example of acting-out in the sense that it is used in western psychiatry occurs in masquerade and possession cults. Such cults have many other functions besides healing—i.e., religious and political functions. It is clear, however, that healing is often important. A chronically ill patient or a patient with an unusual kind of illness may be directed to become initiated into such a cult. During possession or masquerade the patient may act out a wide variety of roles depending upon the spirits associated with his cult. The roles may include very aggressive ones, or self-punishing ones, or the patient may play the role of the opposite sex. With the Gelede cult of the Yoruba, Prince (1965) writes: "During the annual festival, the men masquerade as women, wearing women's clothes and flaunting prominent bullet-like breasts. Some look grossly pregnant, and others carry wood carvings of children on their backs. All wear grotesquely carved wooden masks, some of which are frightening: the mask called *Ogede*, for example, is about five feet high, a black wooden cylinder, with breasts, straight outstretched arms, long black hair, and huge alligator mouth. . . . In action, the figure towers some eight feet tall, presenting quite a terrifying appearance, especially at night when the more important parts of the festival take place."

SUMMARY: THE CONE OF AUTHORITY

In summary, primitive psychotherapy makes no attempt to provide the patient with insight into his own personality or to render

him independent. On the contrary, the common technique is
to place him within a cone of authority as it were—he is assigned
to the care and control of a benevolent spirit. Important elements
in the procedure include the human representative of the benevolent spirit (the healer-priest with superhuman powers); the
healer's demonstration of his powers; the charade demonstrating
the destruction or transfer of evil; and, in some instances, the
periodic acting-out of asocial impulses. In exchange for protection and succor, the patient must provide the spirit with food
or other offerings, must behave in certain prescribed ways and
follow certain taboos. There is an exchange of freedom for
protection. In these systems independence is looked upon as a
vice, and the spirits punish the miscreant with illness or other
bad luck; in primitive psychotherapy, insight is the prerogative
of the healer and not of the patient.

I could perhaps best develop this concept of the cone of
authority by means of a figure. Consider a cone of light at the
vertex of which is an omniscient spirit who is the source of light.
All men within the cone of light are healthy, fertile, and prosperous; in the darkness beyond men are dying, or sick and prey
to all manner of anxieties. To enter the cone of light requires
purification, and to remain requires obedience. Halfway to the
base of the cone is the circle of healer-priests who because of
their proximity can communicate directly with the spirit, but the
common man who rests at the base of the cone can communicate
only through the healer. Under special circumstances, the spirit
may descend from the apex and mount or enter the healer and
speaker of spiritual things to the men below; or the spirit may
mount the laity directly, generating within them and their
companions-in-light salubrious actions.

PSYCHOTHERAPY OF THE POOR

Many of the poor need psychotherapy; indeed, most studies
show that there is an especially heavy loading of psychiatric

disorder in the Class V (Hollingshead) population, which, of course, contains the bulk of the so-called multiproblem families.[7] However, the poor are often unable to engage in insight types of psychotherapy. A wide variety of primitive cultures provide psychotherapy within a complex religiomagical structure that I have called the cone of authority. The logic of our argument would suggest that we ask ourselves whether some such cones of authority are within our own social structure and to what extent they can be developed to provide a more effective psychotherapy for the poor.

Evangelical Religious Groups Christian evangelical religious groups fit well to the pattern of cones of authority. The "holy spirit" presides and the religious leaders are the intermediaries; conversion represents the movement from outer darkness into the cone of light; sometimes the holy spirit descends upon the leaders or the members.

Christian groups moreover have a philosophy that is especially suitable for psychotherapy. Whereas in primitive groups entry into the cone of light can usually be attained by sacrifices of animals and other gifts with minimal submission to behavioral control (they may only be required to follow certain taboos, etc.), Christianity requires the "sacrifice" of the whole personality.

In primitive groups, the priest demonstrates his superhuman powers by sleight-of-hand tricks or the behavior associated with possession. Western religious groups do not appear to use sleight-of-hand tricks; possession with glossolalia still plays some part, and the handling of poisonous snakes and consumption of strychnine practiced by some groups in the American Southeast (La

[7] The general practitioner and the clinic psychiatrist have a role to play, of course, especially with the new developments in psychotropic drugs. But these drugs are stop-gap measures. Tranquilizers are valuable in managing crisis situations and returning the individual to his status quo but have little use in bringing about the radical behavioral changes required to integrate the multiproblem family, the alcoholic father and the masochistic mother. Personality transformations are often called for rather than the relief of anxiety or depression.

Barre, 1964) are rather unusual but striking examples of evidence of superhuman powers. For the most part, however, Christian sects base the proof of the superhuman element upon the "miracle" of personality transformation. The conversion experience or the mystical state and the personality changes that issue from them supply the proof of supernatural intervention.

Some of these groups have developed interesting techniques. On summer nights, usually on Sunday, small bands of congregants of lower-class evangelical groups move out into the streets in the low-income districts of our cities. They sometimes carry a portable organ and a banner. They select a corner, located strategically near a saloon or brothel, and hold a service of singing, lay testimonial, and exhortation. They warn the by-stander of the dangers of remaining in "outer darkness," encourage him with the simplicity of conversion, and testify from their own experience how they found their way into the light. Occasionally an alcoholic or other disturbed person will be induced to submit himself to the cone of authority.

Such activity has social implications: the congregants are usually members of Class IV, with stable blue-collar occupations and often close-knit, if authoritarian, families. Their Sunday-night religious operation is essentially a reaching down into the Class V strata and an attempt to redeem a Class V "sinner." It is also a psychiatric operation—an attempt to raise the alcoholic to a higher level of mental health through belief and submission rather than through insight and independence. This technique is, of course, closed to the psychiatrist because, among other reasons, he does not subscribe to that world view, and the magical and authoritarian implications are contrary to his scientific and democratic canon.

Similar religious activities occur among the rural poor. Consider the following examples collected during a mental-health survey in a rural area of Canada. L. is a 50-year-old, partially literate New Brunswick fisherman who lives in a shack one hundred yards from the sea. A father of six children, he earns some $2,000 a year by fishing in the summer and collecting unemployment insurance during the winter.

> I can't say that I was a very bad man. The only thing was that I had a very mean temper and cursed and swore from morning till night. I gambled a bit.
>
> One time about six years ago there was a preacher fellow from Lotville (fifteen miles away) who used to come and hold prayer meetings in my brother's place every Saturday night. He lived just across the valley. My wife got it into her head that we should go. I refused because I didn't have any decent rig—just an old pair of overalls was all I had. She kept bugging me and said she wouldn't go if I didn't. Then my niece came and started bugging me and finally with both of them bugging me I went. I was just in my old overalls.
>
> The preacher made us kneel in a circle holding one another's hands and he made up the last end of the circle. Each one of us than had to pray, one at a time. I said that I didn't know how to pray. The preacher said, "Just do the best you can." And I did. Then the preacher looked square at me and said, "Do you believe in the Lord?" For some reason I said I did.
>
> I didn't feel anything that night especially, but for the next three days I noticed that I had stopped cursing. It just happened—I didn't do it myself and I knew it was the Lord's work. I asked my wife—she used to curse and swear as bad as me—and she said she had stopped cursing too. And we were both quieter with the children. So we went the next Saturday again and finally we were baptized.

Subsequently, the wife's personality change seemed to fade and she reverted to a former pattern of promiscuity. She left L. and went to live with a local storekeeper. The next excerpt illustrates the potential of the religious conversion in preventive psychiatry:

> When my wife left me it drove me half buggy. I had the six children on my hands and shortly after that they all developed the measles. For about four months I couldn't sleep and I smoked a whole package of cigarettes every evening—just sitting and thinking. I felt all at sea and didn't know which

way to turn. I couldn't eat and I lost weight—went right down to nothing. Then one night it came to me. I prayed and put the whole thing on the Lord. I said, "You know what she's doing Lord, but I don't," and he took the whole thing off my shoulders. I don't think about it any longer. I went to the law of the land and to the welfare and they weren't able to do anything about it. I found there was Someone who could do something about it and I put the whole thing over to the Lord. My worried mind was relieved instantly and I haven't worried since and that is over two years ago. Another thing, if it hadn't been for the Lord I would have killed her and him too. I know how I would have behaved before I was saved. As sure as I am sitting here I would have killed them both and taken the consequences.

A second example is that of a 50-year-old countrywoman, one of the healthier women in a depressed area. Her husband is a carpenter and they augment their income by caring for six young welfare children. Their own seven children are now grown up. This case is presented as an example of the cure of a psychosomatic disorder by a priest and also as an example of the supportive value of the milieu within the cone of authority. There is a kind of psychological "weightlessness" provided by the priest and bolstered by the fortuneteller.

I had a stomach ulcer when I was a child. My father and my father's mother had it before me. My belly would pain and once I vomited blood. It might last for three days. I got tablets from the doctor which would make the attacks shorter, but the attacks were stopped altogether by Father Deveau. Some of the neighbors around knew about my attacks and said that I should go to Father Deveau. When I went to him I was having an attack at the time and he prayed and gave me a medal to wear around my neck and also a small piece of cloth that was part of the mantle worn by St. Martin who is the patron saint around here. The attacks stopped immediately and I haven't had an attack since that time.

After that I took more interest in holy water, that is, water blessed by the priest. This water is quite magical and you can keep it all winter long and it won't freeze. I have done it myself. I had a quart of it, it would evaporate but wouldn't freeze. I used this water on one of my welfare children. It had been beaten half to death by its mother because her husband went off with another woman. It had a damaged brain because of it and when it walked it had to sort of go on its toes. I rubbed its feet every day and now he can walk much better.

I never worry about money. The Lord will always provide for me. If anyone is in need I always give money to them and know it will be returned to me with interest. I could go and spend my last cent and in a few days all my money would come back. Once an old lady asked me for a quarter in the streets of Lotville. I gave her a quarter. On the same day a friend of mine saw me and said, "You don't come to town very often. Here I'd like to treat you to some ice cream." So he gave me a quarter for ice cream. That was the way my money came back that time.

Once I went to a fortuneteller when I was a young woman and she told me about how my life would turn out, what kind of man I would marry and said that I would never be in want, and all this turned out to be true. I have a fortuneteller I write to in California. I saw an advertisement in the paper about getting a magical cross for 25 cents. My husband told me I should write for the cross. And I did. This fortuneteller claims to be able to locate lost objects. One of the neighbors also writes to her—several do, for that matter. This man was drunk one time and his wife asked him for some money. This man told his wife where the money was in the wallet and to take one dollar. The wife took all the money and hid the wallet thinking her husband was to drunk to remember and would think he had lost his wallet. When he sobered up he wrote to this woman who told him to look under the cushion of a certain chair. He did look there and sure enough there was the empty wallet.

I lost my own wedding ring and wrote to her asking for help. I had to send $2. She wrote back saying that I would find my ring in the clothes closet. Well, we didn't have a clothes closet. I looked through my place where I keep my clothes but never found the ring. Sometimes she is wrong but mostly she is right. Some of the people in town tell me I am selling myself to the devil by dealing with fortune-tellers, but I don't see anything wrong with it.

Required Research What is needed is a series of studies focused upon the therapeutic efficacy of the cone of authority.[8] Such studies should be done both upon primitive groups and upon western evangelical groups. In the Kiev volume, for example, are descriptions of therapeutic practices, glossaries of indigenous names for psychiatric disorders and etiological beliefs, and we are told that the systems are therapeutically effective. What we now need are descriptions of the patient populations, their psychiatric histories, the types of various disorders treated, and some indication of the efficacy of treatment and relapse rates.

We want to know more about the varieties of world view held by the various western evangelical groups. For example, I have been studying a spiritualist church in central Montreal. This church has an active membership of some 75 lower-class congregants. The distinctive element in the world view of this group is the belief that departed spirits can communicate with the living through a medium. The medium performs publicly, bringing messages of solace and advice from deceased relatives. In studying this group, we expect to find a disproportionate number with histories of depression and recent bereavement. It is possible that such a church assists its congregants in coping with death through the reinforcement of the mechanism of denial.

The Yoruba diviner may refer his patients to a wide variety of cult groups that have symbolism and world views especially suited to the needs of various patient groups. The Gelede cult provides therapy for impotent males who believe they are suffering from the malevolence of witches. The cult provides a situation for the acting-out of the fantasy of the identification with the castrating and devouring mother. Other cults provide coprophagic and sadistic outlets. Studies of our own evangelical and paramedical healers might reveal a parallel diversity of format.

[8] It is, of course, one of the firmly entrenched tenets of contemporary psychiatry that symptoms removed by suggestion, and unaccompanied by insight, will recur under some other guise. Studies in primitive groups would seem to call this tenet into question. Perhaps symptoms recur not because there is no insight, but because there is insufficient collateral support.

Consultation with Lower-Class Healing Groups Let us suppose that operational studies of these lower-class evangelical groups support our hypothesis: that such groups do or could play a significant role in the management of lower-class psychiatric patients or disintegrated families. The question then arises, what attitude should official medicine and psychiatry take toward them?

In current writings on community psychiatry, much attention is devoted to the subject of consultation between the psychiatrist and other individuals or groups that handle the psychiatrically disturbed. Such consultation is usually based upon the insight model, however, and is therefore irrelevant to our present discussion. Yet some type of consultation seems to be called for.

For example, a recent newspaper article reported the case of a faith healer in rural Ontario who was taken to court because he had advised one of his congregants to discontinue her insulin injections. The woman was a severe diabetic and died in coma. This example points up one important type of consultation required. It has to do with understanding the limits of the therapeutic efficacy of psychotherapy. Clearly every individual or group involved in the management of patients should have medical or psychiatric consultation to assure that these limits are recognized.

On the positive side it is possible that if the community psychiatrist could develop a relationship with a number of such groups, he might feel confident enough to refer some of his patients to them. This, it seems to me, is the genuine function of consultation: mutual understanding and trust between the psychiatrist and the community leader. It is not that the community psychiatrist should teach the leader to be an amateur psychiatrist but that both should attempt to discover their limits and special strengths and "render unto Caesar that which is Caesar's."

portrait of a rural village

Rena Gazaway

It is my intent to take you backstage with poverty. I shall hope to sharpen your insight and increase your sensitivity to some of the forces that are at work. These forces are subtle indeed, but I feel they are highly significant in the perpetuation of the way of life of a segment of our society. The forces are so complex that the problem may well defy solution.

Poverty is a mask for a much deeper problem—a way of life of people who appear to have no immediate hope or desire for a way out. They grow up in a culture that permits them to hide from themselves as well as from others not of their own kind. Hiding, by whatever method, limits their social anxieties and frustrations. The intolerable burdens of the escape route into the cruel, menacing world beyond their hollows offers few or no attractions. " 'Tant worth walkin' into," they tell me, because few are eager to make the break and none wish to sacrifice their in-group status in the neighborhood.

If the dweller in the branch were to win his way into the material plenty of our American middle-class life, he would immediately inherit the economic, social, and psychological tension of his urban counterpart. He would find himself surrounded by growing affluence, which has made many onetime luxuries commonplace. His social position might well prove much less comfortable than he had expected. Income-tax returns, job pressures, family squabbles, and neurotic concerns would take their toll. He would enter a dehumanized environment in which one is no longer a person but a number. He would find that our affluent society provides us with books, time to enjoy a wide variety of pleasures and hobbies, and opportunities to travel. He would also see that this empty modern living produces confused values, even though we have money and leisure. He quickly senses a lofty, disinterested attitude.

A community becomes sick in much the same way as a person. This neighborhood is critically ill, and the symptoms are there for all to see. Unfortunately a complete medical checkup will not reveal the causative agents as it does for a person. The so-called poverty programs may inject a little light into the long, dark night, but they will certainly not cure the cancerous erosion, slow the process of dying, or find effective solutions for poverty amid affluence, ignorance amid learning, and hunger amid plenty. It is conceivable that such programs may increase the evils they were designed to reduce. The workers in this massive attack on poverty still have to deal with real, live people who are already doomed to become the dregs of society. I have been told all too often that "winning the war" will be easy once we have destroyed the many myths about poverty. Poverty is no myth.

DESCRIPTION OF THE COMMUNITY

Let me tell you some of the details of a neighborhood in misery. This branch[1] or "holler" strings along for a mile in a narrow valley between high mountains. There is no road but the creek bottom, which also serves as an open sewer, a garbage receptacle, and a path for those who wade or rock-hop out. Many times each year the water is so deep that it is impossible for anyone, even the adults, to get out.

This neighborhood began in 1920 with the settlement of a few families. Now more than 250 persons live in the shacks perched

[1] The term *branch* means a creek, a brook, a branch of a river. Dr. Gazaway also calls it "the hollow," and some members of the conference call it "the gulch."—Editor

close to the bank of the creekbed. There are 55 families. Nuclear families represent five extended families and four gnerations.

Kinship patterns, of which they have little awareness, are astounding. The second person to establish himself and family in the hollow is now 65 years of age and has 168 kinsmen living in the Branch. This is 71 percent of the total population. Of his 168 relatives, 61 percent are blood kin. He is related to 62 percent of the families and bears 199 relationships to persons with 16 last names.

A woman who is 54 years of age bears more than one kinship to several of her kindred—a total of 364 relationships. To 56 persons she bears four or more different relationships, to 25 persons five or more, and to six persons six or more. She is wife, second cousin, and half first cousin to her present (seventh) husband.

A young woman, age 25, is married to a 57-year-old man. She grew up in the Branch. Her maiden name was R. Of the ten R. family units, she is related to eight. There are 16 families with the name of E. Although there are four different E. groups in 16 individual family units, she is related in some way to each of four main E. groups and to 15 of the 16 E. families. A listing of her kin shows 14 family names. At her young age she is related to 71 percent of the families in the Branch. Her blood kin are 53 percent of the total population, and her total relationships are 306.

Lest you think I am stacking the deck with these four people, 51 of the 55 families are connected to at least one of the four persons. Of the 51 families, two have kinship to all four persons and 23 families are kin to three of the four individuals. Only, four families, with a total of nine members, have no direct relationship to any one of the four individuals. This neighborhood, then, has close kinship ties. There is not one person who is not connected in some way to another family. There are 12 marriages known to be between double or single first cousins, and this number will rise if some of the current "courtin'" terminates successfully. The median age is in the sixteenth year; the average age in the twenty-second. The average birth rate over the past five years is 44. The county birthrate was roughly 31 in 1961, while that for the state was 23.4. The five-year fertility ratio was 1,130 for the hamlet, while the county's was 750 and the state's 576. The parity of the married women shows the historical pattern of having large families still being followed. While 15- to 24-year old married women had an average of two babies compared with 1.4 for the state, the 25- to 44-year-old women had rates double the state figures. Three out of four of the children in the present generation were born at home, mostly with the assistance of granny midwives. The infant mortality rate of 104, averaged over the past five years, was almost four times the state rate for 1961. The stillbirth rate, far more difficult to measure accurately for such a population, was similarly high (Tapp, Gazaway, and Deuschle, 1964, p. 512).

THE MISERY OF POVERTY

A few true stories may illuminate the way these people live. A family bought a secondhand range which retails new for $77.95. As the fourth owners, they were charged $100. They paid $15 down and agreed to pay ten dollars a month. They paid the seller $10 to have the stove hauled up the Branch. When they put the pipe on and started to build a fire in the stove, there was no grate. The father went back to the seller and was told that when the stove left the store the grate was in it. Since he could not use the stove, he stopped making payments. Six months later the stove was repossessed. The grate was replaced at the store, and immediately the stove was sold for $75 cash. The seller, who continued to bill the family for $10, wrote me a note saying it was only fair the buyer pay this, since it was the difference between the repossessed value and the original selling price.

Another man bought a secondhand television set, which retailed new for $177.95 complete with wiring, antenna, etc. He paid $269.80, figured as follows:

Purchase price	$211.04
Insurance and carrying charges	18.76
Wiring, antenna, installation	40.00

The purchaser thought the downpayment of $71.04 was payment in full. When he failed to make additional payments, the set was repossessed two months later; he was given no credit for his initial payment but continued to receive monthly statements for the $269.80, in addition to harsh words and repeated threats. Some time later I visited the home of the next owner of the television set. He had paid $152.66 for it.

Another family was in desperate need of money when a sick child required hospitalization and expensive drugs. When they went to a finance company for a loan of $500, they received $422.66 in cash. Even though the signed agreement stated that the interest rate was 2½ percent per month, the monthly payment of $23 produced a credit of only $14.04 or less toward the liquidation of the debt. I was told by the owner of the finance company that $8.96 or more of each payment went for interest. I continued my effort to find out how the 2½ percent interest was calculated. He told me, "I'm not strong on figurin' but when I check these things I'm might near always right." The interest rate turned out to be approximately 36 percent. For $422.66 cash received, the borrower paid $305.26 in interest, carrying charges, etc., for a total cost of $727.92.

Although these people are willing to work, they live in a county where an antipoverty program that would pay them $1.25 an hour was rejected. Why? The farmers and miners who pay as little as 50 cents an hour are not willing to have "their" workers depart for higher wages while their tobacco remains uncut in the fields and the coal stays unmined in the mountain.

Many of these people speak an English that no one out of the hollow understands. Their vocabulary and speech patterns almost make it a foreign language.

G., the head of a family of six, will work at anything to earn money to support his family. He had so little education that he can be classified an illiterate. His service in World War II was terminated by a dishonorable discharge, whose unfavorable connotations he refuses to understand, telling me with considerable pride, "If aes talkin' talk I ken catch I never did nerray a thing theys tellin' me tos." His record shows that he was in the Army 670 days, of which he was AWOL 611 days. But to this day he does not know what that means.

The first year I was in the hollow G. was employed by a well-to-do resident of the county to clear up an auto junkyard. A man whom he did not know would come around irregularly with a check, paying him supposedly at the rate of one dollar an hour. G. could never be sure he was not getting cheated, but the check would have "payment in full to date" written in the lower left-hand corner. I was aware often of whole weeks of time not paid, and of inaccurate calculation. In one instance he had received no pay for two weeks, and for the 120 hours he worked in 12 days he received $90 instead of $120. He showed me the check; the dates for which he was to be paid were correct, but the payment was not. I commented to a man who knew quite well what was going on, "G. seems to think he isn't getting all his pay." He answered, "Sure he is; but if he wasn't, he'd be too ignorant to know."

What can you tell a man in this kind of situation? Do you increase his concern by saying, "That guy still owes you $30"? Had I said that, my relationship with G. from that point on would have deteriorated; too often I had heard the response, "You's callin' me dumb?" Although many of the people realize what is going on, none of them tolerate your calling attention to the fact.

I would frequently stop and talk with G. while he worked. One day I said, "You're gettin' mostly done." He responded, "Yep," and told me that the man came, looked over what was left to be done, and said, "Reckon it'll be a couple more weeks. I'll be back." He never returned to pay for what was finally three weeks of labor, but he left G. a bill for $300 for acetylene he had used for the torch he bought to cut up the cars in small enough pieces to load on a truck. He had cashed all the checks and did not even know the name of the man who had signed them.

I had no trouble getting it, but the same people who so freely told me who G.'s employer was, kept telling G. that they did not know his employer's name.

G. and I often talked about "doghole" coal mining, and he would recall the dangers that he must ignore if he is to work. He would spend all day in the mine, first on one side of his body, then on the other, "hand-diggin' " out a seam of coal 18 to 24 inches high. He describes vividly how he learned "to crawl fast like a mole" to get back to the seam.

G. and a number of other miners, all out of work, were recently asked if they would like to work the seam out on a contract basis. They were told that a foreman would be required. Unaware of the working of the contract, and assuming the owner would provide the foreman, they each worked two weeks, long hours each day, in a cut only 30 inches high. Each was to make $95 a week.

When pay time came, each man was told he had to kick back 75 percent of the money to pay the foreman, who had seldom gone inside the mine. The owner was there with money to cash their checks, and G. ended up with about $30 for two weeks in the mine. In revealing this, G. was a little ashamed; the fact that he had been made a fool of seemed to bother him more than the loss of his money.

Another miner, S., with a family of seven, works regularly in the mine six days a week; his total paycheck is around $95. If he were killed his family would receive insurance of $14,000–15,000, but if he were injured he would get nothing and there would be no compensation.

Let me tell you about another man, aged 56, with a 36-year-old wife who looks 56, and five children. He had worked 28 years in the mine, never "missin' a day the's open." One day he kept hearing the ceiling cracking but "yous gets use to it." But this day a huge rock came down, pinning him to the floor from the knee down. Despite the pain, "I figger I gotta get out," but his attempts to extricate himself were futile. No one missed him until all the men had assembled outside and the driver of the car in which he was to go home said they'd better go back in and look for him. They finally got him out through the 2½-mile-long tunnel. His ankle was crushed. For this injury, which now prevents his kneeling, he was paid $1,400 after deducting the legal fee. He is now unemployable because of his disabling injury. Mining is all he knows. Yet, because of his age, the only income to which he is entitled is $14 a month for a 10-percent disability acquired in World War II. Fortunately, his ambitions and needs are extremely simple. He harbors no bitterness toward anyone, no resentment for the things that have happened to him.

The Branch is within an hour's drive, on good highways, of four hospitals. Nine physicians work at or near these hospitals. In addition, a health department is located in the county seat just 11 miles away. The excellence of this complex of services seems to have little impact on the health problems of those in the Branch. Many of the people feel that the doctors have not proved they can diagnose and treat disease. Also, the Branchers cannot afford to buy the medicine the doctors prescribe; or if they do buy it, they fail to take it as prescribed because they cannot read the directions on the label. For some unknown reason they feel that a physician should be able to bring immediate relief, and yet when they use a folk remedy they are willing to suffer long and painfully while they wait, often futilely, for improvement.

Among the Branchers a few are able to break out of their old way of life. We need to know a great deal more about why certain ones can rise above early conditioning to attain success, status, and economic independence. Does the environment make the people or do the people make the environment?

The Branchers are a sensitive people, suspicious, fearful, anxious, and doubtful. Yet few cry out for help in extricating themselves from the prison of their self and their setting. They simply do not trust the outsider; they do not believe that he really means what he says. They view any suggested change with skepticism.

Resentment and bitterness are hard to find. Hate, contempt,

and disgust are never evident. Physical abuse of children is rare. I have never seen the people get angry or upset when events fail to work to their advantage. Those they consider archfoes are the ones who try to change their way of life. Trapped on the periphery of a society of affluence, they have learned to live with trouble and those things which cannot be changed or helped, without fear and frustration. Believe me, if I endured such conflicts and contradictions, I would seek the nearest psychiatrist's couch, even though I had no income.

Most of the Branchers have many enviable characteristics that you do not see until you live with them. Often what appears from the outside as irrational belief and behavior becomes intelligible when viewed from within. Things must make sense to them. New items of information must somehow be fitted into their cultural matrix if they are expected to understand and accept.

What I have experienced in the last three years has strengthened my feelings about the deprivation of their lives, their environment, and their evident rejection by the outside world. It has caused me to understand more acutely that few are willing to face the grim facts of the reality of one of our most critical domestic problems. I see young parents and their children engulfed by corrosive forces that will pattern their futures, strifle their hopes, and prevent the children from escaping the fate of their parents.

SOLUTIONS TO THE PROBLEM OF POVERTY

What can we do about such a deplorable way of life? President Johnson has said that these people are "trapped in inherited, gateless poverty." Although we may question the motivation behind proposing an antipoverty program in a presidential election year, let's take a serious look at the steps being taken to eradicate the causes of chronic poverty.

The expressions "war on poverty" and "combat poverty" are

unfortunate; they give the impression that we intend to destroy a people, or at least destroy their way of life. One hollow-dweller said to me, "Em fellers better not come in har with no guns 'specten a war, fer we en't fitten thar battles. We's en't wanten no war. We's done no law breakin."

I'm told that various professional groups will form "shock troops" in the war on poverty. Had anyone been willing to troop through a few of the hollows with me, he could have become fully qualified by firsthand shock at what we saw, smelled, and heard.

The so-called experts I've talked with, government officials and economists, seem to think that it will be easy to bring these people out of poverty. One of our great American delusions is that we can solve any problem by passing a law and appropriating money. One expert told me that we'll solve the problems of the people I've described by making recreation areas in Eastern Kentucky, building expressways, and encouraging tourism and industry. He tried to reassure me, "The poor will some day be helped by these projects." But I think these things are little more than veneer. The persons we wish to change are completely identified with their way of life, and poverty is an integral part of it. An official told me, "You just don't understand these people and what they need. When Congress votes all these new programs we can act effectively." While I think that optimism is good, I also think it is unrealistic; the problem lies deeper than the officials realize. One of my economist friends tried to quiet my fears. "This year our income after taxes was up 8 percent. The gross national product is at an alltime high. We are selling more automobiles than ever before. In spite of the cancer scare we're smoking more billions of cigarettes. Wages, corporate income, dividends, these are really worth bragging about."

But what of the almost eight million people drawing welfare payments of one kind or another? The total increases by one million persons a year, or thereabouts. When my enthusiasm seems limited, my economist friend reassures me, "You worry about such trivial problems. Just give us time. We'll get these people out of the hollows. They will be educated, and we will find them jobs. We have the bills passed, and we have the money. Most assuredly, we can break the cycle of poverty." But I still contend that the problem of poverty is far bigger than the economists realize.[2] Those who so vigorously suggest that we lift these people out of deprivation may be blindly contributing to their fall, long before they learn to fly.

We can't buy our way out of poverty, in spite of the probability that President Johnson's Great Society will never run out of money. An appropriation of $1.3 billion, much as it is, will not even begin to break the cycle of poverty, unless there is a tough followthrough to see that all the money actually goes to the very poor. And it isn't doing so now!

Let's face it: ten major programs in the government's massive war on poverty have not even come close to achieving their original first-year objectives of providing actual benefits to the poor. Even scaled-down objectives are not being met. Those responsible for extending the program another year and doubling the funds seem unaware of or unperturbed by the shortcomings. They shy away from any effort to assess the success or failure.

In one of my recent visits to the hollow I was asked, "Is it true that some people make a hundred dollars a day to fight poverty?" I lost no time in changing the subject, but what were my thoughts? I recalled the appointment of a director of an antipoverty program who was snatched from a $7,500-a-year job, consistent with her ability, and was given a salary of $22,500. A consultant in her

[2] The *New Yorker* once reprinted without comment someone's statement that poverty is basically an economic problem. Evidently the magazine's editors thought that the statement was so obvious as to be humorous. But what seems obviously true is often false. On Labor Day weekend in 1966, almost exactly one year after this conference was held, the New York *Daily News* bore the banner headline: JOBS AND JOBS GO BEGGING HERE. Yet life in Dr. Gazaway's hollow was unchanged, and the University of Kentucky's medical clinics were still full of physically healthy people from Eastern Kentucky who were unemployed and seeking compensation. It is clear that there are some individuals, and even some whole subcultural groups of people, who remain unemployed even when the economy is booming, and when manpower is scarce. Such people may take a job, but it doesn't last long. For an explanation we must turn not to the economist but to the psychologist, the psychiatrist, and the cultural anthropologist.—Editor

office, who was "vital, vigorous, and very helpful to her administration," received $100 a day. She also received $75 a day as a
consultant for two large government agencies and $250 a day
from two private foundations. When challenged, she replied
that she felt she was making a real contribution to the poverty
program, because she provided her services at her cheapest fee.
In addition to the $100-a-day consultant, one employee earned
$65 and another $60 a day. If I had these monthly salaries—
$1,875, $2,000, $1,300, and $1,200, totaling $6,375 per month
—I could work miracles in the Branch. I would be so busy that I
would never be seen out of the hollow. In the words of the
director, I could indeed facilitate, expedite, and energize the
hopeless, the uneducated into an action program that would
astonish the experts.[3]

The premise at the national level seems to be that we, as
affluent Americans, can afford the luxury of ignoring the real
problem, for the people who seem to profit most from the programs are not those in poverty but those in plenty. As my hollow
friends would tell me, "Em at has, gets." How true!

Well, what causes the trouble? And what do we need to do
about it? Poverty is described as a "cycle" that produces personal,
spiritual, social, and material deprivation. At what point in the
cycle do we need to intervene? It seems clear to me that the
basic problem is that people exploit each other. The real problem
is not the poor but the attitude of their fellowmen toward them.
Is the problem inside the hollow, or outside?

In every county in the mountains where poverty exists, there
are a few rich and powerful people who control county affairs.
They stay rich and powerful by exploiting the poor. Sociologists
have ignored this fact, and the national administration doesn't
want to face it. The patterns of exploitation and injustice have
denied security and status to those who live in poverty. This is

[3] Dr. Gazaway does not describe her own program. It includes building a
paved road and a sewer into each hollow, as well as running water. People in
the hollow, when asked what they most need, say a paved road, though, as Dr.
Gazaway points out, it is not necessarily what they really need most.—Editor

not a racial problem, in spite of what you hear. The people of the Branch, and most of the other rural slum villages of Eastern Kentucky, are 100 percent white. Many people seem inclined to deny to others the very security and status that they so avidly seek for themselves. Is it our ambivalence and inconsistency toward the system of poverty that produces the pathology? When we are not concerned with the continuing, systematic exploitation of the natural resources of the area (coal and timber), and with the exploitation of the poor people themselves, are we realistic to expect change?

The Community Action Programs at this time are called "planning" or "demonstration" projects, and at best they will provide employment to a few of the poor. Those who see this part of the effort as the core of the antipoverty war are not aware of the depth of political bitterness and of the lack of community initiative. Community action on a county basis won't work, because the powerful people in the community don't want a change; they don't want to have to stop exploiting the poor.

People who are hiring the poor to work in the coal mines or in the fields at 50 cents an hour don't want "their" workers lured away to work elsewhere for $1.25. When I first went to work in the hollow, I visited the powerful people in the county. They told me that if I was foolish enough to spend my time in the hollows, it was all right, so long as I didn't bring the people out of the hollows. And the nearby public school tolerates truancy in the children of the hollows: there is a tacit understanding that the school would just as soon not have the children.

People in power have played a key role in establishing permanent poverty in our society. The very life of people in poverty is controlled by the rich and influential persons, usually in the immediate locality.

Those really concerned about the poor put their faith in the poverty programs. They are willing to accept some change so long as the status remains basically unchanged. The elite preserve their institutions intact. Most of them will enthusiastically accept any change that guarantees noninterference with the economic structure and avoids any basic alteration in the balance of power.

If we are to help these people, we must begin by recognizing that theirs is an alien culture, an alien way of life. They don't do as we do, they don't see things as we do, and they don't have the same values, ideals, and goals. A government program designed to help people like ourselves won't help them. Yet a government official, sitting in his air-conditioned office, told me that these people will have to fit into the programs, since it would be impractical to make programs to fit their needs. No wonder these people feel alienated. As one man in the hollow said, "We's liven hard, but there's em at's not understanden." These people have some awareness of our way of life. They've seen American middle-class life on television. But they have no feeling that it's anything they could ever possibly live. It's not part of their life space.

Can we properly say that those in poverty are underdeveloped people? In some ways they are highly skilled. The individual in this hamlet is adept at making the best of a hopeless situation, not because of any inborn powers that he has, but because of a lifetime of practice in coping with life in the inconceivably meager situation in which he exists. His standard of living is his lot in life, and improvement is not a goal to which he aspires. His survival depends on his ability to make do. In the misery of poverty he can buy a car for less than $100, keep it running on three cells in the battery, a makeshift carburetor, and no brakes. He need never give thought to a driver's license if he cannot read. He knows better than to take the test.

These people have mastered the art of doing without. They have learned to adjust to that over which they have no control. They do not have ambitions or plans for the future. No one ever hopes to be a doctor or a lawyer. None dreams about a vacation, much less identifies an area that would offer something to his liking. Parents don't encourage their children to get an education, to prepare themselves for a job, particularly if the job might take them away from home. They don't aim to "rise," in our sense of the word. We must bear this in mind in considering the government programs. These people lack the training and skills that are marketable, but more regular school attendance will not assure a quality education. Many of them will be incapable of taking part in a plan that would move them from a culture of poverty into the American way of life.

Some people say that poverty is an economic problem, and that you can cure these people's poverty by putting money into their pockets. But to say that is to ignore the fact that these people have a different culture, different values, a different way of life. If I were a poor housewife and someone gave me money, I know what I'd do. I'd put it first into the immediate needs of health and sanitation, and what's left I'd save for a college education for the children. But these people wouldn't do that. Making plans for the future is not part of their life. No matter how much money is put into their pockets, they'd spend it right away, probably be cheated on the prices, and have nothing left at the end of the week. Their standard of living would rise slightly, in a superficial way, as long as they continued to receive money, but they'd still live in a poverty way of life, even while receiving and spending a big income. They wouldn't spend the money on health or education, and they wouldn't invest it in a way that would improve their standing in the long run. The week after the money stopped coming in, they'd be living in the same utterly miserable poverty as before.

These people have some admirable qualities, and I am fond of them. The hollow man's capacity to accept his troubles without storing up resentment is indeed a phenomenon that defies explanation.[4] He has worn someone else's clothing, lived in deteriorated shacks, worked at low-paying jobs, and yet his deprivations have not motivated him to change. He would be the last to trade his lot for that of anyone else in the world. The

[4] As Dr. Wittkower and other psychiatrists will point out later, the apparent lack of resentment and hostility is misleading. The hostility is there, though the people deny it, avoid expressing it, and even make themselves unaware of it. The hostility comes out as bodily symptoms, technically known to the psychiatrist as conversion reaction or hysteria.—Editor

concept of courage and persistent effort is missing from his way of life, but his existence is dependent on faith, and he firmly believes that faith alone will move mountains.

Some people say that poverty is the root of all troubles. Some people are quick to generalize and say that poor people have a greater incidence and prevalence of mental illness, alcoholism, drug addiction, illegitimacy, desertion, and delinquency. This is a highly unfair generalization.

Day after day these people are reminded in many little ways that they are different. Each one is meshed in a web of misery, and the men of each succeeding generation are less capable of sustaining themselves and their families. It becomes even more impossible today as the pace quickens with automation. Perhaps our current revolutionary processes are creating a bigger group of such people, no longer needed, no longer contributors, people paid not to work.

Under such circumstances, do we really believe that our society is worthy of respect and emulation? Are we right in seeking to spread our way of life to other peoples through the Peace Corps and our many other efforts abroad?

Our government is spending $20 billion to put a man on the moon. Is this right, when we have failed to eradicate deprivation? We have been unable to free ourselves from the political, economic, social, psychological, and cultural misery and the human waste of poverty.

You cannot put a monetary value on misery, hopelessness, hunger, want, despair, and squalor. Money is inadequate compensation for human suffering, for being cold in winter, being thirsty in summer, having no lights, being dirty because there is no water or money to buy soap, being hollow-eyed and tired from loss of sleep because of bedbugs. You cannot compensate a child for all the joys he has missed in his early life in poverty. You cannot pay a person for his loss of human dignity.

discussion one

Already in this first discussion some of the issues that are to preoccupy the conference begin to take shape. Dr. Gazaway's moving picture of a rural slum hamlet in the Southern Appalachian Mountains is the focus of the discussion. Asked how she proposes to help the people of the Branch, Dr. Gazaway tells of her mildly successful efforts to rear one 14-year-old boy whom she took out of the Branch to live with her in Cincinnati. She tells other stories to show how the values and goals of the Branch people differ from our own.

Dr. Opler suggests letting the people organize as a community in their own indigenous ways, whatever they may be. Dr. Lewis objects: the capacity for organization beyond the extended family is not an asset that these people have. Indeed, that lack of organization is one of the marks of the "culture of poverty," in contrast to other areas such as India, where there is poverty, but organization, and hence no "culture of poverty."

Dr. De Vos takes issue with Dr. Gazaway's view that the source of the trouble is the outsiders who cheat the Gulch people. Mentally healthy people won't submit to cheating, he says. Something is psychologically wrong with these people who let outsiders take advantage of them; it is maladaptive.

Dr. Gazaway objects to calling her villagers mentally unhealthy, or even to calling them unhappy. She says that the people would be happy and contented if outsiders would leave them alone, and not take advantage of them. But she also calls for spending federal money to change the people, to educate them and relieve their misery. Dr. De Vos tells her that she contradicts herself.

Dr. Lewis remarks that when an anthropologist designates a group of people as a culture or a subculture, that is, a way of life that perpetuates itself, it need not be true that the people are happy, nor that the way of life is satisfying.

This opening discussion raises two great issues: 1) Are there some objective, scientific ways in which we can judge that a subculture or a way of life is malfunctioning and unsatisfactory, by criteria and evidence from the group itself which do not depend on the personal (or subcultural) likes and dislikes of the observer who makes the judgment? 2) Under what circumstances, if at all, do we have a right and/or a duty to intervene, to try to change a group of people and their way of life?

OPLER: I can think of a lot of parallels to the Branch in big Northern cities. I presume that what you're saying is that we need step-by-step programs that are based on a knowledge of the people, rather than the present abstract and unreal ones. How would you go about it?

GAZAWAY: First, recognize the limitations of those of us who are outside. And really get to know the people in the hollows. Let me give you an example. If some stranger walked up to your door and knocked, what would you do? I'd peek through the little hole in my door and ask, "Who is it?" What do they do? They say, "Come in and set a spell!" This happened the first time I walked up that hollow, when they didn't know me from Adam.

[Dr. Gazaway went on to say that of the 150 or so children in the hollow, only one family would let her take a child out. The boy lives in her home in Cincinnati. She is always battling teachers and principals about him, and feels frustrated that they reject her judgment of him. He had never worn underwear nor used a flush toilet. The school in Cincinnati wanted to put him in a class for severely retarded and handicapped children. She fought and got him put into a normal fifth-grade class at 14 years of age (he had been in the seventh grade in his home village in Kentucky). He can't do fifth-grade arithmetic, but she was shocked to find that she can't either, with the new math. The children at school called him a hillbilly. She told him to call such a person a buckeye (nickname for Ohioan), and gave him a buckeye to carry in his pocket, to explain, "I'll show you what it is: It's a nut!" Even the teacher called the boy "Grampa" because he was older than his classmates. Dr. Gazaway showed a strong emotional involvement in the boy's problems, and a willingness to fight his battles. She explained that she grew up in an area in the Ozarks much like the Gulch.

Dr. Gazaway went on to say that the people of the Gulch like their houses. With holes between the floorboards, housecleaning is easy: the trash is swept through the cracks. In the winter the children use the cracks, and don't need to go out in the cold to the outhouse. The people wouldn't change their housing for anything.]

GAZAWAY: But the one thing they don't have is water. Now I can't see why some of these millions of dollars can't somehow provide these houses with water. Some people say that if they had water they wouldn't know what to do with it. Well, I've eaten food that has been cooked in that branch water, which is pure sewage, because it is all they have. The children gather trickles of water in the branch with a pop bottle, and a family gets about one bucketful of water a day.

[Dr. Gazaway told the story of her efforts to improve the people's housing through the FHA winterizing program. One family, the most hardworking in the hollow, got more than its money's worth by doing the labor; of the $1,000 given them, $855 went for materials. Another family also got $1,000 but hired a contractor, who charged them $590. The contractor cheated them by giving them an old toilet and taking the new one himself. Screen doors were installed, but have never been shut since. When the authorities complained, the housewife answered, "I didn't want 'em in the first place. They were on the list, but I ain't aimen to keep 'em closed. Because the dogs can't get in. And I can't jump up and run every time they come to the screen." Anyhow, the people don't mind the flies. And besides, the father has lung disease and complains that screen doors keep too much air out and make it hard for him to get his breath.]

KIEV: What are the channels through which money from Washington goes to an area like this, and how much money is left from a given sum when it gets to the people?

GAZAWAY: I haven't seen any get there yet, but I know where it stops, and I think all of you do, too.[1]

KIEV: I don't know. That's why I asked.

WEINSTEIN: You say that these people have no philosophy of life or pattern of behavior. I don't see how you could work meaningfully with these people or communicate with them yourself, unless you were aware of their philosophy of life.

GAZAWAY: Their religion, which is about 98 percent Holiness, teaches them that right now may be the end of time. Two minutes from now you may not even be here! That keeps them from looking ahead, because they really believe it. In anything they do, they plan only for the immediate present. For instance, they don't have regular meal patterns, but if they have food in the house in the morning, they eat it. And they have no thought of another meal. If the time comes around, and they're there, they scrounge up another meal, if they can. What we miss, I think, is that we look at these people from a middle-class frame of reference. I'm studying five satellite families from the Gulch that have moved to Danville, Cincinnati, Indianapolis, and Lexington. Many of the things that we have, they have no desire for. For instance, when they look at television and see all the things you spray on your hair, and the curlers you use, and so

[1] Asked to elaborate, Dr. Gazaway sent a clipping from a newspaper. It referred to a series of articles, "Politics in Poverty," in the Scripps-Howard newspapers, revealing that two professional employees of the Letcher County Economic Opportunity Committee had made affidavits charging mismanagement and misconduct in administration of the war on poverty in that county. The newspaper series charged political abuse, nepotism, and mismanagement. The clipping went on to say, "Since the articles appeared, the employees who made the sworn charges have been sacked, and federal officials are scouring the county in an effort to identify jobless men who complained that they were subject to political pressure as the price of continued enrollment in war on poverty programs."—Editor

forth, it means absolutely nothing to a person who doesn't have a comb and never combs her hair.

OPLER: The Indian Service made plans for the Creek Indians to organize a democratic tribal council in which everyone voted. When the plan failed, an anthropologist was allowed to come in at last; he advised them to start with the Indians as they were. He explained that if you let the people organize by themselves, according to their own framework, you may get somewhere. And things just busted loose! Now, in the Gulch, what are the assets? Is it the community feeling? Can they organize locally?

LEWIS: I don't think that the capacity for organization is a native asset. This is the diagnostic structural dimension of what I have called "culture of poverty." The highest level of organization that you find in the native situation is usually that of the bilateral family. That's why you never find the culture of poverty in clan societies, nor in India with the caste system, where in spite of poverty, there is built-in organization, which leads to an entirely different phenomenon. What Marvin [Opler] is asking for is to tackle Gazaway's Branch at its weakest point. To organize beyond the extended family is probably their lowest asset in terms of the native cultural values.

OPLER: I realize that they're worse off than, say, the Creek Indians, in not having what the Creek Indians had, a submerged cultural reservoir that wasn't working but could be made to function again. But if you think that assets of people start and stop with family systems and social organization, I disagree. Society is made up of more than that. I think that a lot of other things are cooking here. But I don't yet see them, except that Dr. Gazaway talks about hospitality. She seems to feel that there are positive things about these people, there are assets; I want to know what they are.

DE VOS: There is another view that can be taken. What I feel is being left out is that this is a maladaptive pattern in the modern world. Its psychological structures are maladaptive; and they don't change very easily. You brought one boy out; and I'm sure that he was selected. You used him as an illustration of what can be done about it. But I think what you demonstrated is that this is *not* what can be done about it, because of the great difficulty you had with one case that was already selected. This kind of living creates its own problems; they don't come only from outside. You've documented a number of exploitative uses of these people by outsiders who've learned to manipulate their inadequacies, which are: they can't handle money, and they can't handle anger. It's maladaptive that they can't even seem to get angry about it. Look at it from a psychological standpoint. The fact that they are being exploited, that predators are feeding on them, shows that somehow they've lost the adaptive mechanisms for self-protection. They may be suspicious of the outside, but they're helpless in the economic world. They're like deer, which can't protect themselves from predators. They seem to have no defense mechanisms built up to cope with their exploitation. I think we need to turn the picture around and look at it from this standpoint: what's wrong with these people that they keep letting outsiders take advantage of them? Why can't they learn to cope with interest? What happens in their upbringing that leaves them incapable of coping with such things?

FINNEY: Dr. Rena Gazaway has done remarkably fine work in her study of the people of the poverty-stricken rural village in Eastern Kentucky. She has come to know these people intimately, and she tells us about them vividly and poignantly. Her combined training in nursing, education, and social science has been of great worth to her, but her greatest asset has been her very warm human understanding and sympathy for these people among whom she has lived.

On June 23, 1964, I spent the day in the Branch with Dr. Gazaway. The country is hilly. She drove her car up the creek-bed, which was nearly dry. It serves as the only street, as well as the open sewer. By that time Dr. Gazaway had been spending much of her time in Gazaway's Branch for two years, and the people in the hamlet knew her well. She arranged for us to have lunch with the family that lived at the very top of the gulch. That family, Dr. Gazaway explained, in spite of some troubles, seemed to have more strengths than any other family in the Branch. Their children went to school more than the children of any other family, even though, living at the top, they had to walk a mile and a half, while the family nearest the highway had less than half a mile to walk.

After lunch, Dr. Gazaway lingered and told me to walk down the gulch without her and to get acquainted with the people I met along the way. A teenage boy and a teenage girl of the family with whom we had lunch walked with me. At most of the houses that we came to, I introduced myself or was introduced by my two companions. The houses were old and decrepit. There was no running water. Some of the houses had small vegetable gardens. Though it was a working day, men were at home at every house. I asked the men what they did for a living. Typically the answer would be, from a man in his forties, "I haven't worked in quite a few years now: my health hasn't been good enough." At one house several healthy young men in their early twenties were sitting on the front porch, swinging. When I asked about his occupation, one of the young men explained to me, "I'm a coal miner. I haven't worked for more than a year now. The mines aren't hiring." It did not occur to him to change to another line of work or to move to another place.

Before and after this visit, Dr. Gazaway told me about the way of life of the Branch. It is not an old community. It was settled within the last forty years. People drifted in, wandered up the creekbed, and built shacks as cheaply as they could. They consider that they own their land. At least nobody is trying to collect rent from them. Land titles are vague, because the land has never been surveyed. Some of the people have their land registered in their names in the county courthouse, unsurveyed as it is, and some of them pay their real estate tax once a year to make their claims good. The property is assessed very low, and five or ten dollars a year may be all the tax. County officials do not foreclose on those who fail to pay their taxes. Indeed, the county officials prefer to ignore Gazaway's Branch altogether.

Almost nobody in the Branch is steadily employed, and nobody really expects to be. Some get odd jobs from time to time. It seems likely that if any man in the Branch became steadily employed, others in the hamlet would criticize him for putting on airs and trying to be better than his neighbors.

Dr. Gazaway told me that the only way the people of Gazaway's Branch compete with each other is to see who can get the biggest pay for not working. There are several sources of pay to the needy, some from the county, some from the state, and some from the federal government. "Commodities," supplied by the county, is about the least. Veterans' compensations and pensions are among the better ones, as is aid to the blind. Almost every family in Gazaway's Branch gets some form of welfare payment, and those that do not are awaiting action on their applications.

Dr. Gazaway knows of a family in the Branch in which the father's ability to work is doubtful. When his first marriage ended, he hastened to marry a young woman and impregnate her. Both husband and wife were in a great hurry to produce five children, the maximum number for which they could be paid ADC (Aid to Dependent Children), twenty dollars a month for each child. Now to you or me it may seem that twenty dollars a month is not nearly enough to support a child. But the people in Gazaway's Branch figure that they can support each child for less than that, and use the profit to support the adult members of the family. So the poorer the people are, the eagerer they are to produce children and get the subsidy. Apparently some change in the system is needed here.

For some kinds of welfare payment, a person must be sick. Some of the complaints are very vague: "I've been feeling poorly lately." Some people have organic disease, as one might expect among people who have low standards of hygiene and sanitation. Tuberculosis spreads, especially within families, because the infected persons refuse to have checkups or treatment. The people of Gazaway's Branch don't trust doctors, even when the medical services are free. When they do see a doctor, it is usually to ask him to sign a paper testifying that they are permanently disabled and need a pension. Though I have not examined people from Gazaway's Branch, I believe that many of them have hysterical conversion reactions, which we see very commonly at our hospital in people from that part of Kentucky. Conversion reactions are supposed to have a primary gain, which is an emotional satisfaction, and sometimes a secondary gain, such as a financial compensation. The secondary gains in these people are clear enough. The primary gains seem likely to be those of dependency, the emotional satisfaction of being taken care of, and more specifically of forcing other people to take care of them. Of course there may be other primary gains, other emotional needs such as oedipal ones in specific cases, but if so we don't usually learn about them.

Hysterical conversion reaction may be considered as an unconscious form of malingering in which a person fools himself as well as fooling other people. True cases of malingering also are known in Gazaway's Branch.

The relationship that has grown up between Dr. Gazaway and the people of Gazaway's Branch is worthy of heed. Some of them believe that she will get the outside world to spend money to help Gazaway's Branch. (What most of them say they want is a paved road into the hollow.) Whether they believe this will happen or not, they see her as a friend. She is a rather high-status friend: she can talk to the county judge as an equal, as none of them can. And yet she doesn't put on airs; she feels at home with the people of Gazaway's Branch and talks to them as one of them, one who knows their language and understands, not as an outsider.

And indeed, Dr. Gazaway has tried to get money to improve Gazaway's Branch. I have sat as a member of a committee representing various departments of the university, including experts in nursing, education, public health, engineering, law, and other fields, to work with Dr. Gazaway's proposals for the Branch. She has sought a grant of five million dollars. The proposal includes building a road, building sanitary sewers, and other public works. Efforts to obtain money under the Johnson poverty program or from other sources were unsuccessful.

Many of us on the committee, too, wondered how we could justify spending five million dollars to improve a community of two hundred people. The county judge says that Gazaway's Branch is only one of thirty similar villages in the county, neither the best nor the worst. And that county is only one of scores of counties in Appalachia. How can we justify pouring all that money into Gazaway's Branch, and not into any of the other thousands of rural slum hamlets in Appalachia? It could be justified, if at all, only if it could show which methods worked and which methods failed to work, so that we could know which ones to generalize and apply elsewhere. It would not be too hard to decide which results to count. Children finishing school and men steadily working and taken off the relief rolls would be a joy to see. A general increase in health and prosperity would be worthwhile. But let us suppose that the measures are applied and some good results happen. When a number of costly measures have been applied at the same time, how are we to tell which ones have brought the good results about? It is necessary to be selective, because we can't plan to spend five million dollars in every impoverished community of two hundred people. From the welfare point of view it would be easier to divide the five million dollars among the two hundred people, giving $25,000 to every man, woman, and child, and to move them to some other parts of the country where the roads and sewers are already built.

In how she feels and what she does toward the people of the Branch, Dr. Gazaway is like a good parent. She is a warm, loving, affectionate parent, who is pleased when her children are happy and sad when they suffer. She is also something of the disciplinary parent, who urges them, scolds them, and even, on rare occasions, forces them. Once she went to the county judge and got him to order a tuberculous man to a hospital for an examination. The judge was known never to have exercised that prerogative before, but evidently felt that he would not be criticized for doing so when it was on petition from Dr. Gazaway.

Like any good parent, Dr. Gazaway protects and defends her "children" in public and scolds them in private. She has often expressed to me her annoyance that these people will not do the things that are obviously for their own good. They will not send their children to school, but prefer to keep them at home. They will not take the simplest precautions of health and sanitation. They resist change, and they continue to do self-defeating things, which perpetuate their "sick" way of life.

When she is feeling frustrated or exasperated, Dr. Gazaway remarks to me that she herself came from a family and a village much like this in the Ozark Mountains, but her family, by persistent effort, pulled itself up out of poverty. She wishes that she could get the people of Gazaway's Branch to do the same; and indeed she is always pushing them to do just that. In terms of the three personality factors that I have described elsewhere, Dr. Gazaway's family succeeded because its members were low in the A factor (that is, they were not neurotic and self-defeating, but were self-advancing) and were high in the C factor (that is, they were compulsive, consistent, and systematic, and could plan to get their satisfaction from anticipation of the future rather than immediately). In contrast, the people of Gazaway's Branch stay in misery because they are high in the A factor; that is, they feel severely disappointed in their dependency needs and their wishes to be taken care of; they picture the world as unrewarding, and they perpetuate this picture by behaving in masochistic ways that bring defeat on themselves. And they are low on the factor of compulsiveness: they don't plan far ahead, they don't keep working consistently toward distant goals.

When a person feels altogether deprived and cheated by the world, he may get revenge by making himself utterly helpless, so that the world is forced to take care of him, to subsidize him at the minimum subsistence level. This is a neurotic and masochistic satisfaction. A person who takes this course cripples himself and hurts himself more than he hurts the rest of the world.

Dr. Gazaway wavers between seeing the people of Gazaway's Branch as innocent victims of unscrupulous outsiders, and seeing them as people who defeat themselves by their own actions.

Three weeks ago Dr. Gazaway remarked to me somewhat as

follows. "Those people in Washington think they can solve the problems of poverty by giving people money. But I asked them, 'Money to spend for what?' They answered, 'To spend for the things that you and I spend for.' But that doesn't work. When you give them money they don't spend it for what you and I spend it for. They don't use the money for their own good. Pretty soon the money is all spent and there is nothing to show for it. And in a few months' time they are just as poor as they were before. Giving them money won't solve the poverty problem, unless you mean to keep giving them money month after month forever. What we need to do is teach these people to use money in a way that will benefit them."

Having heard that, I expected Dr. Gazaway to come to the conference today and tell us about the Branch as a community in which the people are defeating themselves. Instead, she has switched. She has told us about the Branch as a group of people who are being cheated, who are being taken unfair advantage of by shrewd and unscrupulous people outside. And I am sure that there is much truth in what she says. These are only two aspects of our self-perpetuating cycle of misery. Nor is Dr. Gazaway being seriously inconsistent with herself. Like a good parent, she is defending her "children" here in the rather public situation of this conference, and waiting to scold them when she is alone with them. Let us join with Dr. Gazaway in examining the self-perpetuating cycles of this self-defeating way of life, and ask at what phases in the cycle we can intervene.

Any intervention is bound to meet some resistance. The accompanying diagram shows why. The upward direction is discomfort, and the downward direction is relief or satisfaction. Consider the diagram as a cross section of terrain. Any people settles on the way of life that is locally the most satisfying (or, in our model, lower than any immediately surrounding point). Even a highly dissatisfying way of life such as that of Gazaway's Branch is chosen because it is less dissatisfying than other choices that lie immediately around. (Perhaps these same points could be made more elegantly through approach-avoidance conflict dia-

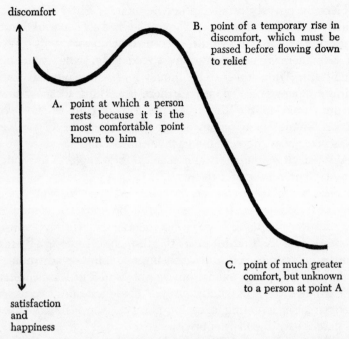

discomfort

B. point of a temporary rise in discomfort, which must be passed before flowing down to relief

A. point at which a person rests because it is the most comfortable point known to him

C. point of much greater comfort, but unknown to a person at point A

satisfaction
and
happiness

grams, or through Lewin's topological and vector diagrams, but the terrain cross section seems to make the point.) What we would like to do is help the people of Gazaway's Branch find a more satisfying way of life. To do so, they must first cut themselves loose from their existing satisfactions, and go through a temporary rise in their anxieties and dissatisfactions. This is a schematic representation of the reasons why people generally resist changes, especially when they cannot see clearly where the changes are leading them. The present dissatisfactions are at least known, and known to be tolerable, and one may not be sure that a change will be for the better.[2]

[2] Furthermore, as we know from the study of masochism and self-defeating behavior, when a person has learned to find rewards and pleasures only in a context of suffering, the suffering itself becomes a reward, an incentive, or a learned (secondary) drive, and so the person is motivated to keep producing his own sufferings in a so-called repetition compulsion.—Editor

As an example, we can be sure that any comprehensive plan prepared by any reputable authority to rehabilitate Gazaway's Branch will include an end to truancy, requiring the children to attend school. The parents will oppose any changes for the same reasons that they have been keeping the children at home already, whatever these reasons may be, perhaps because they like their children's companionship and see no value in education, which they didn't have themselves; perhaps because they sense that their children, if educated, would become alien to them. The children, too, can be expected to resist being forced to go to school when they are used to staying at home. We believe that in the long run the changes will bring greater satisfactions to these people's lives, but in the short run they will bring dissatisfactions. The same may be true of health and sanitation measures. The same may be true of getting adult men back to school for training so that they can qualify for jobs. The same may be true of getting people to think of themselves as healthy and able to work when they are used to thinking of themselves as sick and disabled. It is too much to expect these people to take the initiative to break free of their self-defeating ways of life. It will take people like Dr. Gazaway to inspire them, to push them, to lead them, and to help them tolerate the temporary increase in discomfort that must accompany the way to a healthy and more satisfying way of life.[3]

DE VOS: You said that Dr. Gazaway's family got out of the situation. But it was not so much getting out of the situation as getting the situation out of themselves.

FINNEY: Right.

OPLER: Immigrant groups that I've studied show many stories like that. People took advantage of them. And yet they pulled themselves out of it. There were reservoirs in the culture that

[3] The increased discomfort is temporary provided that masochistic, self-punishing urges have not become deeply set and fixed. Masochism is difficult to eradicate by new learning, and a person with this neurotic sickness may fail to learn to find healthy satisfactions in a way of life that is objectively more rewarding, even after long exposure to it. In terms of the diagram, he has a deep valley and a higher ridge to overcome.—Editor

were tapped—including, in the case of the Japanese, sweating it out, working hard, mobilizing their energies for particular purposes. You can't tell me that these people of the Gulch don't have assets, or that their "aspiration levels" are simply bad. How do they compete with each other? What gives them prestige?

GAZAWAY: Who can catch the first groundhog in the spring? They'll lay off work, and they'll troop through the hills to see who can catch the first groundhog. Who catches it with gloves on, and who catches it with gloves off? They spend the whole summer trying to see who can catch the biggest rattlesnake, the one that has the most rattles. And sharing gives them prestige, too. And my living among them gave them prestige.

LEWIS: On the basis of your intimate understanding of this community, your close identification with them, and your knowledge of so many specific families, how would you characterize their way of life and their mental health? Do you feel that these are sick people? Or that they have excellent mental health?

GAZAWAY: With this audience you're really putting me on the spot. If I take mental health and divorce it completely from the psychiatric frame of reference, I think they do have a degree of mental health.

LEWIS: Do you think their way of life is really satisfying?

[Dr. Gazaway hesitated.]

LEWIS: You didn't sound it. I felt that you identified emotionally with a terribly oppressed, exploited minority group who weren't getting what they deserved, and I assumed that you felt that it wasn't a very satisfying way of life, this little culture that they have.

GAZAWAY: Well, I think it isn't, really. It depends on whether you define the word *satisfying* in our frame of reference, or in theirs. They are happy, if people don't come into the hollow. Now, is that mental ill-health?

LEWIS: They are content with their lives?

GAZAWAY: Midst those of their own kind.

LEWIS: They're not anxious to leave the hollow?

GAZAWAY: They hate leaving. I could tell you of a family that

I'm studying now in Cincinnati which lives in one of our most deplorable slums. [Dr. Gazaway told a story of a woman who complained of the cockroaches, "When I lived in the hollow those were my roaches. But I don't know *who these* belong to."]

LEWIS: There are a few theoretical points that we can tease out of this situation. We in anthropology have perpetuated a myth by our terminology and our definitions, namely, that whatever we call a culture or a subculture (a way of life that persists from one generation to another) is a satisfying way of life. Well, I've discovered in my studies of slums in many parts of the world that this culture, or subculture, of poverty can persist without being satisfying to its members. The reason they don't do anything about it is not that it's not tension-producing, anxiety-producing, and so on, but that the alternatives (as Dr. Finney said) are even more anxiety-producing. As you've described life in the hollow, it probably doesn't seem a good way of life even to the people themselves.

GAZAWAY: I agree with you. The county that I'm talking about is dry; in the hollow if a man wants a drink he has to get moonshine, or liquor that is illegally brought over the county line, usually by the officials, and drinks it at home; in Cincinnati he would go to a bar. And when he's not at home the wife can't find him, unlike in the hollow. Their world is one block square. They're afraid of city lights and traffic. No car goes up the hollow faster than five miles an hour. In the hollow they don't have to worry about things that are real problems for them in the city.

DE VOS: What is mental health? In some definitions it's the capacity to adapt to new situations, not to be caught in rigid, inflexible patterns. Isn't it a sign of mental ill-health in the community that they seem to lack the capacity for adaptation?

GAZAWAY: If you get down to specifics, they're very adaptable. They're flexible. If they have food, they eat it. If they don't, they don't eat.

OPLER: If your fingers are burned whenever you touch the outside, that's good enough conditioning to stay in the hollow. You've intimated that there are meaningful relationships inside; not ones that we'd find delectable, but we're talking about what the people live by. We have to start with them where they are, what they respond to.

GAZAWAY: There's never been a suicide that I can find in any of the hollows. There are two or three persons I'd call psychotic. But they are accepted in the community. The others don't take them to a doctor. They'll hide them in the hills if they think anybody's going to come after them. To them, they're just different.

HUGHES: Let's narrow the question of mental health down to the matter of short-term versus long-term gratification. Given the conditions in which these people live, a denial of the feasibility of long-term planning is adaptive. You don't know whether you'll have food for lunch, so don't count on it. Eat what you have now. But we generally say that planning for the future, thinking in terms of long-range gratification rather than taking every gratification now, is part of good mental health. Some of it is necessary for survival of the species. I should think that even in the hollow, though what they do may be adaptive in the short run, it is a maladaptive or unhealthy way of dealing with the total life situation. There is more that is possible. They don't reach their full potential.

FINNEY: I've heard it said before, that for anyone who is poverty-stricken the necessary and practical point of view is to take the short-range point of view, *carpe diem*, to grab each enjoyment while you can, and not to take the long-range viewpoint of thrift. But I'm skeptical, because I've heard just the opposite to explain the thrift of the Japanese peasant: that anyone so poor as that has to take the long-range viewpoint, has to be thrifty to survive.

DE VOS: In state mental hospitals, some people adjust to institutionalization. They adapt very nicely to being taken care of; they resist being sent out. Is that desirable? I think not. Your people in the hollow are like that. If their life habits are such that they can't cope with some things outside the hollow, the wider society can take one of two stands on it: either intervene or let them be. But you're trying to take both stands at once. You want to get the poverty program in to them in order to change them. Yet when we suggest the idea of change, you turn around and say that we shouldn't try to change these people, that they are adjusted. Well, you can't have it both ways. You can't ask us both to change them and not to change them. Either you must accept their way of life as a pattern that can be encapsulated and stay as it is, or if you want to change it you must look at the whole situation, both what these people are doing to themselves and what outsiders are doing to them.

FINNEY: George, what you're pointing out is masochism; it's neuroticism. You're saying that people punish themselves, make trouble for themselves, cripple themselves, create their own deprivations, or at least perpetuate them needlessly, when they don't have to from any outward necessity, only from within themselves. That's one of the hardest points for a behavioral scientist to get across to a social scientist. By a behavioral scientist I mean a psychologist, or a psychiatrist, or a psychoanalyst, or perhaps a cultural anthropologist, someone who studies the interactions of persons in small face-to-face groups, and who knows something about the motivations, the control systems of individuals. By a social scientist I mean an economist, or a political scientist, or perhaps a sociologist, someone who studies the interactions of nations, or of economic systems, and can do so without needing to know much about individual human beings. The social scientists generally assume that each individual will do whatever is in his own best interest, at least if enough information is available to him. Under that assumption, if someone is suffering, it must be because someone else is harming him. As behavioral scientists we know that this isn't so. People don't act rationally in their own best interests; people do things that hurt themselves; people will sacrifice their so-called objective economic interests in favor of satisfying some emotional needs. Those needs may be either values common to the culture or values specific to the individual. In either case they may or may not be neurotic and self-defeating ones. The cultural anthropologist or the psychiatrist may tell the economist that offering "rational" economic incentives isn't enough to change people's ways of doing things. But the social scientists won't listen to us and won't believe us. That's why our national efforts to help people or to influence people in Southeast Asia, in India, and in Africa are failing. Our government programs rely on economic measures and pay no heed to what the cultural anthropologist, the psychiatrist, or the psychologist could contribute. Man does not live by bread alone. But maybe the only way to become convinced of the powerful masochistic motives that govern human behavior is to practice psychotherapy for a while.

MARGETTS: Dr. Gazaway, these people of the hollow probably don't regard themselves as poverty-stricken at all. You do.

GAZAWAY: I have no qualms about the poverty program getting in there. It won't get near!

[Someone asked whether the schools perpetuate those values. Dr. Gazaway said that rural Kentucky has the poor teachers that have stayed behind, while the good teachers have gone elsewhere for better pay. In the Headstart program this summer, Cincinnati has an intensive program based on a multidisciplinary plan, while in the rural Kentucky county children and teachers simply showed up with no plan. Many children don't begin school until they are 9 or 10 or even 11 ("drop-in," as well as dropout).]

DE VOS: You keep shifting base. First you say, let's be relativistic; there are virtues in their way of living; let 'em keep it. Then you say, let's educate them, let's make them attend school and learn a better way of life. By educating them you'll change their culture; it's unavoidable. You can't have it both ways. You must take a stand on what you want, on what way you want to interfere with these people. And then, if you take the position that education is needed, you must look at what there is in these people, psychologically, that keeps them from getting educated.

FINNEY: Dr. Gazaway, you were thinking along the same lines a couple of weeks ago. Today you said that the trouble is that the money isn't trickling down to these people. But before, you told me that if you could pour money into these people's pockets, the problem still wouldn't be solved, because they'd keep the same values, they wouldn't plan ahead or save any money to advance themselves or educate themselves, and that unless you put them on a permanent subsidy they'd be back in poverty as soon as you quit pouring the money in. Now if that is so, the conclusion is clear. It is a mistake to treat the problem as primarily economic and social, to deal with it by social science engineering, and to try to cure poverty by pouring money into people's pockets. Instead, we need to treat it as a psychological problem, a motivational problem, and we need to deal with it by behavioral science engineering. That means putting the primary emphasis on changing the individual human beings, their attitudes, skill, values, wishes, goals, and ideals in life. That's something that can only be done in face-to-face groups, by conventional education, by individual and group counseling and psychotherapy, and perhaps by newer methods yet to be sharpened.

GAZAWAY: Those are the two sides of the coin. Both are true. I don't know how much good money would do, if they don't know how to spend it or how to save it. I don't know which you do first: give them a chance to make money or try to teach them how to handle it. But I know that when they do have some money, someone charges them an excessive amount for what they buy.

DE VOS: That's exactly what needs to be examined. You told us that the storekeeper sells food to everyone at different prices.[4] I'm sure he's a good psychologist and knows how much he can victimize each individual. He knows those who will resist and those who won't. If you look at his prices for each person, you can get a pretty good assessment of the psychological capacities (of certain kinds) in each person in that community, because some

[4] He refers to Dr. Gazaway's narration while showing slides, not included here.—Editor

people won't tolerate exploitation and others will. Resisting exploitation is part of the defense structure of an adaptive human being. If they're being exploited, there's deficiency in a psychological capacity.

GAZAWAY: Okay, but they exploit each other, too. It's not only the people on the outside that do it.

DE VOS: All right! Now you're telling something that you haven't mentioned before. Exploitation is part of the community pattern itself. Dr. Gazaway is like a kaleidoscope. Every time you shake her you get a different picture.

FINNEY: You've also told me that these people of the hollow exploit the outsiders, too, in cheating their way onto the relief rolls, isn't that so?

GAZAWAY: They have all kinds of techniques that are very effective.

DE VOS: Then one of the things to look at is, who gets victimized? There you have all sorts of mental health problems. Why should one fellow get victimized all the time? There's something wrong with his psychological workings. If others learn to cheat, you'd think that he'd learn to cheat more effectively in that culture.

FINNEY: Let me make another comment on Dr. Prince's paper. Ray, you mentioned Schofield and his "Yavis" syndrome. I think he's not altogether fair to psychotherapy as a profession in our culture. Let's examine his points one at a time.

Young? Yes, patients in psychotherapy do tend to be young. That's natural, because psychotherapy is a kind of education. I say that with some trepidation, because we all know that psychotherapy differs in some important ways from classroom education; a didactic approach won't work. Still, in a broad sense psychotherapy is a way of helping people to learn, to change some of the long-lasting tendencies in a person that govern his responding in certain ways to certain stimulus situations. We prefer to give psychotherapy early in life for the same reason that we prefer to give classroom education early in life: so that a person can benefit from it sooner and longer. When a person gets some education late in life we admire him for it, but we also feel that it's a shame he didn't get it earlier.

Attractive? Fortunately, not all of us find the same persons attractive, or the same persons unattractive. And, also fortunately, some of us have the urge to help the unfortunate person whom most people have found unattractive. In general, it's helpful if a therapist likes his patients, so long as this liking is not a strong personal attraction or emotional involvement.

Verbal? Intelligent? Certainly. In deciding which persons to encourage to undertake a learning process that depends partly on the use of words, it's quite proper to consider the individual's capability for this kind of learning. The treatment should fit the person treated. Psychotherapy is not the treatment of choice for everybody. We don't put everybody into psychotherapy any more than we'd put everybody into graduate school.

Successful? I think Schofield missed the point here. A person who is fully successful doesn't need psychotherapy. Psychoneurosis is something self-defeating, in which a person blocks himself needlessly from the success of which he is capable. What gives us most pleasure is to work with a patient who can become successful as a result of our treatment. It's a great satisfaction to work with a patient who has a potentiality for success, but who is unwittingly blocking himself and making trouble for himself, because of emotional problems. When you see a person like this blossom out in psychotherapy, grow out of his emotional problems, and begin to manage his life more successfully, it gives you a strong feeling of satisfaction: you know that as a psychotherapist you are doing some good in the world.

If Schofield means financially successful, it is true that the economics of private practice is such that most of the patients are fairly well off; but psychotherapists find every bit as much satisfaction in publicly supported clinics, in working with appropriate patients who are not well off financially. It's true that such patients tend to be the underpaid white-collar workers, but some of them are blue-collar workers, too.

I once ran the community mental health clinic at Urbana and

Champaign, Illinois. A certain portion of our patients were poor, starving, struggling graduate students, or their wives or children. Young people struggling along ambitiously with little or no income, trying to get ahead, making sacrifices in the present for the sake of the future. That's a poverty-stricken group that is seldom noticed. It's a group I have a lot of sympathy with.

minority group
identity

George A. De Vos

Comparative psychological anthropology today is uncovering functional parallels among various societies in the psychological effects of minority-group status.[1] There are to be found, in many social settings, differential responses by particular minority groups to socially defined patterns of occupational and social success or failure. These success patterns are inescapable definitions that hold for the total society of which any particular minority group forms one part. More and more, national-political entities must cope with the social and psychological effects of their pluralistic ethnic composition. The vicissitudes of history are producing more situations in which one finds a national society composed of both advantaged and disadvantaged minorities. Many of these situations of advantage and disadvantage can be traced rather directly to the unequal distribution of economic and political power. But it is an oversimplification to attempt to analyze all disadvantaged or advantaged status positions held by minority group members solely in instrumental political-economic terms. The internal psychosocial dynamics—the social self-identity patterns, collective and individual, which develop within minority groups—are passed on as subcultural patterns. Being reinforced and internalized in this way, the patterns persist even when they can no longer be considered as reasonably appropriate responses to the current objective situation. They must, therefore, be seriously studied as subcultural patterns, if we are to understand the course of events occurring in further social change.

Since the subject of this volume is related to questions of the disadvantaged, I shall not deal even indirectly with those mechanisms at work in situations in which an ethnic or social minority finds itself in some form of advantage by means of economic or social innovation (Hagan, 1962). Rather I shall concern myself with the relative failure in one social group—the former outcastes of Japan. As among similar traditionally disparaged groups elsewhere, one finds in this group relatively poor scholastic performance, as well as a number of difficulties arising from a type of social self-identity that raises barriers between members of this segregated enclave and the ameliorative or sanctioning social agencies set up by the majority society.

Hiroshi Wagatsuma and I have recently (1966) published the results of our investigation of the Japanese former outcaste ethnic minority in Japan. Our results indicate, in a number of dimensions, parallel functioning between this minority group and that of the American Negro in the United States. Both groups show various forms of social deviancy and relative failure in the attainment of occupational and educational success. Both groups suffer disadvantages and debilitations that result from the direct effects of discrimination. And, more important for our purposes, both groups also show internal debilitations resulting from the "mark of oppression" found branded on the very personality of many members of these groups which have suffered discrimination through a number of generations (Kardiner, 1962).

Like American Negroes, the Japanese outcaste schoolchildren make lower scores than their classmates on intelligence and achievement tests. Yet the Japanese outcastes are no different racially from other Japanese. This finding suggests that the low scores of American Negroes are the result of subcultural psycho-

[1] This paper is based on a more extensive presentation of materials (De Vos and Wagatsuma, 1966). Our research on delinquency and social deviancy in Japan was sponsored by a grant of the National Institute of Mental Health, Bethesda, Maryland. Some phases of our primary research on the Japanese outcaste were made possible through the able assistance of Mr. Yuzuru Susuki.

logical factors and not of biological, racial ones. Also like the American Negroes, the Japanese outcastes are less likely to find jobs than are other young people of equal achievement in school (especially in the low achievement range). And when one does get a job with a promising future, he is likely to give it up for personal reasons.

Both Japanese and American cultures stress hard work, thrift, ambition, persistence, and achievement. It is an implicit assumption in both present-day American and Japanese economic-social ideology that all members of the society assume the value of personal goal achievement as a means toward the realization of social goals, and that all children will be motivated positively to equip themselves for upward social mobility—or, if they are already of a family of higher status, to seek actualization through their own efforts toward a continuance of this status. Status, in both America and Japan, is, generally speaking, considered to be something that one attains rather than that which one receives by means of some hereditary ascription.

As a number of social scientists have pointed out in comparing the ideology with the actuality, social mobility for some groups within American society is a fairly uncommon happening. There are psychological as well as sociological limiting factors that differentially prevent some groups from realizing such commonly held implicit goals of achievement. Even assuming that there is indeed no full sharing in all groups of the social definitions of success, deviations from optimal expectations are especially apparent in some ethnic minorities. There may be barriers of caste or social segregation; or there may be geographic-social barriers that have led to the isolation of particular communities. The latter situation, in turn, leads to peculiarities in early and later socialization experiences that make it difficult for members of such communities to function effectively in roles defined as successful by the outside majority society.

It is therefore sometimes much too quickly assumed that difficulties encountered by a given isolated or segregated social segment result from their not sharing the general values of the society by which they are judged as functioning poorly. The contrary may actually be the case. Members of an economically or socially depressed group are often painfully aware of their plight and may indeed feel considerable self-disparagement over their collective or individual incapacity to alter conditions. People with a minority self-identity may defensively, in some overt ways, deny any acceptance of the achievement values of the majority, but their very behavior often belies their claims. They may be having trouble just because they have come to be influenced by the ideas and standards of the majority. The majority has become a reference group for them, and they care what the majority thinks, though they deny it.

Wagatsuma and I (1966, pp. 222-40) have discussed how one must be equally aware of a number of social-psychological determinants of behavior related to the continuity of minority groups as socially segregated entities in a pluralistic society. Besides the obvious continuing influence of the discrimination exercised by the majority toward the minority are five interrelated factors within the minority group which help maintain apartness from the majority.

Differential socialization occurs within the primary family and within the intimate social group. Differences in basic socialization (or upbringing) can radically influence how the social world is perceived and how individuals are able or unable to cope with the socially sanctioned demands of the majority group about intellectual and motor behavior. Coping mechanisms or defense mechanisms are part of the basic ego structure or personality structure of the individual, and so these things also vary from one group to another, depending mostly on the methods of child rearing.

These factors determine how role expectations are defined by the majority society and within the minority social group itself. These role expectations help guide behavior from one generation to the next. A person tends to do what other people expect him to do.

These expectations are continually guided by a third general factor, the influence of the "reference group" on the individual. The influence of the immediate reference group depends on a number of complicated identifications occurring during childhood socialization, including the degree to which moral structures are internalized early, and their degree of rigidity. The nature of early internalizations that have formed a person's character help determine the manner in which his behavior can be influenced by the way that groups of people around him define the situations.

Another perspective on minority-group behavior is gained by considering it in terms of self-identity. Self-identity is shaped and supported by the nature of the social reference group, as well as by a basic continuity in the modified functioning of ego mechanisms which were developed within the primary family. Social self-identity (or the way that a person sees himself relating to other people) helps determine the choices that a person makes among alternative means of coping with his environment.

Finally, there are what I have termed differences in "permeability" related to the defensive functions of the ego which allow a selective impermeability to experience to occur in relationships between majority- and minority-group individuals. Individuals within a minority group who are in contact with members of the majority society are nevertheless progressively shaped into a given minority social identity by the selective taking in of social experiences. An automatic means of maintaining social distance operates in maintaining one's self-identity. The individual becomes automatically impermeable to potential ego-disruptive influences that would occur if he too readily identified with the behavior of the majority group. The individual in this manner protects himself from internal conflicts that would occur, for example, if he were being "reached" by a teacher in school. Many minority children are impermeable to what a majority teacher seeks to instill in them.

Hiroshi Wagatsuma and I found all these variables operative in the social plight experienced by many members of Japan's former pariah caste, which now numbers more than two million. The parallels to social degradation suffered and the modes of response taken show a number of interesting similarities to those of the American Negro minority.

THE JAPANESE PARIAH: A HISTORICAL INCIDENCE OF CASTE

Before discussing these similarities further, I think that some introduction to the nature of caste in Japan is necessary (Price, 1966). In today's Japan there are at least six thousand urban and rural ghettos, numbering over two million inhabitants called in neutral, nonpejorative Japanese, "special communities" (*tokushu Buraku*), inhabited by *tokushu Burakumin* ("people of special communities"). The contraction *Burakumin* ("community people") has become the neutral term now applied to these former pariahs. Feelings about the former Japanese outcastes today are every bit as strong as attitudes held by many Americans toward Negroes; they resemble also the attitudes of members of higher castes in India toward the former untouchable groups (Isaacs, 1965).

The present day *Burakumin* are subject to many covert forms of social and economic discrimination. We have documented (1966, pp. 113-28) the impoverishment in these communities and also the types of job discrimination practiced toward members of urban ghettos. Socially, attitudes toward intermarriage are no less severe than those held by whites in this country about the marriage between a white and a Negro. They share in a general negative stereotyping. They are considered by the majority Japanese to be intellectually dull, disorderly, rude, violently aggressive, and physically unclean. They are considered to be alien in origin to the majority Japanese and to be somehow of biologically inferior stock. Yet historical or physical anthropological investigation finds no basis for this belief.

In 1872 the outcastes were granted citizenship. Henceforth, the "new citizens" (*shin heimin*) were to be counted as human beings in the census, whereas before they were tabulated separately as a distinct subhuman species. As far as can be determined the *Burakumin* are descendents of generations of outcastes whose origins shade off into prehistory. The outcasting phenomenon in Japan is a continuous one. It is interesting to note that the *Burakumin* now form a larger proportion of the Japanese population than they did at the time of their emancipation. This increase is not solely from greater birthrate, but must also be attributed to the fact that individuals become outcastes if they continue to associate occupationally and socially with members of an outcaste group.

During the feudal Tokugawa period and immediately before the beginning of Japanese modernization, there were two kinds of outcastes. The *Hinin* ("nonpeople") were itinerant entertainers, mediums, fortunetellers, mendicants, and prostitutes. They assisted with the execution of criminals and the disposal of corpses. Sometimes they were engaged in seemingly nonpolluting occupations such as the building of gardens and houses. The *Eta* ("full of filth") were hereditary occupational groups who had ritually impure activities, many of which centered around the killing of animals and the processing of leather. Some other occupations, such as basketmaking, were also classified as outcaste activities, for obscure reasons.

MINORITY STATUS AND SOCIAL DEVIANCY:
THE CASE OF THE BURAKUMIN

It is cross-culturally apparent that one of the general effects of continuous social discrimination toward a subordinate minority group is to induce the continuance of a separate social self-identity. This self-identity may include potentials either for retreat from contract or, if contact with the majority is necessary or expedient, for an assumption of deviant social roles vis-a-vis the majority society. These deviant roles often contain a great deal of covert hostility expressed toward any form of authority exercised by members of the majority group. Such feelings are continually reconditioned into automatic responses as they are reinforced by generations of experience of exploitation.

Patterns of discrimination practiced against the former Japanese outcaste did not, of course, disappear once the outcastes were theoretically integrated as new citizens. They continued to suffer degradation at the hands of some government officials, the police, and teachers in the schools. Traditional patterns of interaction could not be changed by acts of reconciliation and good will on the part of some majority-group members. Nor is their lot, generally speaking, much better as a result of the enlightenment of the civil authorities and educational personnel. A "psychological lag" is apparent within the outcaste group in spite of the considerable lessening of overt forms of discrimination on the part of majority citizens.

The adverse effects of differential socialization experiences still contribute to early psychological disadvantage. Children brought up n some of the urban *Buraku* are exposed to conditions of social life that are internalized and perpetuated rather than overcome. Such disadvantage deepens with age and with the development and reinforcement of debilitating negative self-attitudes. In school performance one finds indirect evidence of mute resistance and defensive disinterest of *Buraku* children in the learning process documented in a number of Japanese studies.

The reason is not that the Japanese outcaste community does not value education. It is wrong to assume that members of all disparaged disadvantaged minorities simply find no advantage in education and do not encourage their children to do well in school. In some groups at certain times, such as among the American Indians, there is obvious resistance to school programs on the part of the community. The resistance often occurred because such programs were systematically set up to "improve the Indian" and, in effect, were seeking to destroy what minority cultural values remained and to alienate children from their parents. On the other hand, one can also document the active desire for education in urban American Negroes, Mexican-Americans in California, and other groups such as the Maori in New Zealand. Yet children from these groups continue to do rather poorly in school.

To illustrate, Margaret Clark (1959) cites some case material that presents very poignantly how the Mexican-American peer reference group demands disinterest or hostility toward school subjects. Such disinterest goes against the expressed attitudes and hopes of parents. But it takes place because teachers and the entire educative machinery are identified with the outer "Anglo world" by minority-group children. Patterns of resistance negate the learning process for most. In addition to the influence of the reference group in this negation, factors of differential socialization, minority-role expectations, social self-identity, and the automatic selective permeability of experience cited above can be found implicit throughout Clark's material.

These various factors were either directly or indirectly documented in our interviews and secondary materials gathered about the *Burakumin* in Japan (De Vos and Wagatsuma, 1966, pp. 260 ff.). A number of studies done by educators and psychologists in Japan demonstrate the relatively poor grades, achievement scores, and performances on IQ tests by children of this minority group. For example, in one comparison reported by Tojo (1960) approximately 350 fifth- and sixth-grade school children, living in a community near Osaka, were tested with the Tanaka-Binet. Twenty-three percent of the majority Japanese children had scores of 125 or above, whereas 10 percent scored below 76. Among the *Buraku* children on the other hand, 2.6 percent scored above 125 and 37.6 percent scored below 76. This study—and others—patently demonstrates the functional intellectual debilitation of the *Buraku* child brought up in a *Buraku* ghetto.

There is apparent in some urban *Buraku* (but not in others) a differential socialization experience. The child experiences and witnesses from his earliest years a different sort of life style—a different use of intellect and ways of conceptualizing his world. He learns a different set of behavioral expectancies. There is, for example, open witnessing of sexual behavior by children in many situations. The sexual environment is perhaps not as chaotic and hostile as that reported by Oscar Lewis (1966) among the Puerto Ricans in New York, but certainly the early experiences of *Burakumin* children are far different from those occurring among middle-class Japanese.

The general role expectations of outcastes (as in the parallel case of American Negroes) become defined in such a way, both by members of the majority group and by themselves, that it takes a great deal of extra zeal and energy to counter these negative expectations and to play an unexpected role in society. Such extra exertion is not required of a member of a majority group who aspires to the same role. A succession of rebuffs or temporary failures experienced by a youth seeking an occupational career is likely to produce acceptance of failure more readily by an outcaste, who has already learned to expect failure, than by a member of a majority group, who interprets such setbacks as unusual and indeed temporary, to be overcome by persistence.

The subtleties of how, as well as when, a social self-identity becomes established are difficult to document. We have no direct evidence of how this process occurs among *Burakumin* children. We do have, however, some retrospective data on how some individuals at a fairly early age become self-consciously aware of their outcaste status. We also have some indirect evidence of both conscious and unconscious negative self-images and how they interfere with optimum psychological functioning (De Vos and Wagatsuma, 1966, pp. 231-40). The *Burakumin* data are consistent with the findings in respect to the American Negro reported by Kardiner and Ovesey in *The Mark of Oppression* (1962).

One of the defensive maneuvers readily available to a minority-group individual is to give up trying—either to sink into some form of diffuse apathy, or, if more mobilized by hostility, to discredit the generally held goals. Self-identity with a submerged group that is characterized by the majority of society as worthless makes it easier to set up deviant standards for oneself. A general pervasive apathy may become part of one's social self-image that finds constant ready reinforcement in similar attitudes held by one's peers. Conversely, to continue to try or to accept the goals set up by the majority culture is to develop a self-image that isolates the individual from his own group without insuring any direct acceptance on the part of the discriminating majority.

As among minority groups in the United States, the rate of truancy and of dropping-out of school are exceedingly high among the *Burakumin* (De Vos and Wagatsuma, 1966, pp. 263-65).

PROBLEMS OF PASSING

We can cite a number of stories of a painful psychological state experienced by the *Burakumin* person who tries to "pass." He lives in a situation of painful hiding, fearing exposure if he should be in any way identified with other *Burakumin.* A *Burakumin* poet, Maruoka Tadao expresses it well (De Vos and Wagatsuma, 1966, p. 250):

WHY FLEE?

At one time
Alone, in a land of strangers,
I denied my childhood home.

Peter denied his Lord thrice.
How many more times did I deny
My humble place of birth?

Constantly threatened by an unknown lurking shadow,
An oppressive weight cutting off my breath,
I dwell alone, in a strange land,
Fearing to meet my kind, like a crab,
Ready to scurry away in dread of contact.

The passing *Burakumin* cannot easily marry for a variety of reasons, the principal one being that the family records of the prospective bride and groom are usually compared by a go-between before any steps are taken, and it is therefore extremely difficult to conceal an outcaste origin. In other respects, too, the problems of passing, even should one achieve educational success, outweigh the advantages for many *Burakumin.* There are many reported stories of the personal tragedies that occur among those who dare to take this path out (De Vos and Wagatsuma, 1966, pp. 241-57).

Deviant Attitudes Toward Civil Authority Members of traditionally despised minority groups develop less incentive to internalize a conformist attitude toward civil authority and legal codes. Deviant standards can sometimes, on the symbolic level at least, balance out against the overt advantages of the majority. Such deviant ways of getting back at the majority become part of a covert heritage. Ways of outwitting or getting around authorities become part of the defensive maneuvers that are learned and practiced toward majority individuals perceived to be in positions of official power. Wounded and injured self-esteem is salved to some extent by "advantaging" oneself at the expense of the majority group in small ways. It should come as no surprise, therefore, that welfare programs are manipulated by members of the minority group, as well as by the majority society.

Not only is such deviancy true to some extent in regard to programs of economic welfare among the urban *Burakumin,* but this attitude, to their own detriment, makes for an impermeable defense against programs of public health when other people initiate such programs on behalf of the outcastes (De Vos and Wagatsuma, 1966, pp. 269-71). As a result, health authorities are puzzled by both the resistance and the apathy that they encounter in trying to treat the large amount of trachoma and other eye diseases endemic in some *Buraku* communities.

A number of outcastes eventually follow deviant careers as members of outlaw gangs or as prostitutes—occupations in which past family affiliations are not as closely scrutinized as in regular jobs. A higher delinquency rate among minority-group youth is another symptom of the development of such deviant social attitudes. In an investigation of the case files of the Kobe Family Court, we found a delinquency rate three and one half times higher for children of outcaste origin, and seven times higher among Korean children, than for the majority group (De Vos and Wagatsuma, 1966, pp. 266-69).

The high rate among Koreans is not surprising since they, too, are a generally disparaged minority in Japan, suffering many of the handicaps of the outcaste, although the idea of contamination and its unconscious psychological meanings are less prevalent in the social attitudes held toward Koreans (De Vos, 1967). As with the Mexican Americans, some identity is possible with another nation and its culture. Historically, no other identity is possible for either the outcaste or the American Negro.

The outcastes, in a psychodynamic sense, play the same role in the psychological patterns of some majority Japanese as do the American Negroes for a segment of the white population. One essential characteristic of caste relationships, as distinct from class relationships, is an attitude of physiological revulsion conditioned into the majority group which helps maintain a system of social segregation (De Vos, 1966).

One must emphasize that deviant courses of action occur only among a minority of outcastes. Although the majority are apathetically resigned to their lot in life, an increasing minority are advancing occupationally. There are notable cases of achievement and accomplishment, as well as failure. Government careers are not closed to *Burakumin* today in Japan. Many of the educated do, in fact, obtain bureaucratic positions of one kind or another or are active in politics. Some manage to rise far as a result of their professional merit. Some become teachers. The point to be made is that the inducements toward deviant roles and the problems of whether or not to "pass" become serious internal sources of conflict for the outcaste individual who has escaped the first level of a diffuse apathy and psychological retreat—the same emotional response that debilitates and stunts the potential of so many who inherit a position of disparaged status in society.

Radical Political Activity   There is a long history of political militancy among the Japanese *Burakumin* which has in course of time tended more and more to solidify into a fixed leftist-Marxist orientation (Totten and Wagatsuma, 1966; Wagatsuma, 1966). The movements carried on by *Burakumin* leaders throughout

Japan with the assistance of sympathetic majority citizens were set up soon after emancipation in 1872. But these early movements were local and unorganized. By 1903 a fairly large-scale organization, "The Greater Japan's Citizens' Integration Society" *(Dai Nippon Doho Yuwai Kai)* was established. It aimed at uplift through self-improvement in morals, manners, and sanitation.

After World War I a more militant "liberation movement," The Levelers Association *(Suiheisha)* was inaugurated. It adopted a red- and black-flag of social martyrdom—"a blood-red crown of thorns on a black sea of darkness." The *Suiheisha* saw its purpose as an active counterattack against any overt acts of discrimination by publicly shaming the offender or bringing legal action wherever possible. Between 1924 and 1930 a struggle for power within this organization eventuated in its control by avowed Marxists who sought an alliance with farm and labor unions. The fight against discrimination was incorporated almost wholly as far as theory and strategy into what was perceived as the broader context of "class struggle" and "the fight for the proletarian revolution." After a surprisingly ready acquiescence to military suppression during the 1930s, *Buraku* organizations were disbanded until after the defeat of Japan in World War II.

As part of the postwar democratization of Japan, political activities among the *Burakumin* were readily reactivated. A series of events quickly alienated the outcaste movement from American occupation officials, and the movement again turned wholeheartedly to a Marxist identification (De Vos and Wagatsuma, 1966, pp. 68 ff). The original *Suiheisha* flag was revived, but to the crown of thorns was added a red star. It is estimated that about 30 percent of the urban outcastes today are either directly or indirectly controlled by a leadership with a far-left political ideology. Affiliation with leftist union movements is somewhat one-sided. In many instances little more than token support is given to special *Buraku* problems by majority Japanese union members. Even in these leftist unions there is a separation of the outcastes, notably like that seen in the "integration" of

Negroes into labor groups and other organizations in the United States. The Marxist assumption that the outcaste problem is simply part of the class struggle is belied by a failure of Japanese workers to support actively, much less identify with, their outcaste brethren. Majority workers will not readily let down the psychological barriers of caste that separate them.

Those outcastes who find a Marxist political orientation unacceptable are presented with the problem of finding alternative organizations that have an effective program against economic discrimination and the inadequate public housing and sanitation provided in their districts. They find it difficult to find adequate leadership that is not polarized politically. A number of outcastes have joined the *Sōka Gakkai*—a somewhat rightist "clean government" organization related indirectly to a *Nichiren* sect of Buddhism. Ironically, while the outcastes have been accepted as individual members, this sect chooses to remain silent about their membership, since they do not want to discourage the proselyting of new members from the majority group.

One sees nevertheless that political action has become a psychologically integrative outlet through which the Japanese outcaste seeks to express his discontent over discrimination. Such movements attempt to change the social attitudes of the majority and at the same time to maintain the individual's sense of self-identity. The vast majority of outcastes today are not interested in simply being absorbed into the majority society. What they are seeking is some way to gain acceptance and to raise the level of self-respect of the entire group. The effect of keeping records on the Japanese outcastes has been to make of them, in a curious sense, a racial minority in spite of their entire lack of physical differentiation. That is why I have called the outcastes the "invisible race" of Japan.

A careful study of the history of political activities of the Japanese outcastes reveals parallels with what is occurring today within the American Negro civil rights movement. Some of the political activity of the *Burakumin* carries a deep swell of underlying bitterness and discontent. There is a group mobilization for the externalization of feelings resulting from early inner experiences of what happens both to parents and children in each generation and in later social interaction. An activist outlet is a counterbalance to apathy and nonreachableness in regard to education, public health, and welfare. Unfortunately these political activities are often misguided and become too readily at times simply expressive vehicles for the externalization of inner plight. Realistic objectives are sacrificed for ideological certainty. Dogmatic fragmentation vitiates unified action.

Further cross-cultural research should help point up the social psychological processes at work both within and between minority and majority groups in pluralistic societies. Such research may offer no direct suggestion for programs of amelioration, but a full presentation of comparative findings may in some instances prevent the sanguine application of partial palliatives that temporarily conceal more profound underlying issues. The case of the Japanese *Burakumin* deserves careful comparison with other instances of caste segregation in any further exploration into the psychohistorical consequences of social disparagement. They are yet another example of what I have termed the "psychological lag" to be found in every changing society. That is to say, the effects of a particular social condition continue long after the social structural elements producing the condition have changed. The "karma" of exploitation continues as an internalized pattern, very often unfortunately buried alive within the bosom of the primary family of exploited groups. For this reason one must develop programs of intervening in early childhood to help lessen the psychological inculcation of a disparaging self-image and methods of cognitive integration that inhibit a person from further social learning. At the same time, one must in no way diminish or disregard programs aimed at reducing the negative sociological forces of distantiation and disparagement that are at work within a pluralistic society.

psychosocial treatment of psychoneurosis

Hart Ransdell,
Tressa Roche

RANSDELL: We shall attempt to describe the environmental effect of chronic unemployment on mental health in the Appalachian male. We shall try to show how idleness and misery produce deterioration in the mind and body, which manifests itself in neurosis. In the year we have been in Pikeville, countless men have come into our clinic with very similar neurotic and somatic symptoms. These symptoms are so much alike that the psychiatrists in the hospital and the professionals who come to the clinic have begun to call the illness the "Eastern Kentucky syndrome."[1] Harry Caudill, in his book *Night Comes to the Cumberlands*, describes it as follows: "Like dispirited soldiers who hope to avoid combat, they besieged the doctors, complaining of a wide range of ailments. Their backs ached. They suffered from headaches. They could not sleep. They were short of breath and had chest pains. Their stomachs were upset and they could not eat. Above all, they were 'nervous.' . . . [Their] children, as public charges, could draw enough money to feed the family." These men became our most frequent visitors, constantly coming into the clinic to request some type of service; women have not reported the same symptoms.[2] These men usually range in age from the midtwenties to the midfifties, and most of them have been married. Almost all have applied for public assistance or social security, or are already receiving some form of public assistance. If they are hospitalized, they are usually diagnosed as suffering one of three psychoneurotic disorders: conversion reaction,[3] depressive reaction, or anxiety reaction.

ROCHE: Our experiences lead us to offer some new ideas which we hope may help to change this unhappy pattern of living. Although this study is exploratory in nature and lacking in many of the refined techniques, controls, and other essentials for good research, we have applied certain psychosocial concepts. Fenichel says, "There are certain uses the patient can make of his illness, which have nothing to do with the origin of the neurosis, but which may attain utmost practical importance" (1945). We believe that this neurosis of the Appalachian male characterized by psychosomatic symptoms has, as its secondary gain, the obtaining of the basic needs of food, shelter, and security for the individual and his family, which the public assistance check will provide. Whereas the man's role traditionally is that of the breadwinner, we see in these cases a reversal of roles. The wife is now taking care of the passive, dependent man much as she cares for her children. Over a period of time, she assumes many of her husband's former roles. And today she can be seen in the commodity line, signing up for public assistance and applying for benefits, while he lies at home and cares for the children. The woman becomes fully convinced of the authenticity of her husband's illness—because, you see, she also receives the secon-

[1] The term "Eastern Kentucky syndrome" is also in common use at the University of Kentucky Hospital.—Editor

[2] Since that time, Mr. Ransdell and Mrs. Roche have worked in another county nearby, where women outnumber men in the prevalence of Eastern Kentucky syndrome.—Editor

[3] For the nonpsychiatrist reader, let us explain that conversion reaction, formerly called hysteria, consists of physical complaints (often with a superficial resemblance to neurological symptoms) referring to the senses or the large muscles; on closer investigation, these turn out to have no evidence of bodily sickness. Examples are paralysis, weakness, convulsions, tremors, vomiting, headaches, pains of all kinds, anesthesias, and blindness, when these symptoms have no organic cause. Some psychiatrists regard the symptoms as symbolic of emotional conflicts, and as compromises between gratifying and denying a forbidden urge. Others stress the use of the symptoms as communication, as a nonverbal language, and as messages to influence other people's responses.—Editor

dary gain of the public assistance check. Many times, in our interviews, this was vividly brought home to us. Mr. Ransdell would interview the man while the wife was there. Whenever he directed a question to the man, the wife would interrupt to tell how sick he was: He can't do this, he can't do that. She has taken responsibilities that the man had formerly assumed. Now that the man is not working, he is not the breadwinner, and since he must have some reason for this, he is "sick." It is socially accepted that the man is "sick" and that he "draw," as they call it: that he go on aid to the disabled. He's been to many physicians and is skillful in using terms that he's picked up. These symptoms fall into a general pattern: backache, numbness, chest pains, pains going down the arms. We find the same set of symptoms throughout the area. As the wife joins in, it isn't long before she takes over and comes in to get her husband's medication from the clinic.

RANSDELL: Some background may help us to understand this syndrome. Most of this area was engaged in mining. When a man became disabled in the mines, he was entitled to compensation for his disability—monthly benefits, or a United Mine Workers' retirement benefit. Then came social security; since the worker pays for social security, he feels entitled to its benefits. Then the VA pensions, bonuses, and compensations came along— payments to which he feels entitled. He has earned the right to them. In urban areas, people still don't understand completely the difference among these benefits. In this rural, isolated area, it's much less understood. When public assistance came along, the general feeling was that it was another program with benefits to which one was entitled. I've been on house visits with some of the public assistance fieldworkers. We often hear, "Well, my neighbors draw, why can't I? This is something I'm entitled to." I think Erich Fromm might say that this is a socially patterned defect. This man is not at odds with his present environment; what he does is acceptable.

FINNEY: You mean that every good citizen should draw public assistance?

RANSDELL: Yes. I think the most vivid example occurred the

first time I went with one of the public assistance workers. It was the most amazing day I have spent: we would stop at the hollow and see the people running out of their houses, knowing quite well who we were. There may have been a hundred other cars like it in the neighborhood, but they knew the difference.

We've tried many treatment techniques. Fenichel says that the question of how to combat or prevent the secondary gain of a neurosis becomes a main problem of the treatment. For us that was the understatement of the year. Among the approaches we have tried is hospitalization. These men enter the hospital with all their usual symptoms. Within a week or two the symptoms clear up, but immediately upon the men's return to their old environment the symptoms reappear. One man who went to Eastern State Hospital had a diagnosis (and this is rare) "without mental disorder." When I saw him in Pikeville a month later, he told me that one side of his face had gone numb. He had difficulty in speaking, and mentioned pains in his back. Out-patient treatment followup, tranquilizers, and antidepressant medication have all failed. If we refer the patients to Vocational Rehabilitation, they won't follow through with the program because they don't get enough money for a family of ten or twelve to live on. Individual therapy has repeatedly failed, as nothing has been found to substitute for the compensation, the secondary gain of the neurosis.

A new program of the department of economic security began in Pike County in January 1964. It is formally called "Aid to Families of Dependent Children—Unemployed Parents," and colloquially called the "trash program" by men in this area.[4] Basically this program is designed to serve unemployed fathers who are unable to find employment and have no other source of income. In 1964, of 711 men who applied for the program, 361 were declared eligible. The men are assigned to work on public projects, and work supervisors are furnished by the appropriate state unit. They do such jobs as cleaning trash off the sides of the highways, painting buildings, and remodeling

---

[4] It is also commonly called the "Happy Pappy" program.—Editor

schools. We found, however, that this program is not the answer. We would say, "Go over and apply for the work program," and try to help them see that it would be the best thing for them. They would say, "No, no, I'm too sick to work." The wife would support them. "You aren't there. You don't know what he's like at home. He's not able to work."

To quote Fenichel again, "He who has succeeded in getting advantages out of his illness does not give up easily."

ROCHE: There are some individuals who can't resist a challenge. Since the conventional psychiatric techniques had failed, and the work program was not the complete answer, we decided to combine our techniques and try to fit the various agencies' services to the needs of the individual patient. The first job was to evaluate the individual patient, making sure that he did not have an organic disorder. We found that we had much more success if we reached these men early, before they had been unemployed too long, had got in the habit of "drawing," and were content to "jin" around, as they say. We then tried to find out what the man's strengths were: had he worked, had he been gainfully employed, did he have any skills at all that he could use?

We were aware of the inevitable consequences of the dynamic relationship that might develop between the patient and the interviewer, including the possibility of a countertransferencelike reaction.

Many times while Mr. Ransdell interviewed the man, I would sit next to the wife, feeling deeply, aware of her problems and perhaps even identifying with her. She was being asked to give up the only security she had, the check, when she had ten or eleven children (they're very prolific there in the mountains), and what could we offer her in place of it?

I think the way we conducted the interview is important. Everything that we were told this morning not to do, we've done! But we found it worked! After numerous tries, Mr. Ransdell began to take a very direct, authoritarian role. He told the men, "This is what you're going to do: one, two, three, four. You're going over and you're going to apply for the work program." He took a godlike role.

When the wife said, "See, he can't do this, he's sick! I tell you, you don't know what it's like to live with him at home! He can't get up!" I could be supportive and understanding. Soon we saw that we were taking the roles of father and mother. Mr. Ransdell was the strong, direct, disciplining father. I could be the warm, understanding mother figure, who understands how it is. This seems to us to be a very important part of our technique; only with the team approach could we reduce our personal projections and decide what course of action was best for the patient. We fell into these roles unconsciously, and it worked. Being aware of our own personal feelings and how they were affecting our decisions, we could discuss why we were doing what we were and whether it was best for the particular patient. We often asked each other afterward, "Why did you do that?"

The next step was the evaluation of the family, their weaknesses and the assets and strength of the family constellation. Sometimes we used the member of the family with the most anxiety to work with the patient. This will be more clearly demonstrated later when we give our case presentation.

Our next phase of treatment was motivation and coordination with other agency resources. Most of the patients were well known to Public Assistance, whose workers showed a reasonable amount of interest, concern, and discretion in dealing with them. Should we not devote a portion of our energies to giving our patients a good knowledge of psychiatric services and to removing some of the aura of fear and suspicion that surrounded mental illness in this mountain area? But by far the most important thing was to explain our roles and what we are trying to accomplish—to tell them what we were going to do and why, so that we could fully coordinate and cooperate in our services. The need for a public health approach to social and emotional ills has never been clearer.

Here are two cases that are typical of the Eastern Kentucky syndrome patients and of the methods we used in treating them.

Mr. D. is a 52-year-old unemployed miner with eleven children, five of whom are still at home. He has only a fourth-grade education. Mr. D. worked for 23 years in the same coal mine until it closed in 1952. For the next five years, his work was spasmodic. He worked at any mine that had a temporary or part-time job. From 1957 until 1960 Mr. D. did not work, and the family existed on commodities given them by the county and the money that Mrs. D. earned doing housework for neighbors. Mr. D. was first admitted to Eastern State Hospital in 1960 and was readmitted in 1962. He was last admitted July 20, 1963, and discharged in August 1963 with a diagnosis of psychoneurotic disorder, depressive reaction. The admission note states he was "depressed and agitated and saying he was too weak to walk, hurting all over." The discharge summary states that he was in excellent remission, but the outpatient notes two months later read that he was complaining of "pains in my head and back, numbness in my arms." He was treated on a monthly basis as an outpatient. The record reveals that the psychiatrist frequently changed Mr. D.'s medication, but he kept his many somatic symptoms. In October 1964, at the suggestion of a public health nurse and public assistance fieldworker, Mrs. D. came to our clinic, expressing anxiety about her situation. She was depressed and had a noticeable tic on the left side of her face. Mrs. D. said that her husband "lays in bed all day and won't do anything." She reported that he had become worse since their public assistance had been discontinued in May 1963. (He was readmitted to the state hospital in July 1963.) The family had been receiving commodities and handouts from the neighbors.

We had an interview with Mrs. D., aimed at reducing her anxiety and depression. We helped her to bring out her anger at her husband and encouraged her to begin demanding that he assume some responsibility. Indeed, we did more than encourage her. We promoted the change. She said that she planned to leave Mr. D. if he would not take responsibility, and we advised her to tell him of her plans. The following week, a public assistance fieldworker visited Mr. and Mrs. D. at home. The fieldworker explained the work program to Mr. D. and encouraged him to apply for the program. The fieldworker was also supported by Mrs. D.'s efforts to make her husband return to work. Two weeks later Mr. D. was seen at the clinic, and he continued to express many somatic symptoms, but he did not seem as depressed. He was advised by the psychiatrist that there was no reason why he could not work. This sort of coordination is essential: that the public health nurse, the fieldworker, the psychiatrist in the clinic, and those of us on the followup, all say more or less the same thing, "You have to go to work!" He was further told that his recent reapplication for public assistance would probably be denied, since the clinic's report stated that he was mentally able to work. Mr. D. then said that he would apply for the work program and try it; the following day he did so, and Public Assistance processed the case in four days in an attempt to make full use of his "motivation." Mrs. D. later reported that after the first day of work her husband said, "I had a good time, and it's good to be back with men again."

Mr. D. has been working for the past year, and his supervisor reports that he is a hard worker. He still has some somatic complaints, but the symptoms have become less pronounced on each succeeding clinic visit. The work program also requires that these men go to school two days a week, eight hours a day, and work three days. On his last visit to the clinic, he took great pride in telling me that he had been promoted and was now in the fourth grade. His child who is in the same grade, he said, didn't understand his work at all; his textbooks were entirely different, and he felt superior to the child. This case clearly illustrates the necessity to work with the strength of the family and to assume a direct and authoritarian role. It also illustrates the importance of coordinating the efforts of all agencies involved. This importance is more vividly emphasized in the case that Mr. Ransdell will present.

RANSDELL: Mr. W. is a 31-year-old married man with two children under the age of three. He is an employed, illiterate miner. He was admitted to Eastern State Hospital on June 15, 1963, and discharged one week later. On admission, he spoke at length of his many somatic complaints—severe headaches, pain in the chest, and pain in the abdomen. He said that he had been an epileptic and had been taking anticonvulsant medication, but that the family had not been able to afford to continue it. The discharge summary revealed that "within twenty-four hours of hospitalization he became friendly and conspicuously cheerful and socialized well with the patients. However, he avoided work on every occasion. At no time during his hospitalization did he have a seizure." His diagnosis was chronic brain syndrome associated with convulsive disorder, with neurotic reaction. The casework was complicated by the fact that an epileptic was presenting many psychoneurotic symptoms. One month after his release, he complained of chest pains and smothering spells and said he had numerous seizures even though he was taking his medicine. He was followed at the clinic for several months, but there was little change except that he became more withdrawn. His father carried him into the clinic in May 1964 because he said he could not walk. At that time, the examining psychiatrists ruled out the presence of organicity and made a diagnosis of conversion reaction. His recent reapplication for public assistance had just been denied the week before.

In June 1964 one of the public assistance fieldworkers and I made a visit to the patient's home. The patient was sitting in a chair in his father's home. He was unshaven, slow in his movements, and almost mute. The entire family was present and described the patient's frequent running fits. Although the wife was present, the father appeared to be the dominant person. He told the patient's wife, who had just had a baby two days before, to walk fifty yards up behind his house to get the patient's medicine and bring it back down. When rehospitalization was discussed, neither the patient nor his father would agree to it. We then told both of them that it was very unlikely that the patient would receive public assistance if he reapplied. To the father, who seemed more concerned about W.'s financial dependence upon him than anything else, we emphasized the point: "Now look, W. will be dependent upon you for the rest of your life unless you do something."

We suggested to the father that while the patient might apply for the work program at a later date, in the meantime he should start him working around the house. We suggested that he hoe the garden, and that he start carrying coal in from the little mine out behind the hill. Two weeks later the patient was brought to the clinic by his father. He was clean-shaven, neatly dressed, and seizure-free. He began to show some initiative and said he would apply for the work program. That was in June. In August, Mrs. Roche and I made a visit to the home. At that time the patient still had not heard from the public assistance program. This was about the first case in which we had encountered the syndrome, and we were still in the experimental stage. If we had known what we know now we would have tried to get his application processed as an emergency, and he would have been on the work program the next day. But we let it ride, and two months later, when he still wasn't on it, he was quite angry at us and at public assistance. Actually, we felt that it was a pretty good sign that for the first time he was at least showing some anger at us. We went back to public assistance and got the case processed. Two weeks later the patient started working in the city, where he did general maintenance. The patient's father showed considerable anxiety: he accompanied the patient to work each day, bringing him in from the hollow where he lived, about six miles out of town, and waiting in town all day to take him back home. The father began dropping in at the clinic to see us, and we began to have to supply constant support and to interpret the patient's behavior. On the second day of work W. had a "seizure" downtown. Somebody came running to my office and said, "Come on out, one of your patients is lying out on the street, and he's having seizures." I found him lying in the middle of town on the sidewalk; people said he was having convulsions. I looked down at him and said, "Do you want to get up?" He looked up at me and said no. So we picked him up and brought him into the health department, where Mrs. Roche briefed the health officer on the case. The health officer ordered an injection of water and suggested that the patient would be all right in five minutes. Well, within five minutes he got up and walked out. The following day the work supervisor, who'd become quite upset at the idea that the patient was having seizures, said, "No, we don't want him back in this job. He's liable to get hurt." So we had to find another job for him. At that time the health department, where our offices are located, was being painted. We hoped that the security of working in the health department, near us and near medical assistance, would help him. The first day there, after working several hours, he had a weak spell and said he couldn't work. The health officer got quite angry and dressed him down. I telephoned the public assistance worker and said, "I don't know what to do! He's coming over to your office. I'm ready to give up!" The patient, however, was so angry at the health officer that he walked over and said, "I want to try. Those people want me to keep on working. I'm going to keep trying." He asked to be reassigned to the commodity office, where an old friend of his was a work supervisor.

The patient has been working for the past year now. We've seen him often. It's amazing, I think, to see the change in him. He's clean-shaven, he comes into the clinic and shows us pictures of his children that he's taken. He had a tiny one-room house; he's taking the initiative to tear the back off and build another room onto it. He seems happy and gregarious. Work can obviously be most beneficial to the mental health of these people.

SUMMARY

The problems of emotional stress in the face of rapidly changing socioeconomic conditions can be seen vividly in the Appalachian area. The area exemplifies the deadly effects of automation and mechanization. In that respect, it is our contention that Appalachia is years ahead of, not behind, the rest of the nation. The new concepts and programs developed in Appalachia may have to be used in other areas of the nation after automation takes its toll. Most of the existing welfare programs can be applied only after a man has become disabled. Such programs give a man a secondary gain for his illness; this is very difficult to combat. The new programs should be designed to reward an individual before he gets to the point of having no alternative but to become ill. The programs should also recognize that work can create conditions beneficial to mental health, whereas unemployment can be a causative agent in the development of mental illness. It is possible that there will always be problems and individuals like the problems and the individuals in the Appalachian area. Any program should recognize that an individual approach must supplement the general approach; it must not only meet the basic needs of the individual but also provide an opportunity for him to maintain some degree of self-esteem and the feeling of independence.

the games of wooden leg and indigence

Eric Berne

WOODEN LEG[1]

Thesis. The most dramatic form of "Wooden Leg" is "The Plea of Insanity." This may be translated into transactional terms as follows: "What do you expect of someone as emotionally disturbed as I am—that I would refrain from killing people?" To which the jury is asked to reply: "Certainly not, we would hardly impose that restriction on you!" The "Plea of Insanity," played as a legal game, is acceptable to American culture and is different from the almost universally respected principle that an individual may be suffering from a psychosis so profound that no reasonable person would expect him to be responsible for his actions. In Japan drunkenness, and in Russia war-time military service, are accepted as excuses for evading responsibility for all kinds of outrageous behavior (according to this writer's information).

The thesis of "Wooden Leg" is, "What do you expect of a man with a wooden leg?" Put that way, of course, no one would expect anything of a man with a wooden leg except that he should steer his own wheel chair. On the other hand, during World War II there was a man with a wooden leg who used to give demonstrations of jitterbug dancing, and very competent jitterbug dancing, at Army Hospital amputation centers. There are blind men who practice law and hold political offices (one such is currently mayor of the writer's home town), deaf men who practice psychiatry and handless men who can use a typewriter.

As long as someone with a real, exaggerated or even imaginary disability is content with his lot, perhaps no one should interfere. But the moment he presents himself for psychiatric treatment, the question arises if he is using his life to his own best advantage, and if he can rise above his disability. In this country the therapist will be working in opposition to a large mass of educated public opinion. Even the close relatives of the patient who complained most loudly about the inconveniences caused by his infirmity, may eventually turn on the therapist if the patient makes definitive progress. This is readily understandable to a game analyst, but it makes his task no less difficult. All the people who were playing "I'm Only Trying to Help You" are threatened by the impending disruption of the game if the patient shows signs of striking out on his own, and sometimes they use almost incredible measures to terminate the treatment.

Both sides are illustrated by the case of the stuttering client of Miss Black's, mentioned in the discussion of the game "Indigence." This man played a classical form of "Wooden Leg." He was unable to find employment, which he correctly attributed to the fact that he was a stutterer, since the only career that interested him, he said, was that of salesman. As a free citizen he had a right to seek employment in whatever field he chose, but as a stutterer, his choice raised some question as to the purity of his motives. The reaction of the helpful agency when Miss Black attempted to break up this game was very unfavorable to her.

"Wooden Leg" is especially pernicious in clinical practice, because the patient may find a therapist who plays the same game with the same plea, so that progress is impossible. This is relatively easy to arrange in the case of the "Ideological Plea," "What do you expect of a man who lives in a society like ours?" One patient combined this with the "Psychosomatic Plea," "What

<hr />

[1] Eric Berne, *Games People Play: The Psychology of Human Relationships* (reprinted by permission of Grove Press, Inc.) © 1964 by Eric Berne.

do you expect of a man with psychosomatic symptoms?" He found a succession of therapists who would accept one plea but not the other, so that none of them either made him feel comfortable in his current position by accepting both pleas, nor budged him from it by rejecting both. Thus he proved that psychiatry couldn't help people.

Some of the pleas which patients use to excuse symptomatic behavior are colds, head injuries, situational stress, the stress of modern living, American culture and the economic system. A literate player has no difficulty in finding authorities to support him. "I drink because I'm Irish." "This wouldn't happen if I lived in Russia or Tahiti." The fact is that patients in mental hospitals in Russia and Tahiti are very similar to those in American state hospitals (Berne, 1960). Special pleas of "If It Weren't for Them" or "They Let Me Down" should always be evaluated very carefully in clinical practice—and also in social research projects.

Slightly more sophisticated are such pleas as: What do you expect of a man who (a) comes from a broken home (b) is neurotic (c) is in analysis or (d) is suffering from a disease known as alcoholism? These are topped by, "If I stop doing this I won't be able to analyze it, and then I'll never get better."

The obverse of "Wooden Leg" is "Rickshaw," with the thesis, "If they only had (rickshaws) (duckbill platypuses) (girls who spoke ancient Egyptian) around this town, I never would have got into this mess."

Antithesis. Anti-"Wooden Leg" is not difficult if the therapist can distinguish clearly between his own Parent and Adult, and if the therapeutic aim is explicitly understood by both parties.

On the Parental side, he can be either a "good" Parent or a "harsh" one. As a "good" Parent he can accept the patient's plea, especially if it fits in with his own viewpoints, perhaps with the rationalization that people are not responsible for their actions until they have completed their therapy. As a "harsh" Parent he can reject the plea and engage in a contest of wills with the patient. Both of these attitudes are already familiar to the "Wooden Leg" player, and he knows how to extract the maximum satisfactions from each of them.

As an Adult, the therapist declines both of these opportunities. When the patient asks, "What do you expect of a neurotic?" (or whatever plea he is using at the moment) the reply is, "I don't expect anything. The question is what do you expect of yourself?" The only demand he makes is that the patient give a serious answer to this question, and the only concession he makes is to allow the patient a reasonable length of time to answer it: anywhere from six weeks to six months, depending on the relationship between them and the patient's previous preparation.

INDIGENCE[2]

Thesis. The thesis of this game is best stated by Henry Miller in *The Colossus of Maroussi*: "The event must have taken place during the year when I was looking for a job without the slightest intention of taking one. It reminded me that, desperate as I thought myself to be, I had not even bothered to look through the columns of the want ads."

This game is one of the complements of "I'm Only Trying to Help You" (ITHY) as it is played by social workers who earn their living by it. "Indigence" is played just as professionally by the client who earns his living in this manner. The writer's own experience with "Indigence" is limited, but the following account by one of his most accomplished students illustrates the nature of this game and its place in our society.

Miss Black was a social worker in a welfare agency whose avowed purpose, for which it received a government subsidy, was the economic rehabilitation of indigents—which in effect meant getting them to find and retain gainful employment. The

[2] *Ibid.,* 147-51.

clients of this agency were continually "making progress," according to official reports, but very few of them were actually "rehabilitated." This was understandable, it was claimed, because most of them had been welfare clients for several years, going from agency to agency and sometimes being involved with five or six agencies at a time, so that it was evident that they were "difficult cases."

Miss Black, from her training in game analysis, soon realized that the staff of her agency was playing a consistent game of ITHY, and wondered how the clients were responding to this. In order to check, she asked her own clients from week to week how many job opportunities they had actually investigated. She was interested to discover that although they were theoretically supposed to be looking assiduously for work from day to day, actually they devoted very little effort to this, and sometimes the token efforts they did make had an ironic quality. For example, one man said that he answered at least one advertisement a day looking for work. "What kind of work?" she inquired. He said he wanted to go into sales work. "Is that the only kind of ad you answer?" she asked. He said that it was, but it was too bad that he was a stutterer, as that held him back from his chosen career. About this time it came to the attention of her supervisor that she was asking these questions, and she was reprimanded for putting "undue pressure" on her clients.

Miss Black decided nevertheless to go ahead and rehabilitate some of them. She selected those who were able-bodied and did not seem to have a valid reason to continue to receive welfare funds. With this selected group, she talked over the games ITHY and "Indigence." When they were willing to concede the point, she said that unless they found jobs she was going to cut them off from welfare funds and refer them to a different kind of agency. Several of them almost immediately found employment, some for the first time in years. But they were indignant at her attitude, and some of them wrote letters to her supervisor complaining about it. The supervisor called her in and reprimanded her even more severely, on the ground that although her former clients were working, they were not "really rehabilitated." The supervisor indicated that there was some question whether they would retain Miss Black in the agency. Miss Black, as much as she dared without further jeopardizing her position, tactfully tried to elicit what would constitute "really rehabilitated" in the agency's opinion. This was not clarified. She was only told that she was "putting undue pressure" on people, and the fact that they were supporting their families for the first time in years was in no way to her credit.

Because she needed her job and was now in danger of losing it, some of her friends tried to help. The respected head of a psychiatric clinic wrote to the supervisor, stating that he had heard Miss Black had done some particularly effective work with welfare clients, and asking whether she might discuss her findings at a staff conference at his clinic. The supervisor refused permission.

In this case the rules of "Indigent" were set up by the agency to complement the local rules of ITHY. There was a tacit agreement between the worker and the client which read as follows:

W. "I'll try to help you (providing you don't get better)."

C. "I'll look for employment (providing I don't have to find any)."

If a client broke the agreement by getting better, the agency lost a client, and the client lost his welfare benefits, and both felt penalized. If a worker like Miss Black broke the agreement by making the client actually find work, the agency was penalized by the client's complaints, which might come to the attention of higher authorities, while again the client lost his welfare benefits.

As long as both obeyed the implicit rules, both got what they wanted. The client received his benefits and soon learned what the agency wanted in return: an opportunity to "reach out" (as part of ITHY) plus "clinical material" (to present at "client-centered" staff conferences). The client was glad to comply with these demands, which gave him as much pleasure as it did the agency. Thus they got along well together, and neither felt any desire to terminate such a satisfying relationship. Miss Black, in effect, "reached in" instead of "reaching out," and proposed a "community-centered" staff conference instead of a "client-centered" one; and this disturbed all the others concerned in spite of the fact that she was thus only complying with the stated intent of the regulations.

Two things should be noted here. First, "Indigence" as a game rather than a condition due to physical, mental, or economic disability, is played by only a limited percentage of welfare clients. Second, it will only be supported by social workers who are trained to play ITHY. It will not be well-tolerated by other workers.

Allied games are "Veteran" and "Clinic." "Veteran" displays the same symbiotic relationship, this time between the Veterans Administration, allied organizations, and a certain number of "professional veterans" who share the legitimate privileges of disabled ex-servicemen. "Clinic" is played by a certain percentage of those who attend the out-patient departments of large hospitals. Unlike those who play "Indigent" or "Veteran," patients who play "Clinic" do not receive financial remuneration, but get other advantages. They serve a useful social purpose, since they are willing to cooperate in the training of medical personnel and in studies of disease processes. From this they may get a legitimate Adult satisfaction not available to players of "Indigence" and "Veteran."

Antithesis. Antithesis, if indicated, consists in withholding the benefits. Here the risk is not primarily from the player himself, as in most other games, but from this game being culturally syntonic and fostered by the complementary ITHY players. The threat comes from professional colleagues and the aroused public, government agencies and protective unions. The complaints which follow an exhibition of anti-"Indigence" may lead to a loud outcry of "Yes, Yes, How About That?" which may be regarded as a healthy constructive operation or pastime, even if it occasionally discourages candidness. In fact, the whole American political system of democratic freedoms is based on a license (not available under many other forms of government) to ask that question. Without such a license, humanitarian social progress becomes seriously impeded.

teacher education in culture change

William Carse

In the midst of culture change, institutionalized education must prepare to change more significantly than its society. For it is the very institution of education that, in many parts of our nation and of the world, helps to maintain the lack of change. Any casual observer of the schools of Eastern Kentucky, for instance, will realize immediately that little change will take place in youngsters who spend one, eight, or twelve years within their walls. The buildings are as uninspiring as are others in the community. The classrooms are barren. The teachers are unimaginative. No wonder that the end product is an exact replication of the group of adults that walks around outside. For change to take place, these schools must represent the larger world as a desirable place for the child to enter, not an unknown and frightening something beyond the mountains. This paper represents an effort to ferret out some of the restrictions that now inhibit the schools from developing the kind of person who is free to engage in life, and it will propose new roles for teachers, together with new goals for education, in situations that require culture change.

Education is a birth-to-death process, some parts of which are planned (schooling), and other parts incidental to but necessary for living. If the goals can be defined for any moment of life during schooling, then the teacher's job is to see that all the required aspects of the process are planned. I think that the ultimate aim of education is simply the ability of each person to engage in all of life. This transcends and includes such goals as good citizenship, knowledge, appreciation of the cultural aspects of life, or any other of the myriad listings of educational objectives which fill the pages of curriculum guides and books of how-to-do-it for teachers. What I believe to be the goals of education in an age of culture change will be found in the interaction between a person and those things usually listed as objectives. This interaction should be the object of our study, for it is in this interaction that we are allowed to make, or are kept from making, change in our own approach to the world, its people and their productions.

The term *culture change* assumes that one group is different from another or that a group desires to bring about change in its own conditions. Let us look at the first part of the preceding statement: one group desires to assist another group in bringing up to date its current mode of existence so that more congruence exists between the two groups. Let us call the first Group A, the group with an acceptable mode of existence; and the second Group B, the one wanting or needing to change. We can at any time determine the distance between the development of the measurable aspects of a culture within Groups A and B. If Group A has progressed beyond Group B, or more simply, if a difference exists, the task is to determine the distance between the two measured points and to determine the fastest method of bringing Group B to the level of Group A. This same information is needed when we teach the simplest fact to any pupil. Our first task is to determine the pupil's level of understanding or of knowledge; then to arrange the new materials in such a fashion as to allow the child to understand and attach these new learnings to those he already possesses. This is the basic characteristic of all good teachers.

If we look at any aspect of the culture, especially those that we wish to change by use of the institution called school, we know at the outset that in most aspects Group B's behavior differs a great deal from that of Group A. Group B has not moved as far as Group A. The world of Group B has not allowed the same changes that have taken place with Group A. The value systems, and the accompanying attitudes with their behavioral component, have been subjected to constant harassment from the cultural patterns within Group A. The same process or some modification of it must be used if we are to change the members of Group B so that they will approach life in the same manner as members of Group A. In this case, our aim is to change, not to maintain.

When a member of Group B is encouraged, or desires, to enter into Group A, he has several alternatives. He may try on his own to become like individuals in Group A; he may institutionalize himself, so that he can catch up in an orderly fashion by accepting assistance from the institutional staff representing Group A; or he may attach himself to some subgroup of Group A, which will understand and support his lack of congruence with the total group, and plod along at the subgroup's pace, with no real regard for the total membership of Group A.

If a person who, having moved from one culture to another, decides that he will become like members of the other group, we can be reasonably assured that he will succeed. He is open to his experiences, keen enough in diagnostic skills to be able to see the lack of congruence between values, attitudes, and behavior. Seeing this lack of congruence, he makes changes in himself and tests by acting out. Because he is keen enough to measure with a high degree of accuracy the productiveness of these changes in behavior, he is free to reject behavior that is unproductive. If an assessment is positive, he accepts the new society. His adjustment is made.

The person who chooses the second alternative uses the institution that his experience tells him will help him with the changes needed in himself. For most of the world's population, this institution is the school. The school helps the individual to develop congruence with the new society's values, attitudes, and behavior, and to become a contributing member of the society.

For the person who chooses the third alternative, to remain with a subgroup, we can also make some predictions. The psychological studies concerning the results of consistent failure are clear enough for us to predict that his fate is one of rapid deterioration. Since he has not asked for assistance we know that his progress will become slower and slower with each additional impediment. He makes no adjustment to society.

Since great numbers of people do not have the ability to follow the first alternative, that of self-actualization, and we know that the results of the third alternative are disastrous (observe the growth of great numbers of groups with noncongruent values in the United States), it seems that the most economical direction for the society to take is the second: provision of the institution that will bring about the desired change. Since that institution, the school, is actively supported by our society, our task is to improve those parts of it that deal with the members of the groups who need or wish to change.

Since the school, in the final analysis, is no more than its teachers, we must begin our development of the school with changed teacher-education procedures. This new program must produce a teacher secure in his knowledge of the world in general, of his specialty area, and of himself. I believe that honoring certain objectives will educate this teacher.

GENERAL OBJECTIVES IN TEACHER EDUCATION

One general objective should dominate: the development of a teacher capable of establishing congruence between the values, attitudes, knowledge, and behavior of the general society and those of any subgroup, especially the culturally different and the educationally deprived.

The following subobjectives should lead the teacher-candidate to the general objective:

1. The development of a concern about man so genuine that the teacher will engage in the active investigation of the conditions surrounding the group and its members. The desired action implied in the paradigm below must be continuous for each teacher in his educational program and in his professional work.

Genuine concern for the development of each member of
the group into a person capable of engaging in life

leads to

teacher involvement in community activities at all levels

which in turn changes

the group member's perceptions of the teacher (and of
education) to that of a person (or an institution) who cares
enough to be concerned

which then develops

a new concept for each group member about his own worth-
whileness and the possible contributions of the teacher (or
education) to his own development.

Perhaps this can be stated more simply. This subobjective is
involvement, and it implies total commitment. Thus both the
teacher and the pupil remain learners, the teacher operating
at a slightly higher level of understanding than the pupil. If a
successful teaching relationship exists, however, we would expect
all pupils eventually to exceed their teacher.

2. The development of a teacher who acts upon the known
base that desirable change occurs in people who take part in
making the plans for the changes, and who are allowed to put
the new behavioral patterns into action without undue threat of
punishment or evaluation.

3. The development of a teacher who is so deeply based in the
knowledge associated with his selected area of study that he can
act on subobjectives 1 and 2 as a matter of routine behavior.
His knowledge of his specialty will, through his interpretive
actions, have immediate application in each situation. This subobjective will develop a professsional teacher in each knowledge
area. A professional teacher is one who produces within his
teaching specialty upon demand. When he works with the
culturally different and the educationally deprived groups, this
demand is constant.

4. The development of a teacher who is so deeply educated
in the area of human growth and development (knowledge of the

basic organism and its behavior) that the diagnostic skills needed for interpreting cognitive and affective data input immediately lead to action. Stated in another fashion: it means the development of a teacher who has the clinical skills required in the educational setting.

PROCEDURES TO BE FOLLOWED IN TEACHER EDUCATION

Each teacher-candidate selected for education under such a program would be expected to live through the exact replica of the program suggested for the culturally different and the educationally deprived groups. Change of person needs to be evident to the teacher. This means that the staff, or at least certain portions of the staff, must be capable of using the general objectives and the four subobjectives in their contact with the teacher-candidate. The teacher-candidate occupies here the same position as the group with which he will be working, that of a subgroup (nonteacher group to teacher group).

The education of these teacher-candidates will necessarily include the development of knowledge in all areas; of interpretative skills when that knowledge is applied in the teaching situation; of diagnostic skills to determine the reasons that may be hampering a pupil's learning within the teacher's specialty; and of teacher-candidates actively involved in the world, open to their own experiential relationship to it.

Thus the procedures will contain instructional designs that will assist in the development of cognitive skills in each teaching area; interpretative skills in each teaching area; diagnostic skills, stressing the need for this skill in the affective area and its relationship to the cognitive; and an adequate teacher personality through the provision of psychotherapy if needed.

These teacher-candidates would, under the provision of these procedures, develop an extensive understanding of the world of knowledge within their own interest areas and others closely related to it. The instructional design would be arranged so as to take the teacher-candidates as far as they wished to go into their selected knowledge areas. There would be an acceptable minimum of knowledge, but no upper limit would be placed on work in the cognitive areas.

The interpretative skills will be developed as the knowledge base is accumulated. This skill means simply the ability to translate the knowledge into terms appropriate for the pupil in the learning situation. Since the knowledge, considered as truths, cannot be changed for the various levels of teaching, the teacher must know enough about the materials being taught to be able to translate this "truth" into the terms of the most unsophisticated learner. In other words, a teacher for such a situation must be capable of accommodating, to the learner the level of difficulty of the material.

Each teacher-candidate in such a program must become familiar with all the tools of the profession. This includes the tests designed for use in the measurement of aptitude and achievement, as well as those personality tests designed to complement the aptitude and achievement testing. Added to this would be a clinical diagnostic skill that develops only through extensive observations and their relation to the child's world.

Since we would be asking first and foremost for a change in teacher attitude and behaviors, provisions must be made for psychotherapy for those teacher-candidates who request it or for whom, in the view of the staff, psychotherapy is necessary before they can proceed in the program.

There is within the literature of our profession enough material to place the educative meat on the skeleton so far supplied. Again this is essentially a task for the staff.

SUMMARY

Education must shift radically in its approach to people and to knowledge if it is to become an important factor in culture change. Two needed shifts are changes in the role of the teacher and the goals of education. If the teachers continue to act as the sole possessors of knowledge and to evaluate in terms of their knowledge, we can expect little change. It is impossible for any person to keep up with growth of knowledge in all areas. This means that we must tolerate teachers who possess and teach half-truths, or else change the definition of education. I would choose the second course of action. Education must make as its major goal the development of an attitude that extends learning far beyond the school. No man is capable of learning enough during his school life to maintain himself for the rest of his life. Yet this appears to be the most popular view of education, or at least of school.

Teachers must become the symbol of the constant learner, not of the complete learner. Granted that the teacher will be a learner at a more sophisticated level, the teacher and the pupil must nevertheless be learners at the same moment. By this behavior we will become less restrictive in our associations with pupils.

This paper has proposed that we accept a concept of culture change which assumes that any group of people have a behavioral base worth preserving, and that any change should honor this base. Schools must become the institutions wherein change can be made more economically than elsewhere. These changes will be best realized by the teacher who is a learner, who is involved in the culture and the community actions of the people representing that culture, who has great knowledge in a specialty area, who has such exacting knowledge of diagnostic tools that these tools can be applied immediately in any learning situation, and who is capable of developing sound interpersonal relationships with most of those persons labeled learners.

discussion two

The group has now heard several papers. Two, those by Dr. Honigmann and Dr. Prince, have discussed the relationship between mental health and social class, and have asked how psychiatrists and other professionals in our class and subculture can cope with mental health or behavioral problems of the poor. Three papers have portrayed the troubles of specific groups, two in Eastern Kentucky and one in Japan.

Now some conflicting viewpoints begin to appear among the participants. Two psychoanalysts, Drs. Wittkower and Weinstein, have independently concluded that in spite of the apparent warmth and friendliness of the mountaineers, hostile aggressive urges are lurking, ready to come into action. The two psychoanalysts disagree in another way, however: one, following Freud, speaks of primary and secondary gain and of unconscious conflict, while the other, following Sullivan, does not find those concepts useful.

A still more basic cleavage makes its appearance, too. Dr. De Vos makes the point that something has gone wrong within the individuals of the Southern Appalachian subculture of poverty, at least as shown in Dr. Gazaway's Branch: the people may be described as immature, neurotic, or in poor mental health, as their behavior is self-defeating and maladaptive. Dr. Weinstein and Dr. Honigmann object to what they regard as Dr. De Vos's attempt to blame the poor and to hold them responsible for their troubles. They suggest, instead, that we should look for the causes outside, and put the blame on the outsiders (ourselves collectively, as the middle class) for the troubles of the poor.

Dr. De Vos counters that it should not be a question of blame, but of understanding the cause and effect. He maintains that the present system of welfare payments reinforces maladaptive behaviors and not healthy ones. He defines poverty as a loss of role. He says that the lower class is an anachronism, has no future, and must be helped to acculturate, to join the middle class. Dr. Margetts agrees that we must draw them into our own culture. Dr. Honigmann disagrees. He feels that we should help the poor (and people of other cultures) to develop and strengthen their own way of life and not to adopt ours. Dr. Opler tries to smooth matters over, and tells some anecdotes.

It seems plausible to think that Drs. De Vos and Margetts would approve of the treatment method of Mr. Ransdell and Mrs. Roche, while Drs. Honigmann and Weinstein might disapprove. The chairman tries in vain to get some judgments expressed on the matter.

There is some suggestion that "motoric" cultures, stressing gross muscular work, are prone to conversion reaction (hysteria).

FINNEY (chairman): Several points of Mr. Ransdell and Mrs. Roche seemed to challenge some concepts that other people have expressed. What agreements or, particularly, disagreements have we had so far? Dr. Gazaway, will you comment on the attitude toward public assistance in your Branch and how it compares with what the speakers this afternoon said about the attitude toward public assistance?

GAZAWAY: Many of the people in the Branch started public assistance in WPA days and have never got away from it. The second and third generations have never known anything but welfare payments of one kind or another. The other difference that I see is that when the department of community medicine looked at the people of my hollow, almost every family was found to have two or three serious physical sicknesses or disabilities. And that doesn't count the intestinal parasitism. Some have as many as five kinds of intestinal parasites. There is no psychiatric illness, but physically the people are ill. That doesn't necessarily mean that they are sick or disabled enough to qualify for welfare, but they do have physical ailments.

FINNEY: No psychiatrist has examined them, but I'd be surprised if the Branch people turned out to be lacking in diagnosable psychiatric disorder. I believe you told me once, Dr. Gazaway, that the only way the people in Gazaway's Branch compete with each other is to see who can draw the biggest check for not working.

GAZAWAY: Yes, or who can qualify for something that he's not really qualified for. I can give you one illustration of a man who's on aid to the blind. Not only he but his wife and two children are all getting paid for being blind. Yet he drives a new car, which he negotiates around a curve better than I can, and his children are not placed in special classes in school. Well, being only a nurse, I wouldn't be in a position to say, since the doctor diagnosed him, but what actually happened was that two days before he went down to apply he put snuff in his eyes. He was a sorry sight. I've seen others try it. It's very painful. Their eyes are very watery and almost closed. They use other methods to get aid to the blind, and they know how to get on other welfare programs. They compete in it. They compete with one another in drawing supplemental commodities, which are sold if they have value (some of them nobody will buy).

HONIGMANN: We seem to be talking about two sets of people who are trying to outwit each other. The people in Dr. Gazaway's Branch, the Eastern Kentucky syndrome people, are trying to outwit the people who control the welfare dependency aids. On the other hand, the cooperative social agencies are trying to get these people back to work, essentially to realize middle-class values, even though their own tendencies may be something different. These two are warring with each other. It's an excellent description of a kind of class war that I hadn't known of.

FINNEY: The warfare between groups that is often described is true enough, but is only part of the truth. Most often a transaction takes place in which the members of both groups find satisfaction. In a state prison system I found that the staff and the inmates had an implicit agreement, never put into words, to maintain a steady state (von Bertalanffy) in which both could be reasonably comfortable. The continual minor infractions and punishments served to confirm the agreement and continually redefine its limits. Unfortunately, one part of the tacit agreement is that the staff not demand real character change in the inmates, which would be upsetting. Eric Berne has described a like transaction between the caseworker and the welfare client: both parties get a satisfaction from the relationship, and so neither party wants to break it by letting the client become self-supporting. Perhaps in the class warfare that you describe, John, between the welfare agents and the people of the hollows in the Eastern Kentucky mountains, there is also an implicit agreement and a transaction that brings powerful emotional satisfactions to the people on both sides. As a matter of fact I'm quite sure that there is such an unconscious transaction between the poor people of the hollows and the handful of rich or politically powerful families who are called the "power structure" of the county. Both groups would gain from economic and social reforms, such as the President's war on poverty might bring, but both groups are likely to oppose the change, as it would destroy the present interaction of nurturant and dependent, a paternalistic (or maternalistic) relationship that brings emotional satisfactions to both parties. Of course, these are not the reasons they will give for opposing the change, if someone asks them. They'll give more "objective" economic reasons, which are rationalizations.

RANSDELL: I hate to get the two Kentucky groups fighting. I'd much rather you gentlemen battle each other. But I disagree with Dr. Gazaway at some points. The Eastern Kentucky syndrome that Mrs. Roche and I are talking about is an unconscious action to become ill, not a consciously purposeful one. So it differs from what Dr. Gazaway describes. Second, I disagree with the idea that everybody up there is out to get welfare payments. I'm sure that there are many cases of that, but Los Angeles or

Chicago may have more. Furthermore, I do not see these people as a suspicious, fearful, backward group. I see them as being very warm, friendly people who accept you immediately. You can walk into any home up there, and they insist you sit down and have supper with them, and sit and talk. I can just see a stranger knocking on the door of a home in Lexington and saying "I'm a mental health worker," and being invited in for supper! Or walking in and saying, "Where's the neighbor next door?" Why, they'll no more tell you that than the man in the moon.

DE VOS: When did the mines close up?

RANSDELL: The mines have been closing up for the past twenty to thirty years, since the machines came.

DE VOS: There's still a tradition of work there, isn't there?

RANSDELL: Oh, yes. They're producing more coal in the mountains than before.

DE VOS: You haven't got to the second generation yet.

RANSDELL: We're coming to it.

DE VOS: I wonder whether the attitude in the second generation will be what you're describing now in your group or will be more like the Gazaway's Branch group?

RANSDELL: I can't answer that. One thing that we must consider is the strength of many of the people. There's been a migration out of the area. Some counties have lost up to 30 percent of their population in the past ten years. The more motivated, the more educated have left. So what do we have left in this area? The less motivated, the less educated, and people with less initiative.

DE VOS: Selective migration.

RANSDELL: Right.

[He told of a study by a psychiatrist at a miners' hospital, showing that the younger generation of mineworkers fear minework with its risk of injury, while their fathers do not.]

WEINSTEIN: I'm surprised that none of the anthropologists has questioned the supposed friendliness. If a Negro should walk in there, would they be warm and friendly?

GAZAWAY: I can only answer for the Branch. They have no

color sensitivity. I've taken Mr. Powell, a Negro social worker from the VA Hospital, to visit them. He has petrified that something would happen because he was colored. He has a great big Cadillac and insisted on driving it down. Fortunately, he parked it where it could not be seen. We went up the hollow and he was very warmly received; he ate in the home of one of his former patients. There was no reaction to him at all from any of the homes he visited.

WEINSTEIN: I'm certain that it is in culturally defined circumstances that people are warm and friendly. I've worked with Virginia patients. The Western Virginia syndrome is the same as the Eastern Kentucky syndrome. I've had experience with people who are rather impassive and, by your standards, even friendly. But I would trust them no more than I would trust the patients I've seen in this area. Harry Caudill's book tells how Negroes were brought in to break a strike. The local people certainly weren't warm and friendly in those circumstances. You find them friendly because your image has been created before you, by welfare workers over a generation, who have created a receptive attitude.

RANSDELL: I think that it depends on you. If you accept these people as individuals, they will accept you. The first time I went out there to locate a patient, I stopped at the general store and asked if she lived up the hollow, and how far back. They said she lived three miles up, but it had rained, and anyway she wasn't there, she was down the road with her husband. The man said, "I'm going to warn you, she goes off it sometimes, and that's why her husband takes her with him to work. When she goes off, she comes running out of the hollow with no clothes on. She's crazy." I asked directions to the other house. A man who had overheard us said, "I'll take you, if you don't mind me riding with you." For the next half-hour he showed me around and went right in with me.

WEINSTEIN: Why is it that these warm, friendly people have such a high homicide rate?

RANSDELL: I don't know that they do.

WEINSTEIN: South Atlantic states in general have the highest rates in the country. And the rural areas are even higher than the urban areas.

FINNEY: Like you, Dr. Weinstein, I was struck by Dr. Gazaway's statement, "He harbors no bitterness toward anyone, no resentment for the things that have happened to him." And like you, I think it struck a false note. The hostility isn't lacking; it's only hidden. It comes out at other times which, as you say, are culturally defined. I'll go further; I think a person not only hides the hostility from other people, but also, in many cases, hides it from himself, makes himself unaware of it, makes it unconscious. Some of these people may be perfectly honest in denying any resentment.

The other point is the feeling of deprivation. People who cheat are usually people who feel that the world has cheated them, and they feel justified in cheating the world in return. Sometimes this feeling is conscious, and sometimes it is unconscious; there are all degrees and combinations. This was one of the striking things I saw in the Hawaii prisons. The thieves were people who felt that they had been deprived. The feeling went way back into early childhood and must have begun with the interaction of mother and baby.

OPLER: The Puerto Ricans are much like the Eastern Kentuckians in many ways. They have much the same sicknesses, disabilities, and poverty. They also have what they call attacks, and they are classic conversion hysterics.

WEINSTEIN: The Puerto Rican syndrome.

OPLER: Yes. It's also the Puerto Rican syndrome. And they have the same feeling about cheating. They feel that other people cheated them and so they feel justified in cheating to get welfare payments. It's a stereotype to say they all do it, but a certain percentage do.

Now let me tell about the Japanese-Americans in California during World War II. More than a hundred thousand of them were taken from the West Coast and thrown into concentration camps. Whole families were crowded into meager barracks.

They arrived with their suitcases and found bare beds with no sheets. There were no chests of drawers. When I got to Tule Lake, people told me, "The Japanese rob you blind. You put wood out and it disappears." I was so annoyed by these statements of white Haku-jin who had never been inside the Japanese houses that I got Allan Eden of the Russell Sage Foundation to come out and photograph what the Japanese, who are artists with paper and wood, did with this stuff. They used the wood well. They made chests of drawers, inlaid cabinets, and extra cribs for the babies. What was being said about them was unfair. The Japanese felt that they were being treated unjustly, and they were right. Their own surgeon from San Francisco, Dr. Hashiba, a fellow of the American College of Surgeons, was being paid $19 a month. And his surgery was interfered with by an ignorant American USPHS doctor, who was formerly with the Indian service and who had never been certified in surgery. Dr. Hashiba subscribed to nineteen medical and surgical journals, while the other man was an illiterate hack. When people are treated unjustly like that, no wonder they feel justified in cheating; no wonder they steal wood; no wonder they rub snuff in their eyes! They're pulling a sharp trick, getting back at the outsiders, evening it up. That's the way I see it.

[Dr. Opler told about helping with community activities, so that the Japanese could organize "something that meant something to them in their own terms." They made a meticulously detailed Japanese garden.]

I think the only way to avoid the vicious circle of chiseling is to find out the people's interests and help them to organize activities based on them. The people of Eastern Kentucky seem to be interested in houses; maybe some sort of corny local housing redevelopment would be worthwhile, as a community project. Trying to treat these people case by case isn't as good an approach as trying to introduce changes through a community spirit.

MARETZKI: I don't think you can generalize from the Japanese to the people of the Southern Appalachians. I think you're dealing with a different dimension.

DE VOS: Let me take Marvin's story a little further and tell what happened when they got to Chicago. I think that will get back to the point. What we're talking about is the debilitating effect of relief payment versus its possible integrative effect. The Japanese, when they got to Chicago after the relocation, got off relief as fast as possible. They refused to take things from the social agencies. And they got jobs.

OPLER: More than that, George, one step beyond. They went back to Los Angeles and reconstituted Nihombashi ["Japan Bridge," the name for downtown Tokyo].

DE VOS: I think that's what we are talking about. Dr. Gazaway's Branch doesn't sound integrative, because the people are not working at solving the problems. They have a water problem, but they are not making any effort to solve it. When you mentioned that the roofs leak, it seems to me that something is being missed. If the roof has to be fixed to have cisterns, then the roofs have to be fixed! Most cultures that are integrated use the natural resources around them. To me, that is the test whether a culture is integrative: do the people use their natural assets? The Japanese do and the Eastern Kentuckians don't.

OPLER: I agree with you and Tom that Appalachia is not like the Japanese culture. I said this morning that some people have cultural reservoirs that these Appalachia mountaineers apparently don't have in abundance. But I'm looking for the trickle points. My anthropological conscience reminds me that the Hopi Indians did not drill wells. They had the equivalent of a snake-handling cult and danced until the rain came. We're talking about technological and educational differences in the levels of culture.

DE VOS: What I'm talking about, Marvin, is the difference between becoming parasitic and suffering from it, on one hand, and being able to cope with your own problems on the other.

OPLER: The only way to stop the snake dance is to build the water system. Then it will stop.

DE VOS: But the Hopi Indians dealt with it indigenously. They didn't depend on an outside culture to solve their problems.

HONIGMANN: They apparently had cultural values that prevented parasitism. Then the white man started to come in and make parasites out of them.

DE VOS: Exactly.

HONIGMANN: They apparently had cultural values that pre-only to look in Gazaway's Nook, or whatever it is, for the source of it. I think we might look outside.

DE VOS: Exactly. This is something we should talk about: welfare policies and what they're doing to people.

FINNEY: Dr. De Vos is agreeing with Dr. Honigmann in a way, but at another level he is disagreeing. Dr. Honigmann means, "Don't blame the people of Gazaway's Gulch. Feel sorry for them. Blame the outside world, which has mistreated the people and caused their troubles. We outsiders have not treated them well." Dr. De Vos's reply is, "No, the outside world has treated these people too well, has let them get away with too much, has rewarded them too much, or at least has rewarded them for the wrong things, has reinforced the wrong behavior. Though well meant, this lenience and charity is really not treating them well, because it is not good for them in the long run. Outsiders who have been too lenient, too lacking in firmness, have let them get away with too much, and have unwittingly reinforced their dependency and their deceptiveness, by allowing them to cheat their way onto the relief rolls. It is this leniency that has been harmful to them. Instead we should firmly insist on their behaving honestly and self-reliantly, and we should encourage them and reward them when they do so."

WARREN: Let me tell you about a patient that I have now, as an example of the kind of problem, and the difficulty that I as a physician have in dealing with it. I want to rehabilitate this man so that he can work and earn a living again. He won't talk to me! He's satisfied the way he is. With his disability, he has a legitimate, respected position in the community. And he gets almost as much money for being disabled as he could make by working.

I can't beat that system. And I know that that system is wrong. The system should provide only partial insurance. As long as it insures a person up almost to what he could earn by working, the person will rarely want to be rehabilitated and go back to work.

KIEV: It seems to me that when we compare the Gazaway report with the Ransdell-Roche one we can draw a distinction. What Mr. Ransdell and Mrs. Roche talked about this afternoon is a clinical problem, within the field of psychiatry. Their people are selected patients disabled by a diagnosed neurosis, who suffer from a variety of conflicts, many of which spring from within their culture. Their experience, their family relationships, and so on, predispose to the clinical problems they present. I don't think, however, that one can with any firm justification say that Dr. Gazaway's people are mentally ill. They don't meet the conventional simple criteria used in psychiatry. I think that their problems are, to a certain extent, psychological, sociological, cultural, or what have you, but they are not what we know as mental illness.

WEINSTEIN: I think the Ransdell-Roche paper was exceptionally good. In their treatment they disregard the diagnosis, the clinical label, and that's wise. A patient has organic brain disease, but instead of emphasizing it by doing a pneumoencephalogram, they minimize it. Psychiatrists have a kind of prejudice that these people with conversion hysteria are only neurotic, and hence they ought to get better; while with a psychosis, we're much more tolerant. We feel that conversion hysteria is the simplest of all neuroses and theoretically should be the most amenable to treatment. As a matter of fact that's one of the diagnostic criteria. I've worked all over the world. I've seen psychoses that last only six weeks, after which the person is all right. It makes me wonder. Maybe the neurotics with conversion hysteria are just as sick as psychotics. A doctor often has a great intolerance. He begins by expecting a quick cure, and then he gets very resentful if his patient, who doesn't have a single delusion, still won't get better. That is one of the remarkable things about the Ransdell-Roche study: they've cut through all this. They've dealt with the problem in a practical way, in terms of behavior, and not in the esoteric terms of psychiatric diagnosis.

KIEV: That is one thing. Another significant point is that, when we look at poverty (and I think this is a middle-class discrimination), we look at the hovels and the poor latrines, and we call them the causes of mental illness, in the sense in which it was used this afternoon. But that's not demonstrated at all. If you examine the literature you find that if these people work to improve their economic standing and become more technologically advanced, the incidence of psychiatric disability is likely to go up. I think that here we have an unusual opportunity to do research in psychiatric epidemiology. As poverty programs move into these areas, as agricultural and other extension programs bring greater prosperity to these areas, and educational opportunities grow, one can begin to count the increasing cases of psychiatric illness.

[Several people talk at once here.]

KIEV: Here is an opportunity to introduce ways of measuring the effects along with the programs.

DE VOS: That's what bothers me. I want to know what programs are effective. First, establish the baseline; then decide whether to interfere. Will our interference do more good than harm? And if we decide that interference seems to help rather than hinder, and we decide to interfere, we next need to ask in what way we should interfere. There is a Pomo Indian group up at Clear Lake which for the past twenty-five years has been coming apart. They no longer marry. The reason is the rules of the administration of welfare programs, aid to dependent children. You can't marry, because your relief check is cut off if you do. So nobody marries anymore. The men disappear when welfare workers come around. Before, they used to work, but no one works any more, even when work is available. This is an example of a welfare program that does harm and not good.

KIEV: Instead of giving welfare handouts, should we introduce some program like TVA that will provide jobs and other opportunities so that the people can develop within?

DE VOS: My basic question is, what is the man's role? If you define the program so that he has no role, you create a social problem. The role doesn't have to be work; work isn't the only solution. In fact, as automation reduces the work needed, we must find something to take its place—some activity that defines an adult male and that takes the place of work, because obviously we don't need unskilled labor any more. Either that or a person has to join the middle class, and work. In the past the people on the bottom worked the most, and the upper classes practiced leisure as much as possible, finding ways of not working; but now the work pyramid is turned upside down. The higher you go, the more you work. It's a curious reversal of the whole social structure that's going on. The higher you go, the more techno-logical you get, the more time you are required to put in working. It's the professors, the scholars, the scientists, the medical doctors, and the business executives who work long hours, not the blue-collar men. You see, we're here, we're working at this conference. You've got us working long into the night. We're not working an eight-hour day here. We're here for three days, and you're getting at least a fifteen-hour day out of us. [Laughter.] That's because we're "distinguished visitors."

FINNEY: Think what an honor it is!

DE VOS: The middle-class virtue that we have grown up with is a work role. That's the middle-class conception of the honorable thing that a male adult does. And what these Kentucky mountain fellows are doing is reclaiming their self-esteem in terms of a work ethic.

HONIGMANN: They have a work ethic.

DE VOS: They've had a work ethic.

HONIGMANN: They've had it. [Laughter.]

DE VOS: And they can go back to work and solve their problems by a work ethic. Now I don't know if a work ethic is the solution. Frankly, I don't think that a work ethic will be the solution, in our society, in the long run.

WEINSTEIN: There are societies in the world that don't have this value and don't need this excuse.

HOCHSTRASSER: I'd like to add a footnote. The welfare programs in Kentucky until recently have been confined to four categories:

aid to dependent children, aid to totally and permanently disabled, aid to the blind, and old-age pensions. There wasn't any general welfare until the commodity program came in very recently, and now the unemployed fathers' program. So the only way anyone could get welfare payments was to qualify for one of those programs.

DE VOS: You had to earn it by being disabled.

HOCHSTRASSER: I've heard case after case of families in which the father is hiding out so that his wife can declare that he has left her, thus making her eligible for Aid to Dependent Children. I think that a social-cultural context in which people have only these welfare programs has bad results.

DE VOS: What happens to the kids growing up here? Their idea of the father's role is that he hides out until the check is paid. That is pathological, it's unhealthy. But we're failing to examine it. The mythology in Washington is that if you put money into a program you will solve the problem. If you put enough money into the space program, you will solve all the technological problems. The same philosophy is applied to these psychosocial problems; if you put enough money into the war on poverty, somehow you will come up with a solution. And I question this. This is a kind of rain-dancing in Washington. It's a superstitious, unscientific, unrealistic, magical gesture based on empty faith.

FINNEY: You're making the point that government programs often have a harmful effect by inadvertently rewarding behaviors that are the opposite of what we want.

DE VOS: Exactly.

FINNEY: Rewarding sickness instead of health.

DE VOS: Exactly.

FINNEY: That came strikingly to my attention last summer when I visited Alex Leighton and his group in Stirling County. At one of his meetings it came out that fishermen in Stirling County were refusing to accept work in the winter months, because they were drawing unemployment checks. If they went to work on a fishing boat in the winter months, they might only work a week, depending on the weather, before they were out of work again.

And if they were out of work again, they had to wait another three weeks before they'd be eligible to resume getting their payments for unemployment. Obviously, to work a week and then go without income for three weeks to make up for it wasn't worthwhile. The thing that was worthwhile was to avoid working in the first place. And that's what these people did.

Of course, we have only talked about the secondary gain, the financial one. Let's not follow the economists into the trap of assuming that people act only on rational economic motives, for secondary gain. You and I would work whether it paid well or not. And we'd work even if we were rich enough not to need the money. Our compulsive consciences require it. People act from combinations of motives, biological and interpersonal, conscious and unconscious, conventional and personal, religious and esthetic, altruistic and self-centered, short-term and long term, puritanical and hedonistic, realistic and neurotically self-defeating. We shouldn't be surprised when people fail to do what is to their economic advantage.

WITTKOWER: Would you allow me to approach the problem from an entirely different angle, the psychoanalytic angle? The speakers this afternoon spoke of the secondary gain, the financial reward of being disabled. Now, the emphasis on secondary gain raises the questions, what is the primary gain and, even more important, what is the primary loss or what is the primary frustration? I wonder if the speakers could tell us something about the primary loss and the primary frustration? The second point is, they spoke about conversion hysteria. Conversion hysteria means the dramatization of an unconscious conflict. Now, what conflict do they dramatize? I think we can guess what one conflict is, because you described mostly motor symptoms. I don't know anything about your patients in Eastern Kentucky, but the situation in many ways is similar to that of the Peruvian Indians who live up in the Andes. On examination they are exceedingly friendly, warm people, who have a great deal of hostility underneath. And my guess is that the Appalachian people also are not so friendly; that they are merely friendly on the surface, that there is a great deal of hostility underneath. Dr. Weinstein spoke about the rate of homicide. This claim of disabling symptoms conceals the unconscious impulse to strike. I wonder whether there is any evidence to support this idea.

ROCHE: That's what we came to you for—answers. [Laughter.]

WEINSTEIN: Well, I question the whole concept of unconscious conflict; that people have unconscious wishes, needs, drives. I think they are unconscious only of how they *show* them and how they affect other people. The same person can be quite friendly at one time and quite hostile at another. That doesn't mean that he has been repressing it, being unaware of his hostility all the time. I think that these people respond by extremes. There is an access all to one or all to the other. A stranger is good or he is bad.

There's one other issue that I hoped Dr. Honigmann would bring up, because it is in reference to his talk of this morning. It's the ins and the outs. We talk of these people trying to get something for nothing, and that we're rewarding sickness and poverty. Well, actually, in our culture I think we reward wealth and success much more. If a man gets paid, say, under the soil bank for not growing something, or a business firm gets a large reduction on its income tax, these are much larger benefits than these people are getting. And I wonder if the behavior we call dishonest—cheating, lying—is not simply a caricature of what we ourselves are doing all the time. We shouldn't be condemning those people with our moral judgments.

DE VOS: Let's get away from the question of the ethics of this matter. We are simply talking about cause and effect. I don't think this is a moral issue, necessarily; I think that this is just a question of what you do in this situation. What is available to you? How can you get something? Now, if a welfare policy teaches people that you can get something if you behave a certain way, people will do it. Some will even put tobacco snuff in their eyes periodically, to be examined and ruled legally blind, though that is rather far out. Most people aren't that ingenious: they stop short of this sort of thing. Gazaway's Branch is a fairly recent community, from what you've described. I'll give it a value judgment. It's growing like a tiny cancer. It's producing it own norms, while it grows as something parasitic on the larger society. It's a little parasite culture that depends on the checks that are coming in from the outside. The people are not learning to put roofs up for their water. They are not learning to cope with their environment. Instead, they're learning *not* to cope with their environment.

FINNEY: You're saying that this parasitism is an unhealthy condition. It's a sick condition of society. In the long run, it's not good for the people of the Branch, and it's not good for the people of the larger society. It's a situation that cripples people, that keeps people from growing and reaching their full potential, from living a mature life.

OPLER: A comment on that. When you compare Gazaway's Branch unfavorably with Japanese culture, or Hopi culture, you must remember that these others have had centuries of culture-building, while Gazaway's Branch is a quickie, growing, you say, like a cancer. But I think patients, wherever you find them, are important objects to study, and I think Dr. Wittkower's question is a very significant one to pursue. I remember running into conversion hysterias in great number in Portland, Oregon, at the Morningside Clinic and Hospital. That was at one time the only federal psychiatric installation for Alaskan natives. They were Athabascans; there were Eskimo and frontier whites. And their mental health did vary. These are acculturating communities; this isn't like the Greenland Eskimo. (Mental health in Greenland was better than in Alaska, where there was quick and exploitative cultural contact, which brings about kinds of breakdown.) The thing that is interesting for Eric's question is that in the cultures that valued mobility, and where people were supposed to hunt and gather and keep on the move and function with their muscles, the way out was conversion hysteria. It was like Biblical kinds of conversion, as I read the Bible; that is, you got lame, or halt, or blind, and somebody could cure you by moral suasion of some sort or by water injections or magical gestures.

As I read the Bible, those are cases that psychiatrists today would call hysteria or conversion reaction.

I then studied the Ute. Their classical syndrome was conversion hysteria, too. Again there is a demand for vigor and mobility, to keep going and keep pushing against pretty bad odds. I began to study some of the Ute cases in which the shaman did dream analysis out of Freud, or did sleight of hand, or, as somebody mentioned this morning, the equivalent of water injection, so that the patient can get up and proceed on his way.

But there is one more thing that interests me greatly, and it's along the lines that Eric mentioned, the primary and secondary layers. (Let's leave aside this whole business about unconscious, and so on. That appears to be grounds for debate in the other corner among the psychoanalysts.) The Ute Indians, with their extended families, don't all get conversion hysterias, but there are significant cases of authority and age pressures and conflict situations in the family, where these neuroses develop, and the shaman *did* produce marvelous cures. Conversion hysteria is a classical kind of neurotic ailment, and it's often open to spontaneous remission. I imagine that visiting caseworkers and people dealing with a case don't know it culturally or completely, as an individual case history. But the person's lot is cast in this little narrow chasm, with all those introverted people. When I speak of the Ute extended family, and then hear your statistics on Aunt Berthy in Gazaway's Branch, who was related to so many people, it sounds the same.

I noticed in the discussion of work, there are them here that likes it, and them that don't. But I would be pretty sure that the kind of work that I saw the tuberculous man doing, hacking up the animals [refers to Dr. Gazaway's slides], or the story I heard about the other one in the mines being crushed by a rock, or others who have crawled through these things and weren't crushed—this is damn unpleasant work. Let's not talk about work as a way out; it isn't. This isn't Hopi Indians planting corn in concert in the arroyo bottoms and surrounding each growing cornstalk with a little wall. Gazaway's Branch is a disgusting way of life. I agree with George on that point. It's a blind alley. I think that those who are arguing that the problem is purely clinical are forgetting that the size of the social group you're thrown in with, the typical conflicts, the typical defenses that are called for, all make a difference. This is Anna O. in the gulch. [He refers to an early case of Freud's.] And for good reasons. Anna O. in Europe was a little bit hemmed in, shall we say, by an aged, sickly father and a hatchet-faced mother. She was supposed to be a good dutiful daughter; she got her conversion hysterias. She got psychotic hallucinations at the same time, too. That was a classical conversion hysteria case, and everyone knows the story of the way out. That lady is supposed to have been one of the first social workers in her country. [Editor's note: Freud reported his cases by pseudonyms. Many rumors circulate about the true identity of his patients.] No matter how much we discuss the way of life, you're still dealing with a real problem. We can move them out of the Kentucky mountains tomorrow, but I don't know where you can resettle them.

DE VOS: This war on poverty is like the Japanese story of Momotaro, a young boy who defeats the demons. He gets a dog and a rooster and the rest and they go off to war against the demons. But you have to know who the demons are, before going to war.[1] What is poverty? I define poverty as a loss of social role. What goes on in these situations is that the adult male doesn't have a role. The women don't have the problem, because they pretty much make their role as homemaker.

FINNEY: You mean that what characterizes the culture of poverty is that the adult man doesn't have a useful role in which he can respect himself and expect other people to respect him.

KIEV: I think it would be helpful if we had some idea of the potential ways in which the government can help these communities. That is to say, are the programs to be welfare programs, merely handing money out, or are they to be tailormade to the

[1] In the old Japanese folk tales, the demons or ogres had skins of odd colors, red and white. They were the Ainu or white people who lived in Japan before the coming of the Japanese.—Editor

particular needs of these small communities? We need to examine what is available, what can be introduced.

FINNEY: Before we close our discussion we need some comment on the program that Mr. Ransdell and Mrs. Roche have described this afternoon. Essentially what we have been told is, "We deal firmly with the hysterical conversion reactions, telling the people that they *can* work and that we insist on their working. We do everything possible to encourage them to work, and often it succeeds." The combination of one strict commanding parent and one warm loving one, working together and not at cross purposes, makes a double bind. I've pointed (1966) to the effectiveness of the same combination in *hsi nao* [Chinese phrase literally translated "wash brain"]. Do we have any comments on that general approach?

DE VOS: You've described how it's better to be unemployed in the wintertime because if you try to work, you're penalized. It seems to me that one of the things here that we should discuss is the effect of such a double system. It's hard to have a work ethic in the summer and an avoid-work ethic in the winter. Isn't one corrosive of the other? When you have a well-established relief policy and a problematical work situation, isn't work discouraged?

HOCHSTRASSER: There are other patterns of response. In the study in Morgan County that I've been involved in, you find seasonal work. Many people leave the county during the summer and live on construction work. They find out about jobs through friends in Ohio, Michigan, and other places, and a whole carload of them will get together. Maybe one can drive and has a driver's license and can read a little bit. They all go off in the car and leave their families behind, looking for a job; some of them are successful. Maybe the wife joins the husband when he has a job. Sometimes the whole family goes. There is a regular cycle that they go through every year. They're in the county in the wintertime, and they're out in the summer. So you see that some of the poor people in Kentucky do seek jobs; you're stereotyping the area unfairly when you say that there is only one kind of response. Your cases are in Pike County, in mining country. Now the county that I'm working in is predominantly agricultural, with a little mining, and the situation is very different.

MARETZKI: There are many contradictions in the situation in Kentucky. It seems to me even from what you've said that there is still a work ethic. Miners can still go back into the mine shafts on their bellies, and scratch around coal. Among the Hawaiians, there is a different ethic. You don't work unless you absolutely have to. But in Kentucky there seems to be a residue of a work ethos. So I'm not sure that the role model is entirely missing.

WIKLER: As for the people described by Mr. Ransdell and Mrs. Roche, if their behavior and symptoms are so easily controlled by the manipulation of secondary gains alone, they don't sound like people with conversion reaction. They sound more like sociopaths, with malingering.

FINNEY: Oh, wait a minute. One of the people that Dr. Gazaway described, the man who put snuff in his eyes, was malingering, and that was a sociopathic act, though I'd hate to label a person from one act. The Ransdell-Roche patients had been diagnosed by psychiatrists as conversion reaction, and probably rightly so; though, like you, I shouldn't have expected them to respond so promptly to secondary gains; hysterical conversion reactions are supposed to have primary gains as well, and the primary gains are harder to reach and deal with. Maybe Mrs. Roche and Mr. Ransdell gave primary rewards, too, satisfying the oral, dependency needs. Superficially, hysterics and sociopaths may be alike in their behavior, but the motives, the dynamics, are different. Both of them deceive people, manipulate people, lead people to expect certain things and then fail to pay off. As Eric Berne would say, both the hysteric and the sociopath play "games." As part of the maneuver to influence people, both the hysteric and the sociopath develop physical symptoms in imitation of organic medical sickness. But there is a difference. The sociopath knows what he is doing, and he does it callously. The hysteric, on the other hand, both in his conversion reactions and in his "hysterical acting-out," fools himself, deceives himself.

He is not aware of the game-playing that he does. Now, Dr. Weinstein, you may not feel that this is an important distinction; you say you don't believe in the unconscious. But it seems an important distinction to me. I'm glad that the diagnostic manual of the American Psychiatric Association separates the hysteric (conversion reaction) from the sociopath. If you can make a hysteric aware of what he is doing, why he is doing it, and how he is manipulating people, it makes him highly uncomfortable. His conscience bothers him. That's not true of the sociopath. And that difference ought to make a difference in the methods by which we can hope to change or influence these people. Of course there are all gradations in between, gradations in the strength of conscience or the lack of it.

Dr. Opler's point that people who cheat tend to be people who feel justified in doing so, who feel bitter about having been cheated themselves, is an interesting one. When I was the psychiatrist and psychologist for the Hawaii prisons and reform schools, I found that so, especially among the thieves. They felt bitter, felt that they had been deprived in life, and so felt the urge to take revenge on the world by stealing from other people. But I don't share Dr. Opler's belief that the source of this feeling is usually that someone really has cheated them in their adult lives. That may be true of the Japanese group, a people who didn't have this bitter feeling until they suffered a real injustice as adults. President Roosevelt, who was supposedly a liberal, did a real injustice to the American citizens of Japanese ancestry, arresting and imprisoning them on the basis of their race and the national origin of their parents. They had a right to feel bitter. But people who feel cheated all their lives are a different story. If such real-life episodes of being deprived do happen, they are only confirmatory episodes that a person himself creates, what Freud would call a repetition compulsion, to confirm and justify a deprived feeling that he has had long before. When you trace it back, you find that the person has had the deprived feeling all his life, or at least since early childhood. So we must conclude that if there really was a deprivation that produced the permanent feeling of deprivation, it must have occurred within the family; it must have been their own parents who deprived them of affection, leaving them feeling unloved. This is what I've found in my work as a psychiatrist, psychologist, and psychotherapist; and I suspect it's true of Dr. Gazaway's hollow-dwellers, and of Dr. Opler's New York Puerto Ricans. The adult-life episodes, the economic or financial dealings, are only a surface explanation for a lifelong feeling of deprivation that runs much deeper.

MARGETTS: We've talked a lot about the outsiders' view of Gazaway's Branch, but I'd rather like to hear about the inhabitants' stereotype of what the people outside are like, outside Gazaway's Branch. What do those people think about us? What do they think about how they might relate to the people outside of the Branch?

GAZAWAY: They have a very limited possibility of relating, because in the first place people can't understand their dialect; and in turn, their ability to understand what outsiders say to them is very limited.

MARGETTS: But what I mean is, if the people in Gazaway's Branch were trying to analyze us as we're trying to analyze them, what would they think of us, how do they see people in the outside world?

GAZAWAY: Well, when they ask me what I do, and I go into some of the details, telling them that I set my alarm clock and get up at five every morning, they're proud of the fact that they get up at four, because they wake up at four. But they can't understand that I go to bed at eleven o'clock while they go to bed at eight or nine. For instance, because I had three or four dresses all of the same kind, they thought I wore the same dirty dress all the time, as they do. I talk about some of the things that I like to do, like hunting. They can hunt, they're much better shots than I am, but they don't have any shells. So when we went hunting, I'd bring the shells, and they'd bring the guns.

MARGETTS: What do they think of a lighted city street?

SOMEONE: What do they think about somebody who drives a nice automobile?

HOCHSTRASSER: They all have electricity.

GAZAWAY: They don't all have electricity in the hollow.

HOCHSTRASSER: Don't you think they've seen city lights?

MARGETTS: If you're trying to reorganize these people, they have to know what they're going to be reorganized into. Otherwise you don't stand a chance. Do they want to be reorganized? Are we to reject them or are we to draw them into an outside culture? Those are the two alternatives. I can't see it halfway.

HONIGMANN: Those are not the only two alternatives. To let somebody alone or to adapt him to our own culture is not our only choice.

MARGETTS: What's the third, fourth, or fifth one?

HONIGMANN: The third one would be to develop them from their own jumping-off point.

[Several talk excitedly at once.]

MARGETTS: What you are suggesting is idealistic and impractical. It will never be done.

HONIGMANN: I would question that.

MARGETTS: I haven't seen one demonstrated like that.

a puerto rican boy

Oscar Lewis

Over many years spent in Mexico in the study of peasant cultures, and more recently of urban slums, I developed a concept, first published in 1959, which I called the "culture of poverty." Michael Harrington, in his book *The Other America*, took the concept up, but I find that he doesn't mean by it quite what I described. He seems to equate the culture of poverty essentially with poverty itself. I try to differentiate them because I think the consequences of the two are very different. What I should like to do, therefore, is briefly to review a few aspects of the definition of the culture of poverty, and then spend most of my time reporting to you on my recent study in Puerto Rico, in San Juan, and reading to you a portion of a book that I am working on now on a Puerto Rican family.

I define the culture of poverty in terms of some sixty specific traits that fall, essentially, into economic, social, and psychological traits. The model is clear. If you have these traits, you have the culture of poverty. They are really bundles of related traits, and within each bundle there are some that I consider crucial. Now the point that I want to make is that poverty doesn't always give rise to these traits. The concept might have been called the culture of X or phenomenon X. Not all poor people have a culture of poverty.

The characteristics that I would stress in defining the culture of poverty are characteristics of a psychological and social nature. The psychological traits I've emphasized are feelings of not belonging, marginality, unworthiness, inferiority, and the feeling that the institutions of the larger society are not there to serve

LIST OF TRAITS OF THE CULTURE OF POVERTY

Economic Traits

Unemployment and underemployment

Low wages

Miscellany of unskilled occupations

Child labor

Absence of savings

Chronic shortage of cash

Absence of food reserves in the home

Frequent daily food purchases in small quantities

Pawning

Borrowing from local money lenders at usurious rates of interest

Spontaneous informal credit devices

Use of second-hand clothing and furniture

Constant struggle for survival

Social & Psychological

Crowded quarters

Lack of privacy

Gregariousness

High incidence of alcoholism

Violence

Violence in training of children

Wife beating

Early initiation into sex

Free unions

Abandonment of mothers and children

Mother-centered families

Predominance of nuclear family

Authoritarianism

Emphasis upon family solidarity (only rarely achieved)

Local residence a kind of small community

Stable residence

Lifetime friendships

Daily face-to-face relations with same people

Extended family ties quite strong

Local community acts as a shock absorber for rural migrants to city

Use of herbs for curing

Raising of animals

Political apathy

Belief in sorcery and spiritualism

Cynicism about government

Hatred of police

Limited membership and participation in both formal and informal associations

Critical attitude toward some of beliefs and values of dominant classes

Mistrust of government and those in high position

Cynicism which extends even to the church

Members attempt to utilize and integrate into a workable way of life the remnants of beliefs and customs of diverse origins

Strong feeling of marginality

Strong feeling of helplessness

Strong feeling of dependency

Feeling of inferiority and personal unworthiness

Little sense of history

Not class-conscious

Others

Strong present-time orientation with little ability to defer gratification

Resignation and fatalism

Male superiority (machismo)

Corresponding martyr complex among women

High tolerance for psychological pathology

Provincial and locally oriented

Marginal to national institutions (social security, labor unions, banks, etc.)

Low level of education and literacy

Relative higher death rate

Lower life expectancy

Higher proportion of individuals in the younger age groups

Higher proportion of gainfully employed (because of working women and child labor)

the interests of these people. I would also stress a family structure that is a bilateral, not a unilateral, system, and extended families, but as social units, not as residence units. In short, there is an absence of organizations beyond the level of the family. When these people live in slums and when there is some stability of residence, they do develop a sense of neighborliness and some sense of identification with the slum, but there isn't anything in their subculture which gives them a sense of belonging to organizations that go on over time.

This criterion immediately eliminates from the culture of poverty poor people who are organized and poor people who belong to trade unions, particularly when the trade unions are functional and give them a sense of identity. Therefore, organized labor, no matter how low the wages, would not meet the ideal type that I am talking about. In India, for example, where you have a caste system and a clan system, the lowest caste is desperately poor; nevertheless, they had a great sense of belonging, and of cultural identification, and a deep sense of tradition. They were Hindus and on most ceremonial occasions behaved just like the upper castes. Their marriage systems were identical, in contrast to a culture of poverty whose marriage system is not the same as that of the middle or upper class. In the culture of poverty we find a great preponderance of free unions or consensual marriages.

The people in the culture of poverty have no sense of history. They know relatively little about the past and about the society they are living in, and, as has been pointed out, they are very much oriented to the present time.

Perhaps I should give a few other examples of situations in which there is great poverty but not, by my definition, the culture of poverty. If you have only poverty, you have people with values and ideas that are very much like that of the middle-class society in the modern world, and therefore it's not a very difficult problem to reach these people. If they are just poor people, all you have to do to relieve their problems is give them some source of income. But when you have a large number of traits which, I think, go together in various bundles, a *culture* of poverty, it is clearly not just a matter of economics. Then you have to deal with a whole value system which is not necessarily satisfying to its members but which does persist and does offer some satisfaction.

I have also indicated that middle-class people (and this would certainly include most social scientists) have tended to concentrate on the negative aspects of the culture of poverty and to associate negative valences with such traits as present-time orientation, concrete and not abstract orientation, and so on. Now I would be the last one to romanticize the culture of poverty. As someone has said, it is easier to praise poverty than to live it. I think, however, that we should not overlook the positive aspects that flow from some of these traits. Living in the present may develop a capacity for spontaneity and for the enjoyment of the sensual, a sense of adventure, and the indulgence of impulse, which is often blunted in our middle-class, future-oriented man. Perhaps it is this reality of the moment which the middle-class existentialist writers are so desperately trying to recapture and which the culture of poverty experiences as a natural, everyday phenomenon.

Now I believe that my earlier works, the *Five Families*, particularly, and the *Children of Sanchez*, indicate quite clearly a whole range of characteristics that are essentially positive characteristics. I also take exception to the trend in some sociological studies to identify the lower class almost exclusively with vice, crime, and juvenile delinquency as if most poor people were thieves, beggars, ruffians, murderers, or prostitutes. Most people in the United States find it difficult to think of poverty as a stable, persistent, ever-present phenomenon because our expanding economy and the specially favorable circumstances of our history have led to an optimism which makes us think that poverty is transitory.

As a matter of fact, despite the national interest in poverty, I believe that people in the United States with most of the crucial traits of the culture of poverty are very few. Although in financial terms 30 percent of the families in the United States are below the poverty line, I estimate that certainly no more than a third of those—10 percent of the whole—have the culture of poverty.

Illiteracy, real or functional, would be one trait that I insist upon as being very important. When you compare the United States on this trait with many of the underdeveloped countries of the world, you see at once what a tremendous difference there is. And there is a different quality as a result of this. So that people having a culture of poverty, I think, represent only a small segment of the poor people in the United States.

My purpose in the Puerto Rican study was to test the concept of the culture of poverty in different national, historical contexts. I developed it from Mexican material and from my reading. For the most part there is very little in anthropological literature that can be used for comparative analysis because I was dealing fundamentally with an urban slum phenomenon, and anthropologists have made almost no studies of the urban slums of the world. I therefore had to rely upon some of the better novelists, some of the autobiographies of people who grew out of the slums, and some of the writers who at one time were slumdwellers. I wanted to test my findings directly in the case of Puerto Rico, and I designed a study as follows.

We began with a hundred families in four slums in San Juan, and we selected families who had low family income of $1,200 or less a year and who had relatives in New York. Thus we could also study a hundred families of their relatives in New York City. We wanted to get some idea of what life was like in San Juan slums and of how it changed or didn't change in New York City, and we wanted to do it in terms of intensive family studies as well as of observed days and reconstructed days, and so on. We now have gathered over 30,000 pages of tape-recorded life histories and other interview material from these families. My book *La Vida: A Puerto Rican Family in the Culture of Poverty, San Juan and New York* is based upon 6,000 pages of tape-recorded life history material of all members of the family. I have broadened the canvas somewhat compared to my earlier works.

In this book, sixteen Puerto Ricans tell their life stories, and, for the first time, I have tape-recorded the life stories of children.

In studying children, we get some notion of what the culture of poverty does to young people at a very early age. I think this is quite crucial in terms of learning theory, particularly in terms of how the culture is perpetuated from generation to generation. What I would like to do here is to read to you excerpts from the life story of a seven-year-old who has lived in the San Juan slum and then moves to New York City. The excerpts that I will read include both the San Juan and the New York City side, but very briefly as you can see. I studied this family quite intensively. I am calling it the Rios family, and the child is called Gabi. Please remember that this is a seven-year-old. I have, of course, organized the material. All the language is his; the organization very often is mine as well as the selection of materials. My idea in this presentation is to give you not only an understanding but some feeling for these people, particularly of family life as seen through the eyes of a child.

What I would like psychiatrists and other clinicians present to do when I am through is to tell me whether this seven-year-old has good mental health or poor mental health. Tell me what you think would be your prognosis for his future in New York City. I think it will be fairly obvious what the culture of poverty does and means to a child of this age.

[Dr. Lewis told the story at some length, mostly by direct quotation of the child's words. The boy kept complaining of neglect and mistreatment; he seemed to do so confidently, aggressively, and perhaps impishly. The story was full of sex and violence, both occurring as impulsive actions on the part of the adults, actions that affected the little boy, and that he could do nothing about. Grownups seemed big bullies to the boy. The attitude toward sex seemed an inconsistent one: promiscuous sexual activity was something that adults did, but which they or other adults must have condemned, because the little boy complained that it was wrong.—Editor]

discussion three

Dr. Lewis's paper stimulates lively discussion by the other participants. Drs. Opler and Lewis compare their findings on Puerto
Ricans in Puerto Rico and in New York, and Dr. Lewis compares
the psychological functioning of Puerto Ricans with that of
Mexicans. Dr. De Vos and others discuss the validity of the
Rorschach and other psychological measuring instruments when
used cross-culturally.

LEWIS: I'd like the psychoanalysts here to tell me something
about this child. Does he sound like a well-adjusted child to you?

FINNEY (chairman): Dr. Wittkower, would you like to comment
on the case? Dr. Opler, are you a psychoanalyst?

OPLER: I have had psychoanalytic training. I don't think you
can analyze this case without seeing the person and observing his
behavior. You have to see him do things, and not only listen to
him. Frankly, from what I have heard, I do not think that this
seven-year-old is mentally ill, but he sounds terribly, terribly old.

LEWIS: That is one of the outstanding characteristics of the
culture of poverty. There is no childhood. The children must
cope with adult problems. They develop an apparent precocious-
ness that is not true maturity. It seems to me that this boy copes
very well with what I call a pathological family situation. His
mother is a prostitute. Not only that, but she mixes her business
with her home life. Her mother says, "The trouble with my
daughter is that she does it for the love of the art." In other
words, she gets emotionally involved and brings some of her men

home, because she is still hoping to find a man who will fall in love with her and accept her and her five children. It seems to me that this child copes beautifully with this environment. The question is, will he be able to cope as well when he is put into a better environment, if that's in his future?

OPLER: In Midtown New York the Puerto Rican children see primal scenes [sexual intercourse of their parents] and births.

LEWIS: Among more than 200 families we have studied in Mexico City and 230 in Puerto Rico, this is one of the outstanding differences—the lack of repression in Puerto Rico, as compared to Mexico. Over a twenty-year period I must have spent eight or nine years in Mexico, in fieldwork, and in all that time I have rarely heard anyone, either peasant or slumdweller, admit that he had seen or heard his parents copulate. In Puerto Rico it's common in life histories to hear detailed accounts. And there's much less effort on the part of the mothers to protect their children from it. Again, there is a high incidence of asthma in Puerto Rico, which in Mexico is almost absent.[1] Perhaps related to that is the fact that Mexican mothers rarely give their children away, while in Puerto Rico it is common at all class levels and commonest among the poor. The poor use informal adoption, the upper classes, formal adoption.

FINNEY: You are referring to the psychiatric opinion that asthma comes from a fear of separation from the mother.

[Dr. Opler comments on such experiences among Puerto Ricans in New York and relates them to seeing cut-up bodies on the Rorschach. Projective findings of this kind, which are usually considered highly pathological, do not correlate with the degree of judged psychopathology among Puerto Ricans.]

LEWIS: The form of expression of aggression in the slums of Mexico City is quite different from that in the slums of San Juan. In Mexico City you rarely try to mark someone up. You are more

---

[1] Marvin Opler remarks later that it is hard to tell whether Puerto Ricans with dyspnea really have asthma (a psychophysiological reaction) because most, if not all, of the clinical picture is from a conversion reaction (hysteria). The same is true in Eastern Kentucky, where the common "smothering spells" are conversions. —Editor

reserved, you are more hesitant to get into a fight, but once you do, your objective is very clearly to kill, usually with a knife or a gun. In Puerto Rico, the objective is much less to kill than to mark up. Cutting faces with a razor is common. One of the motives of some of the people in moving to New York City, strangely enough, is to seek plastic surgery at Bellevue Hospital. Four of our hundred families gave that as the major motive for migrating. Of course, if you do a questionnaire study they will not give you this as their reason. As a matter of fact, if you do a questionnaire study (and we've checked this again and again) the motives become very stereotyped, and they are all economic. They migrate to look for jobs, to better their conditions. But when you get to know the families well and live with them for a year or more, you find out that in almost every case there is some psychological factor, some family factor, some social problem that they have, which they almost never, of course, own up to in a three-hour interview on the first go-around or even on the second go-around. Curious things happen. When we first did the questionnaire study, the uncle of little Gabi gave us a typical answer. But having studied every member of his extended family, we knew enough to ask him if it was true that trouble with the police had led to his move. Actually this was the major cause, according to his mother's account and others. Eventually he told us about it. Eight months later (we knew this family quite well and had visited it a great deal) I had an occasion to go back to redo the initial questionnaire survey. When I came to the question "Why did you come to New York?" he gave me the stereotyped economic answer again.

Now on the Rorschach, Children's Apperception Test (CAT), and other tests, we got a very different picture of this child, a picture of a child in trouble. I have a very brilliant Rorschach interpretation composed of two independent analyses, one by a Mexican who has met the child, and one by a tester at the Harvard Clinic. They tend to agree. Clinicians in looking at my test material always see these people as much sicker than I see them. I don't know whether that is a function of the tests or a function of their occupational perception, but they *always* see them that way.

OPLER: There is a cultural shift in the Rorschach in the Puerto Ricans. So you can't use U. S. clinic standards of Rorschach interpretation at all.

LEWIS: Nor with the Mexicans.

OPLER: The accounts we have from kids are similar—they beat hell out of each other. One of the San Juan slum games that was reported to us again and again was beating with sticks. The guy who wins is the guy who lasts longest, who stands the pain with the most manliness. That's about as masochistic a game as I can think of. But it comes naturally.

FINNEY: Sadomasochistic, and perhaps exhibitionistic.

KIEV: It seems to me that while this young fellow sounds sophisticated and perhaps not mentally ill at the moment, the family background you describe certainly does not sound good prognostically. He may be in a fair setting at the moment, but the first seven years are pretty crucial. His perception of men and women would not offer a good masculine self-concept at the age of 18, or make for trust in women at a later stage if he marries. I think this boy is probably destined for an unstable series of marriages. It would be interesting to compare him with a child who got out of the same situation at an earlier age. You could perhaps do this in quantity to see at what age the most damage is done.

LEWIS: For the first two years of his life he had a fairly stable family. But what saves so many of these children, it seems to me, is the amount of autonomy that is forced upon them very early. They can get away from rejecting or punishing mothers and spend much of their time alone on the street. In multiproblem families some of the children who lose their mothers when they are very young are better off.

KIEV: They may be, in avoiding a psychotic kind of adjustment; but in learning the ability to tolerate frustration, to plan for the future, to incorporate a satisfactory self-image, and identification, I think you don't get these from living in the street.

LEWIS: No, I don't think you do, but there were some positive men in his life, some male images that he could identify with, and he wanted to be like the neighbors. I think the neighbors have saved many of these children. They are so dependent upon neighbors, even for food, in this case. Of course, I wonder that he seems so grown up. He knows all there is to know about life and marriage and everything else, at age 7; I wonder what life can teach this child.

DE VOS: Will you be a little more specific about what the people said about the projective tests?

LEWIS: I'd love to tell you if you want to listen. It's a fascinating analysis.

DE VOS: Do they comment on the specific responses themselves?

LEWIS: Oh, yes. The CAT was very rich. And also the Rorschach.

> Gabi is a boy who has not been able to make the most of his rich intellectual and emotional resources. Despite great environmental poverty and lack of cultural stimulation, his good natural endowment is reflected in his productivity and in his exuberance in the use of color and human movement. His apparent precocity is, however, but a symptom of his uneven development and of the methods he's employing to deal with destructive impulses, and to handle overwhelming tensions. He seems to be deliberately making use of every resource at his command in a struggle to maintain some kind of equilibrium, to come to terms with himself and his environment, to find identification objects. He handles his anxieties by indulging in an uncritical compulsive-like productivity, of playing with concepts in semi-perseverative fashion. There is gross acceleration in the thinking process, which finds expression in deviant ways. His reality testing is poor and often leads to grandiose generalizations. This is reflected in the large number of whole responses, many of them of poor quality. He incurs DW responses, confabulations, position responses, gross poor form responses, transpositions, all indicative of deviant thought processes. His lack of a self-satisfying self-concept and his ensuing need to find himself by way of multiple idetifications is reflected in the large number of human movement responses. An overly large number of

human movement responses, way over what corresponds to his age, with only one animal movement response, represents an exaggerated reversal of expectancy for an 8-year-old boy. [We tested him when he was eight.] It does not represent the healthy internalization of consistent love-objects, but a ceaseless role-playing, a taking on of the roles of adults because of a lack of consistent love objects in his environment. Just as he overreacts to the human aspects of the stimulus, so he is over-profuse in his use of color, more in response to external pressures because of dependency needs that are reflected in oral gratification content, than in a healthy emotional reaction to a satisfying environment. He makes little use of shading, but reacts to the diffuse impression of a blot stemming from its darkness and often in unison with inanimate movement showing his susceptibility to profound disturbance. In anxiety-arousing situations he experiences inner tension and aggressivity.

Well, this goes on and on. It's a long report.

DE VOS: You have a problem here. The type of interpretations that are made of specific material would be quite different if he were a 20-year-old. Certainly it isn't according to the expected pattern of what we get in middle-class culture on the Rorschach. Nevertheless all that human movement is only possible in a highly differentiated ego. This is not a simple problem. It's a rather complex ego structure and it's interpreted as sick because he goes against the expectancies of the normative group.

MARGETTS: Did the interpreters know the age of the child?

LEWIS: Sure.

MARGETTS: For those who are more interested in Rorschach than I am, I'd like to ask, might not that contaminate the interpretation? I don't think that a clinical psychology test is of any use whatsoever unless the tester knows nothing about the person tested.

DE VOS: I quite disagree with you.

MARGETTS: Otherwise the test, as far as I am concerned, is invalid.

DE VOS: No, not at all. The test is another way of getting standardized behaviors. And there is no reason why it has to be used blindly. That is the kind of thing I disagree with completely. If you take a psychological test as a way of eliciting behavior from an individual, this is valid behavioral material. It's sterile to say that the less you know about a person the more you can depend on the test. Blind interpretation is a good method if you are trying to learn about the test, but not if you are trying to learn about an individual.

MARGETTS: Now, wait a minute! Would you get different conclusions if you did it blindly?

DE VOS: Yes. If you did not know the age of this child, you would interpret it quite differently.

MARGETTS: So what good is the test?

DE VOS: It's important to know the age of the child. When you give an IQ test you have to know the age of the child. When you give any kind of a test you have to know the age. Sex is less important. But certainly you can't interpret a child's test like an adult's test. The peculiarity of what you have read is the amount of material you got out of it. It is very difficult for a child to produce movement responses and inanimate movement responses.

LEWIS: Yes, and a great deal of whole responses, very productive, about five per card.

DE VOS: This kid is expressive, it's very obvious, because it is not usual for a child to press thus hard. And that he can't quite control it is very obvious, too. He presses beyond his means. But the thing that's peculiar is that even though there have been studies in which children produced movement responses, it's a poor prognosis for adult stability. Nevertheless, I don't think people have looked at this matter from the standpoint of what you're studying. I think that the kids who produced the *M* responses are probably experiencing the same sort of thing, trying to internalize it, trying to handle it within, because this is what the *M* response and the inanimate movement means. This kid is trying to internalize the material that life is giving him, trying to handle it, to cope with it somehow, but he is only an eight-year-old; it stretches his development capacity to cope with such material. The prognosis is likely to be poor, because the child is just not up to coping with this material. Here is a kid without the usual self-control, without the usual inhibitions, showing a superior mentality, but on an eight-year-old level, in a culture that is not letting him stretch it to where he can handle it better. It is an incongruous picture. Psychologists who come from a clinical setting don't know what to do with things like this.

LEWIS: Some would go by the tests, I've found; others would go by history. Of course, they all say that best of all would be some clinical experience with the child—actual observations.

DE VOS: You see precocious mentality in his attempt to cope with reality. In a sense he is very much reality-oriented. He does not withdraw into mathematics, as would a middle-class schizophrenic child, getting away from people. He is in there coping with people, trying to understand, and trying to see himself in the future. This is a very, very exceptional kind of a kid; no doubt about it.

LEWIS: He is very unusual. He isn't like a child.

DE VOS: If you had got this in an adult, you'd still worry about the disturbance, inner tensions, and so forth. You'd say that the mental processes are not well controlled, but he's got them. Now the DW and the contamination, and so on, in an adult you'd say is schizophrenic or schizoid. But in a child it is very difficult to say what a DW means. Once you get away from the clinic, you find that a lot of people in any normative group produce what would be seen as sick records. I disagree with Marvin Opler, who said that you can't use the same Rorschach norms in another culture. I think it means the same in any culture. A DW is a DW is a DW. Whoever produces it, in whatever context, it means the same thing structurally about the functioning of a person's intelligence. But there is a difference in whether it is adaptive or maladaptive in a particular culture. If you get it in a middle-class American, the chances are that the fellow is pretty disturbed and will be so regarded by others. If you get it in another culture, it may be encapsulated within the context of the culture, but qualitatively, as mental functioning, I think the finding still means the same thing.

FINNEY: Both Dr. Wittkower and Dr. Opler have been trying to say something for a while.

WITTKOWER: From the story the boy obviously normalizes exceedingly well. I would say from the clinical point of view I cannot see anything sick or abnormal in it. But in many ways it is more important to know what he didn't say than what he said. So I would like to ask Dr. Lewis two questions. Of course, I am familiar with your books. But would you first explain how you elicit material, how you interview? And the second question is, if you know the boy (you know him; we only know what you have told us about him), what features in the material that you have presented are, in your opinion, indicative of emotional maladjustment?

LEWIS: Well, take the second one first. What I see as maladjustment in this child, I would put in simple terms. He's so bright that without much thought about detail, without stopping to reason, very bright ideas and observations come to him. This has been rewarded by the adults, and he's been encouraged to talk a great deal, to move a great deal, to dance, to act, to the point where it has become part of his habit system. This is not typical for boys in the culture, because it is associated with femininity. This attempt to develop a male, a macho, begins when the little boy is born, or within a few weeks. All through the first and second years mothers kiss the genitals and play with them in public, holding the child up and saying, "You see this is a complete man," and so on. Well, I think that he has been overstimulated, mostly at home. He has high native intelligence. The only thing that I saw which I consider a symptom is this tremendous overstimulation of his talkativeness, and his relationships with his brothers and sisters. This doesn't seem to me to be too alarming, considering that at age six he has to stay home and take care of these kids, who are quite active.

I use several methods of interviewing. I don't usually use a tape recorder until I have known someone for two or three months. I don't go to the home with a tape recorder. I usually get a complete life history without a single tape recording; this takes many, many months of friendship and a great deal of confidence. After I have all that I think I want, I say to the person, "Now let's do this thing all over again, but this time I want to make a tape recording. It will help me in my study." And that is what was done with this child. With other individuals I use another approach. With this child, for the first two hours, there was no direct questioning at all—beyond, I mean, complete free association. After that, there was a great deal of systematic questioning about every aspect of the family history that I was aware of. By the time I tape-record I know the family well, which gives me a very wide range of angles. After that I use highly directed questioning, getting his version of incidents of which I have already got five other people's versions. In his version of the fight he has a very positive image of the man who was kind to him. This was one of his grandmother's men, the one whom I called Hector, whom he loves and cannot imagine cut up by a razor. He uses denial constantly as a basic mechanism. Perhaps the great length of time it takes is one of the reasons we haven't seen any other books of days or really comparable multiple autobiographies in single families. I think that my method is an entirely different genre of research from the straight single biography, which is very subjective. When I do a family study I'm not really doing a biography. Reuben Hill told me that he's had very bright graduate students go in and try to do days and biographies. They go in with a tape recorder, which often, though not always, ruins everything in advance. I do not even take notes. The whole tape recording is simply a recapitulation, and can only be done if the friendship and the confidence is great enough. In other words, I am really taking a chance, investing a lot of time, getting a lot of data and not in their own words, and then eventually getting it in their own words. Now some subjects need a great deal more organizing than others for the final product.

But any way you look at it, this child is recognized within his own group as having great verbal facility. In my book you see him first as his mother sees him in her life story. Then you see him in an actual recorded day. Besides actual observed days, I have reconstructed more than fifteen days in each of these households. When you see them through all the lenses, besides the way I see them, you realize that truth is a very multifaceted thing.

FINNEY: As I listen to what this boy says, what comes through most strikingly is that he is developing into what would be called a dissociating personality, what used to be called a hysterical personality. It can already be seen at the age of seven. People of this kind use a defense called dissociation, which used to be called repression (and still is, by some people). Some people here have said that it is striking that he is not repressed at all, but I think that is confusing repression with inhibition. He is surely not inhibited; he is not restrained. Indeed, the reason I favor abandoning the word *repression* is that it is so often used with different meanings. This boy is dissociating; that is, he keeps certain ideas from becoming integrated with each other in his awareness, but he is surely not inhibited. Some people say that people of this kind talk a lot and say very little. Some say that such people express their feelings, and others say that they don't. It depends on what you mean by "express." I'd rather say that these people display their feelings but don't reflect on their feelings. They don't look within themselves. Dr. Prince described this same contrast in his paper today. When Dr. Lewis says that this boy uses denial, he is talking about something akin to what I mean. This boy shows another characteristic of such people, too: a strong concern with sex; we might say an overemphasis on sex, with strongly mixed feelings about it. He is both fascinated with sex and scared of it. The same may be said of violence. There is an all-or-none reaction. As Dr. Weinstein said today, access all to one extreme or all to the other.

But there's something else about this boy that has hardly been mentioned, which is, the messages that he is sending, the communication in which he is taking part, the games that he is playing, the ways in which he is seeking to influence the person he is talking to, the payoff or reward that he is getting from what he says. After all, talking is an instrumental act: it is purposive. What inward emotional satisfaction does he get from saying these things to Dr. Lewis? In the form in which it is presented, as a monologue, not a dialogue, we lose sight of it. We think of how his speech serves our purposes, gives us the information we want. Or we think of his speech as simply a window into himself. If we want to see what kind of reinforcements this child is seeking, we need to hear the whole conversation, what Dr. Lewis says as well as what the boy says. And we need to hear it the first time that Dr. Lewis asks it, not as he repeats it months later. Dr. Lewis leaves it out because he is not publishing a study of himself, nor even of the boy's interacting with him, but only a study of the boy and the boy's family. Still, our understanding of the boy himself would be greater if we could see the interplay, how he and Dr. Lewis interact with each other. It may be that the things he tells Dr. Lewis about his mother make sense only in terms of a transaction between the boy and Dr. Lewis.

DE VOS: Yes. This boy and his family remind me of the Mexican-Americans in prison in California. The characteristic modality that I see is one of repression and of very sparse individuals who don't look at motivation at all. They don't go inside and look at why they do something or why people act in certain ways. What really impressed me about the record is this utter lack of interest in motivation. Evidently the Mexicans and the Puerto Ricans are alike in that respect.

LEWIS: I think I agree essentially, but there is also something else to be said. One of the most striking differences between our material on Puerto Ricans and our material on Mexicans of the same socioeconomic level, both urban, is what I would call a much greater thinness of content. The Puerto Ricans are less capable of introspection, of looking into themselves, than are the Mexicans. And I think this, in turn, reflects fundamental differences in the history of the two cultures. I don't think it would be easy to find two cultures within Latin America that are as different and have had histories as different, as Puerto Rico and Mexico.

FINNEY: The Puerto Ricans are less able to look within themselves? Even less able than the Mexicans?

LEWIS: Oh, much, much, much less able than the Mexican urban slumdwellers. This is my overall impression. Puerto Rico and Mexico have some obvious things in common—Spanish is their common language, they were both colonies, and that's about it. Beyond that, you find that in the pre-Spanish period, Mexico had a great flourishing civilization, very complex, with a priest-hood and temples and great ritual complexities, class stratification, and so on. In Puerto Rico and the Caribbean generally, you find very simple food-gathering, in some cases agricultural societies. In Mexico a great deal of the pre-Hispanic culture has been preserved. So you have a mixture of Indian and Spanish. In Puerto Rico the Indians were wiped out; there is no pre-Hispanic tradition, but a Negro combination. You can't compare the status of the Negro slave in the colonial period with that of the Indian under the crown. In seventeenth-century Mexico there were institutional defenses of the native culture in the courts and a kind of native Indian village democracy. From the very beginning, the Mexicans were always protesting. They fought and fought until they developed a tremendous feeling of national consciousness among the growing bourgeoisie. Even the poorest Mexican slumdweller knows a good deal about the great national heroes who fought against Spain. For the Puerto Rican slum-dwellers history begins and ends with Muños Marin. This is their time perspective. If you give them a long list of their writers, politicians, and heroes, they recognize none of them. The same more or less illiterate people in Mexico know much more. In addition, the Mexicans have a revolutionary tradition. Puerto Rico has never had a revolutionary tradition. You have to recognize different profiles within the culture of poverty, which, as might be expected, reflect the history of the country.

As a result of the technique that I have developed, of multiple biographies, observed days, and so on, a study of even a few families reflects a great deal about the national history and society. You cannot explain these differences in terms of the local situations, since they are subcultures, anyway, as was pointed out by John Honigmann. On the whole my feeling is that the Puerto Rican life is a much sadder one than the Mexican, even though the Puerto Ricans have a much higher per capita income than the Mexicans, have achieved great things with Operation Bootstrap, have more than a thousand Puerto-Rican-sponsored factories, mostly with United States capital, and have developed a managerial class. When you go to the slums—and on all levels—you find a greater confusion of cultural identity in Puerto Rico than in Mexico. Muños Marin is extremely sensitive about this and is aware of the problem of cultural identity. About the only thing they have left that is at all distinctive is the Spanish language, which, of course, is not distinctively Puerto Rican, although Puerto Rican Spanish differs from Mexican Spanish. But there is very little you can point to, if you know Hispanic culture in Latin America, which is distinctively Puerto Rican. As a result, almost none of the items mentioned by Marvin Opler in his paper about the Puerto Ricans, which he will read at this conference, are distinctly Puerto Rican; they are Latin American, Mexican, and so on. There are some differences, but you have to say more than he said to tie down the differences between Mexican machismo and Puerto Rican machismo.

The compadre system, for instance, occurs throughout the Catholic world; it's not Puerto Rican. Machismo occurs all over Latin America, practically; it varies between rural and urban, Indian background and otherwise, and other elements in the culture. Respect, honor—these are good old Spanish values, not really distinctly Puerto Rican. Any country has its mythology to justify the miseries of the present by the glories of the past. In Mexico it was the great Indian culture. In Puerto Rico it has been jibaro. But I have done a six-generation study, and the stories of family life and child training in so-called jibaro times, when the jibaro was still not contaminated by American culture, make it clear that it was not nearly as Rousseauan as they would like you to believe.

FINNEY: I am puzzled. You said that the Mexicans were more repressed than the Puerto Ricans. If you use the word as I do, that means that the Mexicans are less able to look within themselves. And perhaps your finding that Mexicans don't report primal scenes strengthens that view; the Mexicans blot such memories out. (Though maybe it only means that the deed is witnessed less often in Mexico than in Puerto Rico.) But then you puzzled me by saying just the opposite; that the Puerto Ricans are less able to look within themselves than the Mexicans are. It seems to me that we have to say, as George De Vos does, that in comparison with Americans both the Mexicans and the Puerto Ricans are people who don't look within themselves, don't examine their motivations, don't bring their urges into reflective consciousness, don't label their goal-seeking actions with words. In Ray Prince's words, they are motoric people who talk readily *as* themselves, but are tonguetied when they are expected to talk *about* themselves. They *express* their feelings but don't *describe* them. This is what some psychiatrists call the hysterical personality. Its mechanisms are the defenses called repression and dissociation, which are much the same thing. I don't like to say "repression" because nonpsychiatrists don't use it to mean the same thing as psychiatrists. When you said that the Puerto Ricans are less repressed than the Mexicans, Oscar, I think you were not using the word in the way that psychiatrists use it. I think you meant that the Puerto Ricans are less inhibited, less restrained, more expressive.

DE VOS: Yes. I was also wondering, Oscar, where the middle class is going in its identification. It must have a difficult time trying to find itself.

LEWIS: Terribly difficult. All the classes have a difficult job because the mixture of Spanish and English is fantastic.

KIEV: Will you comment on the difference between Puerto Ricans in Puerto Rico and Puerto Ricans in New York?

LEWIS: Yes. The main point is the absence of differences. Among the families with a median income of $1,200 a year, and their relatives in New York, I have yet to meet a family that doesn't say they want desperately to go back, unlike most other immigrants in New York. The distinctive thing about the Puerto Rican migrations is that it is a two-way movement at all times. In the 1950s there was an average net migration to the States of 50,000 a year; between 1952 and 1953, 75,000 came up; but that is not the whole story, because almost 250,000 Puerto Ricans were coming and going each year. Migration has been reduced in the 1960s, and in the late 1960s, of course, it will be further reduced. For the first time in 1964 there was a net gain for Puerto Rico.

KIEV: Do you think this is something inherent in the culture?

LEWIS: Well, the economists say it's all a function of jobs, but everything I see tells me that it's all social and psychological. It must be both.

FINNEY: Dr. Lewis, from what I have seen of Puerto Ricans in Hawaii (1963b), that group is more like American slumdwellers than any other cultural group in Hawaii. There are other groups equally poor: the Hawaiians and the Filipinos, for example. Even some of the Japanese are quite poor, though on the whole the Japanese have become a middle-class group. I have encountered many of these people of various ethnic groups in Hawaii, in the reform schools, and in prison. And yet, as I talk with the people of all these ethnic groups, they don't strike me with the hopelessness of slumdwelling American criminals that you find in prisons or reform schools in the United States; except for the Puerto Ricans. They do. There is something different about them. I think it's precisely what you have described as the culture of poverty. The Puerto Ricans, incidentally, have the highest crime rate, and the highest imprisonment rate, of all the cultural groups in Hawaii. I wonder whether the Puerto Ricans acquired a slum subculture, a subculture of poverty, before they came to Hawaii in 1905.

LEWIS: I don't think that's too long ago. There probably was a widespread rural culture of poverty in Puerto Rico for a good part of the colonial period. Puerto Rico was always a second-rate colony, always neglected; slavery began very early, and there was a great deal of the kind of thing we have discussed—multiple spouses, the neglect of children. I think it began quite early, surely before the American takeover. But it would take a lot of historical research to establish that fact for sure.

DE VOS: Is there any section of the society that had a stable paternal structure, say in the upper class?

LEWIS: I think that all the societies in Latin America, even in the culture of poverty, have a full patriarchal ideology, while the reality is matrifocal. It's not that all men are demeaned, it's just that husbands are especially demeaned.

DE VOS: Husbands, excluding the role of paterfamilias.

LEWIS: Exactly.

DE VOS: But the role exists.

LEWIS: But the role does exist. As a matter of fact, I can't conceive of a true culture of poverty developing in what we anthropologists would call a true matrilineal system. I don't know of any example of a culture of poverty in anything but a bilateral family system.

OPLER: We have millionaire Puerto Ricans in New York. There are rich Puerto Rican lawyers who do not have the typical epidemiological rates for Puerto Ricans or for New York. But epidemiologically New York state and Midtown New York are full of Puerto Rican mental health disabilities; the rate of schizophrenia is well known.

LEWIS: It's very high.

OPLER: It's the greatest per capita in New York state.

LEWIS: Where can one get some real figures on this?

OPLER: You can take mental hospital admissions, but, of course, that's not the kind of data that a sophisticate wants. In the Midtown study we predicted that the Puerto Rican group would be the most problematic in the whole community, and they were. (The Hungarians were next.) The Puerto Ricans were so problematical, that Benjamin Malzberg, who makes hospital admissions studies, had to do some serious fantasy thinking about the future of the children of these schizophrenic parents.

LEWIS: But Nat Glazer's view of the Puerto Ricans is very different. Nat Glazer in his book on. . . .

OPLER: I don't think he studied them definitively at all. That doesn't scare me a bit.

KIEV: In Bellevue Hospital, which is the largest receiving facility for the Puerto Rican community, Puerto Ricans are considered white or Negro. There is no category of Puerto Rican. If you want to do any epidemiological study, you have to find them by tracking them down. You can't find it on the records.

OPLER: I want to ask one more question. In interpreting the Rorschach, I agree that the psychologist needs to know the patient's age, and it's even better if he sees the modal behavior, but I think he should be sealed off from the anthropological data. Is he? That's the crucial point. If not, there's no scientific value in correlating the psychologist's report with the anthropologist's.

LEWIS: I had real blind analysis not only of the child but also of the mother. I keep reading and hearing from colleagues, particularly at the University of Illinois in the psychology department. . . .

DE VOS: They're brainwashed there.

LEWIS: Yes, very anti-Freudian, all experimental. Your status goes way down if you use a Rorschach.

DE VOS: That's a sanctioning mechanism that is part of our culture. That's a culture of poverty, too, though of a different kind. An intellectual impoverishment among certain psychologists.

LEWIS: From my experience with people whom I know well— when I made complete biographies of the individual and of others in the family who could give me views of the same people —I am simply amazed how much you can get from a Rorschach in the hands of a really able psychologist, like this Mexican that I'm using. And when you add a Children's Apperception Test it becomes even better.

psychocultural dimensions of social change

Charles C. Hughes

In speaking of "psychocultural dimensions of social change" I wish to make it clear, first of all, that I am rejecting the implication that a dichotomy can be drawn between "change" and "nonchange" in things of the empirical world so far as scientific understanding is concerned. Everything is in flux and all is process, as we have been reminded repeatedly since Heracleitos (and yet so often seem to forget in the conceptualization of research questions). The human organism adapts to a highly complex environment. In transacting the business of life, it changes the very nature of that environment both for others and for itself. If we are to understand more fully—and hence predict more accurately—the processes and directions of social change, we must in all cases view it within such a holistic, adaptational framework. We must consider psychocultural factors, since they seem to be most decisive in differentiating the outcomes to the environmental challenges both in social change and in stability.

This way of approaching the problem is not a new one; in one form or another it is found (at least implicitly) in much behavioral science research. But I think there are good reasons for making this framework explicit in considering individual and social change. For in situations that offer a choice among adaptive possibilities and call for behavioral decisions on the part of individuals, certain features of this conceptual model become highlighted, and the basic workings of the human social process are laid bare. One of the most critical of these basic dimensions is the pervasiveness of ego functions and of "coping" behavior, of what White (1959, 1960) has called "effectance motivation." This principle, in turn, implies—indeed, requires—a comprehensive ecological framework that uses the concepts of communication and information to depict the dynamic processes of human beings, individually and in groups. Further, it is in a context of change, in the psychological variations and complexities of coping behavior, that some of the chief problems of concern to this conference can be grasped most clearly. I refer first to poverty. The basic psychodynamic process in which poverty is rooted is the comparison of oneself with others, resulting in feelings of relative deprivation in one area of life or another. Poverty will always be a feature of the human condition, so long as this process takes place.

A few years ago, in Walt Kelly's comic strip "Pogo," there appeared an epigram with which I want to introduce consideration of this topic and to indicate my philosophical orientation toward disciplines, problems, and the natural world. The issue for the day was differences of opinion, and the conversation between Pogo and his companion went somewhat as follows. Howland Owl, arguing for the relativity of all knowledge, recalled the story of the three blind men of India confronting the elephant, and noted that "each was *partly* right." After a moment's reflection, Pogo opined, "That's right; but you gotta remember that each was *mostly* wrong, and each was *entirely* blind."

I often call this to mind when academic discussions wander into the morass of arguments about words per se. Words are tools; words are conceptual axes to use in carving one's way through the rain forest of interlinked processes that comprises nature. While I have no wish to imply that the several behavioral sciences concerned with problems of change are either "mostly wrong," or "entirely blind," I suggest that a great deal more attention should be paid directly to the ostensible object of inquiry: the elephant. Moreover, the elephant perceived with its full naturalistic attributes of habitat, life cycle, homeostatic processes, internal anatomy, and external relations—the elephant, in short, before it is fractionated by the sharp edges of typo-logical labels and wrapped into neat packages. For often such a job of butchery, while carving nature into manipulatable units, does so by cutting asunder the organically meaningful process—bone, muscle, nerve—instead of performing the dissection at the joint, at the point of articulation *between* two systems.

WHAT OF MAN?

Standing back for a moment from the specifics of argument about particular studies, where do we stand in knowing man, and man vis-a-vis the idea of social change? A good place to begin is a recent summary statement based on an extensive review of behavioral science findings. Berelson and Steiner (1964, pp. 663-66), attempting an overall perspective and appraisal of their labors, would sum up our knowledge in the following way:

> Man is a creature who adapts reality to its own ends and transforms it, in two ways. One is by making instruments to master the world. The other is by distorting his understanding of the world, through defense mechanisms, to protect himself from what he cannot bear to face. He uses language to deceive himself. What he seeks most is approval from other people. Each man is shaped less by nature than by other men.
> [Summarized by editor]

From this descriptive generalization of what man is as behavioral science knows (or purports to know) him, several major themes stand out which are related to the main concerns of this conference: the extensive and often unappreciated influence of the social network, and the socially derived basis of selfhood and

security; the predispositional power of the system of tacit under-
standings and images or codes that orient a society and its members in their striving for psychodynamic rewards; the importance
of multiple modes of information and communication as the
basis of the social order and of the individual's transactions with
this environment; the ubiquity of psychological restructuring of
environmental events and circumstances, of projection and recreation of the world; and, above all, the adaptability of the
human organism, given motivation, time for familiarization, and
the support of one's fellows.

META-METHODOLOGY

Given the central theoretical importance of the subject, it is not
surprising that one of the most pervasive themes of contemporary
behavioral science research deals with one facet or another of
relations between group structures and behavior of the individual
person. Another factor, however, also seems to be involved—
one that, curiously, I find undiscussed in our enthusiasm to be
"objective" and therefore—as if *ipso facto*—"scientific." I refer to
the metaphysical implications of the conceptual dichotomy between the individual and the group. One may wonder what
difference it has made in the development of the behavioral
sciences that the study of human behavior represents the only
case in the world of science in which a given order of nature turns
the spotlight of its intelligence self-consciously inward upon
itself in a search for abstract knowledge, and hence control, of
itself.

The fact that the investigator has the capacity to put himself
in the place of the object investigated (whether entirely accurately
or not does not matter at this point) has a number of "meta-
methodological" implications for the development of behavioral
science. It is not so easy, realistically, to imagine oneself as the
fly under the microscope, much less the gas molecule in a
chamber; but it is possible for a man to share at least some of

the world of perception and feeling of another—although, of course, never with complete congruence. Polanyi builds his entire approach to the philosophy of science on just this acceptance of our humanness, our particular location in the scheme of things, and suggests that "as human beings, we must inevitably see the universe from a centre lying within ourselves and speak about it in terms of a human language shaped by the exigencies of human intercourse. Any attempt rigorously to eliminate our human perspective from our picture of the world must lead to absurdity" (1964, p. 3).

The fact that empathy is possible at all gives the investigator of human affairs a powerful tool. While it is clear that the seductions of projection can lead to faulty assumptions and hence fruitless hypotheses, it must also be recognized that, like any tool, the capacity can be handled either well or badly; and the excesses of psychological introspection should not lead to an overly restrictive "scientism." Well used, empathy—"taking the place of the other"—means simply that the investigator is discerning and acting or thinking in terms of the assumptions and complex patterns of codification which characterize his subject— and not necessarily of those codes or images characteristic of himself.

FIGURE AND GROUND IN CHANGE

It is not hard to discern why the relationship between social change and psychocultural factors in a human population has occupied the attention of many behavioral scientists for decades. Practically, we are, of course, challenged on every hand by the omnipresence of social changes, many highly accelerated, so that transformations in social forms which once might have taken several generations are now accomplished within the span of one, with many problems of adjustment and accommodation. Further, however, understanding the manner in which such changing social conditions—i.e., contextual fields of limitation and opportunity—are perceived by and enter into the psychic economy of individual persons affected, illuminates the basic processes involved in individual societal relationships seen in a more general framework. For the person is the "engine" on which the social order revolves, either toward repetition of the previous pattern, or toward modification of that form, however slightly. It is into this perceiving, synthesizing, creating, and responding organism that the stimuli from the environment are channeled, evaluated, and used as the basis for decisionmaking. The person thus becomes a "behavioral center," to use Cantril's term—the subject and object of feedback processes that consist in large measure of communicative relationships with the environment. Wiener puts it this way: "To be alive is to participate in a continuous stream of influences from the outer world and acts on the outer world, in which we are merely the transitional stage" (1954, p. 122). And Hinkle has noted, "Man's relationship to the world around him is largely a communicative one. He obtains information from the environment, evaluates it, and organizes and directs his response on the basis of this evaluation" (1961, p. 291).

But a man's environment is not an unstructured background for behavioral pathways. The concept of "environment" should not be a residual category, the unanalyzed foil for the complexities of the individual human organism, or the unexamined ground against which the figure of the human personality is illuminated. For the environment itself is prefigured, has points of saliency and structure, all-or-none emphases that function as coercive and orientational frameworks for the perceiving organism. Many psychologically oriented studies of the individual personality focus their search for system inward on the individual and, whether by design or implication, leave the environment a background of random, undifferentiated opportunity. But it is, on the contrary, a background of structured opportunity and obstacle in both physical and social terms. What we have is the gearing into each other of two or more complex systems—personality and the social order—each structured to a significant degree by the guidance framework of a common culture. Perhaps we have something of a "Heisenberg effect" in behavioral science: in order to understand the actions of the individual in a context of social change, we assume stability of the environment; and, to understand permutations of social environment, we assume stability and uniformity of the persons. But surely this is a caricature.

In situations of accelerated social change, the range of possible actions, or "behavioral space," for the perceiving individual is widened, and the need for decisions is heightened. Alternative designs for living, images of conduct, sanctions, and standards bring each other into question. What happens as a result of this joining of alternatives varies, and theoretical expectations of the psychological implications of social or cultural changes have differed. Some investigators, basing their arguments on the "function of the familiar" in the conduct of life, emphasize the effects of congruence or isomorphism in innovation, or the disruptive effects of changes through heightened anxiety and stress, especially if the change is rapid. Others, however, point to the psychological beneficence of change and stress the advantages of rapidity in the turnover of an entire way of life. The evidence, to say the least, is mixed, one reason for which is no doubt the incomparability of indicators employed to assess either disruption or peace of mind. Obviously what is needed is a far greater number of specific studies that incorporate the psychological dimensions of a human population undergoing sociocultural change—and these, moreover, conducted in a framework of comparable concepts having to do with levels and patterns of psychological functioning appropriate to the cultural context.

The Spindlers have recently discussed the new direction that a number of studies of culture change have taken—toward more refined approximations of dynamic relationships, or what one might call the "progressive contextualization" of the research problem, in which the scope of investigation enlarges from a preoccupation with figure to include an analysis of ground. The points made in the following passage (Spindler and Spindler,

1963, pp. 515-16) have a number of implications. Notice the
ease with which it can be translated into a view of culture as an
information source, a complex image, the recipient and the
originator of feedback in the circular processes of man's adapting
to the world.

> Culture, in our definition, is the patterns for behavior, whether
> put into words or not, that are shared by a group of people
> and transmitted to new members. The patterns are modified
> as new people respond to them. The representation of culture
> in each individual is his personality and includes his percep-
> tions, motives, defenses, and controls. In cultural contact, as
> the conditions of survival change, established patterns lose
> meaning and may become maladaptive. Patterns lose effect,
> and behaviors are tried unpredictably until a new pattern
> consolidates. Many societies are in the unsettled transition
> phase now, and psychological studies of their peoples are
> needed not only for the irregularities but also for the pan-
> human regularities in psychological adaptation during cul-
> ture change, a psychocultural approach.
>
> [Summarized by editor]

BEHAVIOR, CHANGE, AND ADAPTATION

But something more than a proliferation of empirical studies is
needed, it seems to me, for elucidating alternative directions of
social transformation. What is required is a broader conceptual
perspective of the transactions between individuals and group.
Instead of asking whether social change fosters either disruption
or adjustment in personality systems, even in the terms suggested
by the Spindlers, let us ask more fundamental questions. What
is the nature of the environment to which individual psychobiological organisms attempt to adapt? What are the salient
features of the adaptive pattern that has been developed under
conditions of either rapid change or relative stability? In other
words, how effective is the adaptation? It is, then, not to much
the "structural" problem of change or no change, as it is that
of the empirical content, the transactive aspects of adaptation,

and the psychodynamic outcome. These are hard to conceptualize in human behavior; for one thing, we have the problem of "cultural relativity" to deal with. Dubos (1965, p. 15) has put the matter nicely with reference to a basic biological framework that, perforce, must include man and all his doings:

> Man's biological nature has not changed since late pale-olithic times. His 20,000 pairs of genes and his drives are basically the same, and the same rituals and symbols can appeal to him. But the manifestations, the structure of his society, changes endlessly as man responds creatively to challenge. A scientific understanding of the human condition will come only from describing and analyzing the pattern of responses that man makes to all stimuli.
>
> [Summarized by editor]

In saying that the problem must be treated not as an artificial question of change or no change, but rather as a more fundamental issue, that of adaptation, I realize that I am not pointing to anything original; for the term *adaptation* has been employed in various settings in discussions of human behavior for a hundred years. But it seems that some curious conceptual gaps exist in the array of behaviorally oriented sciences and that, moreover, much behavioral science research still proceeds as if problems of adaptation were outmoded or were not sufficiently amenable to methodological treatment to warrant attention. Thus we still find studies of traits or factors or items that make no reference, either implicit or explicit, to the role they play in regard to processes of adaptation. We often find rejection of such concepts as equilibrium, homeostasis, balance, on the assumption that because at present we cannot operationally define such vague concepts, or handle them mathematically, their use will not serve any purpose in the study of human life.

Yet surely any discipline purporting to deal with human behavior must, sooner or later, incorporate such ideas as adaptive process, homeostasis or steady state, transactive dynamics, and complementarity of pattern between empirical systems. Human life is a subset of the general class of living matter and is thus characterized—indeed, defined—by activity, exertion, irritability, mutuality of function with an environment. Without activity, there is no life; without interchange with an environment, the essential process and thus the essential structure disappears; the physicochemical materials, which in controlled flow comprise the structure, revert to randomness. As Bertalanffy noted: "Living structures are not in being, but in becoming. They are the expression of a ceaseless stream of matter and energy, passing through the organism and forming it at the same time" (1952, p. 181).

Such a dynamic concept has, in one form or another, informed research investigations in several of the behavioral sciences. In the fields dealing with behavior of the individual, this essential contingency of behavior, this duality of investigator's perspective, is perhaps expressed most clearly in dynamic psychiatry and clinical psychology. Anthropologists, sociologists, economists, and geographers, in studying the relations between group life and habitat, usually arrive at formulations about subsistence and the technological order. Recently the term *cultural ecology* has been used to cover many problem areas investigated in these terms; and the somewhat earlier term *human ecology*, as it is usually employed by sociologists, covers something of the same ground. Within the broad domain of biology, of course, the comprehensive, synthesizing viewpoint of ecology "proper" deals with the dynamics of populations and their adjustment, modification, or elimination by physical environmental influences.

The gap to which I referred a moment ago lies between the individual-centered discussions of personality adjustment, adaptation, and balance-oriented activity on the one hand, and the population-centered, group-focused, collectivity-pointed discussions on the other. Ecologists usually leave their discussion at the level of group and population dynamics, taking scant heed of the fact that each of the constituent members of the group is locked in the same problematic stance vis-a-vis its environment as is the group, considered as the unit. And discussions of individual psychodynamics, centered as they are on individual persons, rarely attempt to extend their basic ideas to the social group.

The conceptual gap between adaptation as the vital dynamic concept for understanding individual behavior, and adaptation as a feature of the social, the collective process, is illustrated in various works. One of Karl Menninger's books discusses the complex process of adaptation at the level of the individual organism, and the many lines of defense and creative reaction developed by the person attempting to reach a satisfactory *modus vivendi* with environmental pressures. Menninger notes:

> Internal and external equilibrium and the automatic maintenance of certain levels of functioning within the organism by various homeostatic devices were elegantly described by Claude Bernard, and later by Walter B. Cannon, in biochemical and physiological terms. This principle can, and in our opinion must, be extended to include psychological and social factors. Some of the interactions of individual and environment take place in ways that cannot be usefully reduced to physical and chemical terms. Organismic equilibrium maintenance and reciprocation between the individual and the outside world take place with the aid of special symbols, feelings, gestures, thoughts, and acts in patterns that are governed by the same general principles of reciprocity and integration which have been described by these eminent physiologists and others in regard to body tissues and body fluids. [1963, p. 78]

The psychologist Robert White speaks in much the same spirit, although with a different language. In his article "Motivation Reconsidered" he discusses the concept of "competence" and "effectrance motivation" as a key, pervasive feature of human behavior that cannot be squeezed into the status of a "drive" or "variable" but is, rather, a transmutable adaptive process that characterizes wide areas of human striving activity (1959, 1960). In their person-centered analysis, regrettably, neither White nor Menninger uses the term *culture* when discussing the fact that most of the instrumentalities an individual uses in his adaptive endeavors—the language, behavior patterns, skills, sentiments, etc.—are derived from the symbolically transmitted system of knowledge accumulated over generations by his forebears.

Nor do White and Menninger make use of the term *ecology* in their discussions of adaptation, not even in the overly narrow and restrictive manner of Lewin and Barker (e.g., Barker, 1960). Yet this is precisely the type of situation that the ecologists of biology and the clinicians of dynamic psychiatry or psychology are concerned with: patterns of interaction and mutual influence between one order of nature and other orders conceived as constituting the environment. At the same time, the ecologists and population biologists do not say much about the role of the individual member of the population in adaptation, ecological chains, niches, and processes, except in numerical representation. This is particularly true when they discuss human populations. One reason for their silence is the difficulty of interpreting human adaptive processes in concepts appropriate to nonhuman animal populations. Once having said that men, too, must adapt; that they do, in fact, adapt with greater or less effectiveness through technology and social organization; and that increasingly they are adapting to a manmade rather than a natural, unmediated world, what is left? Of course, what is left is the complexity of that manmade world, the goals of action not directly related to tasks of immediate survival, and the shifting and subtle symbol systems, perceptions, and sentiments that cannot be fully grasped by simple measurement of energy input and expenditure. Yet it is precisely in this area that the clinician confronts the problems of adaptation and maladaptation—not in obvious tasks of survival.

Not until the development of general systems theoretical approaches, which made it possible to consider communications and information in the framework of adaptation, did the importance of thinking about these basic problems within the same conceptual framework become sufficiently stressed—and the possibility of doing so enhanced. What, then, might we say about communications and information theory in human behavior? Some salient points relevant to the central topic must be dealt with here.

COMMUNICATION AND INFORMATION IN THE SOCIAL PROCESS

What do we mean by "communication"? Does the commonsense meaning—i.e., symbolic transmission of message—exhaust all fruitful referents of the term? In a pioneering work on communication in human behavior, Ruesch very broadly defined it as "all those processes by which people influence one another" (Ruesch and Bateson, 1951, p. 6). Weaver has an only slightly narrower definition: "The word 'communication' will be used here in a very broad sense to include all the procedures by which one mind may affect another. This, of course, involves not only written and oral speech, but also music, the pictorial arts, the theater, the ballet, and, in fact, all human behavior" (Shannon and Weaver, 1949, p. 95). Such definitions, as broad as they are, enlarge the commonsense referent of the term beyond the mere transmission of cognitive messages and take it into the realm of induction of feeling tones, sentiment, and belief. Ruesch's definition, in particular, seems to include types of relationship other than the cognitive-communicative, by which people influence one another. In fact, when he says that "where the relatedness of entities is considered, we deal with problems of communication; when entities are considered in isolation from one another, problems of communication are not relevant" (p. 6), we are very close to a statement of functional interrelation on a physicochemical basis in the ecological sense. In these terms, for example, a food chain would be an illustration of communication. Indeed, there would seem to be good reason for including problems of perceptual and cognitive communication in just this sense as part of the larger class of processes of energy flows and interrelationships.

Returning for the moment, however, to consideration of cognitive and symbolic relations, I want to discuss that aspect of communication most directly and profoundly influenced by man's unique development—culture. Communication as a process is built upon, and implies, a more fundamental accomplishment: codification. Codification can be defined as the systematic and arbitrary substitution of one event for another, or one pattern of events for another, in a communication system in which there is isomorphism, i.e., the overall structure remains the same, although the specific empirical content changes. As a process in human behavior, codification is therefore an illustration of the use of referential symbolism and sign language (for these purposes, I do not make a distinction between the two), so important and so highly developed in human social systems. The use of representative symbols or signs as shorthand indicators of environmental stimuli is not confined to the higher animal orders, although unquestionably the use of arbitrary symbolism, in which there is no organic connection between symbol and referent (as there is, for example, between smoke and fire), is most elaborated in human behavior.

The adaptive or survival function of such symbolism in man's relation to his environment is obvious. A symbolic reordering of the world, made possible by the development of symbolic and therefore conceptual thought, is highly efficient and economical in survival. By constructing within the nervous system spaceless and timeless worlds, man is capable of stopping the recalcitrant flow of phenomena, reversing it, reexamining it, and formulating new courses of action. In our abstract or symbolic space we can act without acting, as Dewey put it. "That is, we perform experiments by means of symbols which have results which are themselves only partly symbolized, and which do not therefore commit us to actual or existential consequences."[1]

The study of communications systems of a physical type has been highly elaborated by communications engineers in the last two decades, and some of the concepts developed have been applied in various guises to human social phenomena. The transmission of symbols of a particular type in a particular physical system was the basis of Shannon and Weaver's original monograph, so instrumental in the development of this new line of thought. Their concept of "information"—that which is transmitted—generally refers to the polar opposite of maximum

[1] Freud also regarded thought as tentative action.—Editor

entropy, or randomness and disorder. "Information" thus means a heightened ordering and selection, a maximum categorization and structuring of environmental events with as little extraneous contamination or "noise" as possible. At the other end, the transmission of information also necessitates a preferential treatment of phenomena, a discriminating approach in which some choice has been made, some alternative rejected in favor of that which was selected. In fact, one technical definition of "information" is "the lowest possible freedom of choice," i.e., unambiguity.

But information is not in itself physical, although it resides in and is transmitted via physical apparatus. But if not physical, then what? Configurations of symbols that, when decoded, comprise meaning. The political scientist Deutsch has a cogent statement in this connection:

> When a spoken message is transmitted through a sequence of mechanical vibrations of the air and of a membrane, thence through electric impulses in a wire, thence through electric processes in a broadcasting station and through radio waves, thence through electric and mechanical processes in a receiver and recorder to a set of groves on the surface of a disk, and is finally played and made audible to a listener—what has been transferred through this chain of processes, or channel of communication, is something that has remained unchanged, invariant, over this whole sequence of processes. It is not matter, nor any one of the particular processes, nor any major amount of energy, since relays and electronic tubes make the qualities of the signal independent from a considerable range of energy inputs. [1953, p. 67]

"That 'something' is information—*those aspects of the state descriptions of each physical process which all these processes had in common*" (1953, p. 68). Ruesch and Bateson say essentially the same thing—that information (in the organism) inheres in an arrangement of nervous impulses and neural connections representing relationships that are "systematically derived from those among the original events outside the organism."

The importance of communications in human social behavior

has led to numerous studies of the forms of communication in society. The most obvious is language and its many derivative forms (e.g., telegraphy). Others are gestures, music, the visible arts, graphic symbolic forms. Insofar as the latter convey patterns of discriminated stimuli which produce an effect in the perceiver, they may be said to transmit "information." It is clear, however, that when we include such types of symbolic communication as graphic or pictorial art in the class of communication forms, we are dealing with a kind of communication which does not exactly fit the model proposed by Shannon and Weaver. For their model presupposes a time line; their symbols are what Langer has called "discursive," as opposed to "presentational," symbols, in which the "meaning of . . . symbolic elements that compose a larger, articulate symbol is understood only through the meaning of the whole, through their relations within the total structure. Their very functioning as symbols depends on the fact that they are involved in a simultaneous, integral presentation" (1951, pp. 78-79).

Whether this difference in temporal mode of symbolic communication makes the form of communications theory developed by electronics engineers irrelevant and inapplicable for understanding human society may perhaps depend on the view we take of argument by analogy. In any case, the model has been widely applied, and in such a way as to make it seem useful in integrating the study of human behavior into a more general framework of patterns of energy allocation and information flow —in other words, into a basically ecological framework.

Deutsch (1953), for example, maintains that cultural information can be quantified and measured and that application of the cybernetic frame of reference to social phenomena is possible. He apparently draws no distinction between semantic and technical problems of symbol transmission. For him, a communication network among a group of people is the most significant aspect of social life; in fact, he defines a community, or a "people" in the ethnic sense, as a group linked by complementary habits and facilities of communication. Deutsch suggests that the complementarity of communication throughout the system can be measured by such devices as psychological tests for verbal comprehension and reading skills; by the efficiency with which people can organize for a joint task; by the rate of learning; by the nature of the patterns of commensality, etc. But Deutsch does not seem to me to suggest any techniques different from those proposed by the students of general semantics for clear understanding of verbal usage, or anything new in the way of quantification beyond what is being pursued now through surveys, tests, and the widespread application of statistical techniques.

What is new in Deutsch's approach, however, is the framework suggested as a background for such tests, a framework that poses problems of a different type in the application of the concepts of communications engineering to social data. In order to consider this more comprehensive level of analysis, one must step away from an ongoing, communicating sociocultural system and approach it with a different scheme of analysis.

In such a scheme, culture can be looked at as an overarching symbol system, a set of choices among the infinite possible alternatives for action available to a group of human beings. In this view, it is not only value analysis that is the study of choice behavior; the same can be said of any culture pattern, from particular methods of child rearing and food preferences to the traditional dogmas of the ethical system. And insofar as culture patterns are preferences for particular (as opposed to random) patterns for action which are passed down from generation to generation, they can be thought of as messages in information terms. Deutsch sees this fairly straightforward translation of culture into information. "A common culture, then, is a common set of stable, habitual preferences and priorities in men's attention, and behavior, as well as in their thoughts and feelings. Many of these preferences may involve communication" (1953, p. 62). "A concept for that which knowledge, values, traditions, news, gossip, and commands all have in common has been developed

by communications engineers. They have called it information"
(1953, p. 64).

> Societies produce, select, and channel goods and services.
> *Cultures produce, select, and channel information.* A railroad
> or a printing press is a matter of society. A traffic code or an
> alphabet is a matter of culture. Society can build walls; cul-
> ture can impose tabus. Society communicates tangible goods
> or inputs of energy called work; culture communicates pat-
> terns. These may be patterns of the arrangement of objects
> in space, from pottery and ornaments to tools and buildings.
> They may be patterns of action, such as games, dances, or
> models of graceful behavior. Or they may be patterns of
> preference, of do's and don'ts, such as standards of morality or
> taste. Or, finally, they may be codes and symbols, that is,
> patterns so arranged as to convey information about other
> patterns, up to the vast extent of what the biologist J.S.
> Huxley called "man's unique biological characteristic of tradi-
> tion." [1953, p. 66]

Ruesch and Bateson (1951) imply similar conceptions of
cultural phenomena when they call a value a "preferred channel
of communication or relatedness," or a preference. Roberts (1964)
has noted that "it is possible to regard all culture as information
and to view any single culture as an 'information economy' in
which information is received or created, stored, retrieved,
transmitted, utilized, and even lost" (p. 438); and D'Andrade
and Romney (1964), discussing current work by anthropologists
in the study of cognitive structures, such as componential analysis,
speak of culture as a shared system of codes for the transmission
and evaluation of information. "The signals constitute the actual
behavior, while the code consists of the rules or shared under-
standings by which the signals are transformed into messages
carrying information" (p. 230). And Boulding (1956, 1964) uses
the information concept with the term *image* in his discussions
of control and guidance features of empirical systems.

Perhaps the most elaborate and systematic treatment of culture
as a normative or orientational symbol system is that of Talcott
Parsons. In his theoretical framework the cultural system is one

of the three basic components of social action, the other two being the social system and the personality system. The orientational, or informational, aspect of the cultural system in the action framework is described in the following:

> [Dr. Hughes quoted at length from Parsons (1951), pages 11, 327, 328, and Parsons and Shils (1951), 159, 162. The editor summarizes it:]
> Human action systems can become highly elaborated because we have rather stable systems of symbols with generalized meanings, something that develops only when a number of people keep communicating with one another. The system of symbols become a cultural tradition. Culture comes to provide standards for ordering the communication. Conventions of the language and of the belief system make possible the complementarity of expectations. Interpersonal generalization is the essence of culture and allows the same way of orienting to appear at different times in the same or different people.

A key term in discussions of information transmission and control systems is *feedback*. This word, too, has been generously and meaningfully applied to human behavior in the context of information flow, especially with reference to the maintenance of levels or patterns of organization and equilibrium. Deutsch notes: "In every system which shows a significant degree of self-control, external action is guided by the interplay of circulating streams of information" (1953, p. 140). Information is thus essential to maintain the integrity of a system, of system boundaries; and the process of transmission of information is then one of a circular flow of behavior and feedback of information, of energy inputs and outputs. To maintain any level of equilibrium in organisms, continuous communicative interaction of multiple types with the environment is essential. The system receives reports of the results of its previous actions vis-a-vis the environment and bases subsequent actions on these reports. Thus communication is essential to the maintenance of a "steady state," or the functionally permissible range of oscillation in total physico-chemical balance. In effect we are dealing here with different aspects of a complex, unified stabilizing process: communication is necessary to maintenance of equilibrium; feedback processes are one important aspect of communication; and feedback is composed of processes of information transmission, decoding, and evaluation.

In this light we can look upon all manifestations of learning as forms of feedback. One should probably distinguish, however, between the simple reporting of information back to the system, and what the system does as a result. Deutsch goes into this matter in more detail, maintaining that even the simple feedback networks can be usefully applied to the basic characteristics of the "learning process" as this is described by John Dollard—drive, cue, response, reward (1951, p. 246). The drive is the initiating state of action; the cue and response are input and output; and the reward or reinforcement is the achievement (by feedback) of reduction of the initiating tension, or the goal. Deutsch continues, emphasizing that the feedback network always implies a goal to be reached as the result of activity, and his passage has many implications for psychiatric theory.

> This definition of a goal, or purpose, may need further development. There is usually at least one such external goal, i.e., a relation of the net as a whole to some external object, which is associated with one state of relatively least internal dis-equilibrium within the net. Very often, however, a very nearly equivalent reduction in internal dis-equilibrium can be reached through an internal rearrangement of the relations between some of the constituent parts of the net, which would then provide a more or less effective substitute for the actual reaching of the goal relation in the world external to the net. There are many cases of such surrogate goals or *ersatz* satisfactions, as a short circuit in an electronic calculator, intoxication in certain insects, drug addiction or suicide in a man, or outbursts against scapegoat members in a "tense" community. They suggest the need for a distinction between more or less direct internal readjustments, and readjustments sought through pathways which include as an essential part the reaching of a goal relationship with some part of the outside world. [1951, pp. 246-47]

But Deutsch's most valuable suggestion, to my mind, is the distinction between the types of feedback that are directed toward achieving a goal, and those directed toward changing a goal.

> Simple learning is goal-seeking feedback, as in a homing torpedo. It consists in adjusting *responses,* so as to reach a goal situation of a type which is given once for all by certain internal arrangements of the net; these arrangements remain fixed throughout its life. A more complex type of learning is the self-modifying or *goal changing* feedback. It includes feedback readjustments also of *those internal arrangements which implied its original goal,* so that the net will change its goal, or set itself new goals which it will now have to reach if its internal dis-equilibrium is to be lessened. Goal changing feedback contrasts, therefore, with Aristotelian teleology, in which each thing was supposed to be characterized by its unchanging *telos,* but it has parallels in Darwinian evolution. [1951, p. 247]

Deutsch continues by offering a scheme of four different levels of "purpose" in feedback nets, especially when these are applied to human beings. They might be conceived as suggesting hypotheses or new insights into the overlapping and multifarious nature of "purpose" in human affairs, especially to be seen in conditions of social change, when activity is often directed more toward acquiring new goals than toward restoring old patterns.

The different orders of "purpose" ascend from the physiological through the layers of symbolic overlay to the derived and acquired disequilibrating conditions. The first order of purpose is an internal disequilibrium of the type that requires an "adjustment" —a tension-reduction activity. The second order combines internal and external conditions; the immediate gratification of first-order purposes is renounced in favor of long-range wants. Such long-range wants (such as self-preservation) have been modified by experience to such an extent that they override immediate gratification of first-order purposes. "A third order purpose might then mean a state of high probability for the continuation of the process of search for first- and second-order purposes by a 'group' of nets beyond the 'lifetime' of an individual net. This would include such purposes as the 'preservation of the group' or 'preservation of the species'" (1951, p. 248). Finally, a fourth, and highest, order of purpose is found in states that offer high probabilities for the very process of *purpose-seeking*, of searching. In this group Deutsch includes all forms of learning, and "all other purposes envisaged in science, philosophy, or religion."

A book by the economist Alfred Kuhn (1963) continues in this same vein. It enlarges the application of communications and information concepts to the study of human transactions. In fact, Kuhn bases an entire "unified approach" to the study of society on concepts derived from general systems theory, communications and information theory, as well as the more traditional social disciplines dealing with allocative decisions that affect the flow of behavior: "The key analytical concepts . . . are *transactions* and *organizations,* each with an extremely broad definition, along with the major supporting concepts of *transformations, decisions,* and *communications*" (p. vii). "Human behavior is viewed as the product of a controlled—i.e., cybernetic—system" (p. viii). In this most impressive work it is regrettable that Kuhn failed to apply some of his own highly stimulating insights to the culture of a group as an information source, a shared pool of information that structures vast areas of behavior for members of the group.

INFORMATION AND ECOLOGY

Let us return for a moment to an earlier theme. Adaptational striving is a key concept in studies both of the individual and of the group. Unfortunately, there is a gap between treatments of this concept in the frameworks of traditional ecology and of the behavioral sciences, particularly those concerned with individual psychodynamics. It seems clear that the concepts of communications theory, especially the concept of information discussed above, provide a unifying theoretical framework for many levels of events. If we broaden typical ecological theory to refer to more than just gross exchanges or flows of energy, and include the idea of patterned transmission of energy which may take the form of messages, the way is opened for integrating much behavioral science research into a more fundamental framework.

In a recent formulation of the ecological frame of reference and its relevance to modern sociological theory (which, refreshingly, goes beyond the restrictive and largely cartographic use of "ecology" in many earlier sociological writings), Duncan (1964) attempts just such a statement. He discusses the fundamental parameters of social existence in terms of a dynamic framework of the flow of materials, energy, and information.

> [Dr. Hughes quoted from Duncan (1964), pages 37, 39, and 40. The editor summarizes:]
> The ecosystem is a natural unit of the various living and nonliving parts. Energy and information also flow, though not in circles. A living system, whether cell, human individual, or society, is a complex structure of matter maintained by energy, which is put in not at random, but patterned, with information and instructions on how it is to be spent. Every living creature is a structure that gathers information and organizes it. Various branches of science are now concerned with information: we read, for example, of cracking the genetic code. The concept of information may become as central in science today as that of the conservation of energy did a hundred years ago.

Duncan then gives some examples of the manner in which the flow of information functions in nature and discusses applications of these concepts in biology. He also implies that the difference between simultaneous and extended transmission of a message does not eliminate the possibility of "noise" in the communication system or—to use other terms—conflict in information.

> Information storage and accumulation are referred to as learning; the retrieval of learned information is the exercise of memory. Both capacities, in however rudimentary form, apparently are possessed by all animals. (The greatest versatility belongs to the species capable of symbolic learning, but symbols are intrinsically social mechanisms not adequately analyzed in the simple individual-environment framework.) The dissipation of information is implicit in the "noise"

generated by competing perceptions, in forgetting, and in the changes of state that render information relevant at one instant obsolete at the next. The total amount of information "applied," therefore, is vastly less than that received by the organism. Death, again, is tantamount to the complete loss of information stored in learned symbol or response sets. [p. 42]

Information, then, does not represent the flow of a fixed quantity over circular paths (materials) nor yet the throughput of an amount supplied at nearly constant rate (energy). It neither obeys a conservation law nor moves in cycles. In virtue of this freedom, information results in transformations of materials and energy virtually limitless in the variety of their manifestations, though it can, of course, accomplish nothing that is incompatible with the laws to which materials and energy are subject. [pp. 44-45]

Again, however, as did Kuhn, Duncan has failed to recognize that there is a readymade concept, culture, designating a major information source in society.

I would, therefore, support the theoretical approach that sees in communication or information theory a set of concepts that addresses itself essentially and without equivocation to the central process on which all life, including human life, is based: the transactions, conceptual and functional, which occur between entity and environment. A general systems or communication theory approach seems to give considerable promise of salvation from entrenched and restrictive intellectual parochialism.

INFORMATION AND SOCIAL CHANGE

But what might this approach indicate about situations of broad social change and their psychocultural dimensions? It indicates a great deal, it seems to me, if we recapitulate the salient elements involved. Social patterns become accepted and perpetuated only by being internalized as motivational elements in the personality systems of individual human beings. To become thus accepted, they must address themselves more comprehensively and satisfactorily to the need-dispositions of the ones who are confronted by the alternatives. For such a change and substitution, there must be a loosening of the hold of traditional culturally defined goal objects. Decisions must therefore be made by the individual among (usually) legitimate alternatives. They must be based on the manipulation of information and the reconciliation, repression, or compartmentalization of conflict (or "dissonance"). Such decisions need not be based entirely (nor even predominantly) on "cognitive" information, but may just as well be based on affective parts of the control and guidance system.

In this light, a recent article by Boulding is highly useful in suggesting some lines of applicability of an informational framework to the study of social dynamics. In the article "The Place of the Image in the Dynamics of Society," he carries further the arguments that he first expressed in his book *The Image* (1956). In the latter work, of course, he was concerned with the role of communication and control functions in systems at different levels of complexity and phenomenal organization. He uses the term *image* to refer to the organizing and control structures, the pattern of information, which guides the processes of energy expenditure, whether in the genetic code, electronic aiming devices, human behavior, or any other system. In the more recent statement, Boulding (1964) discusses in terms of communication theory two characteristics of human social systems which both distinguish them from physical systems and point directly to the heart of the problem of psychocultural dimensions of social change.

> The difference between social and physical systems is not confined to the complexity and order of the difference of differential equations which govern them. Social systems are characterized by at least two other peculiarities which differentiate them very sharply from simple physical systems, such as celestial mechanics. The first characteristic is the predominance of "threshold" systems in which small causes can sometimes produce very large consequences. The second characteristics is that social systems are what I call "image-directed," that is, they are systems in which the knowledge of the systems themselves is a significant part of the system's

own dynamics and in which, therefore, knowledge about the system changes the system. [p. 7]

The idea of "threshold" is a key one in understanding social transformation. It contains implications of discontinuity, rapid reorganization of gestalts, acquisition of insight, sudden and catalytic effects of an ideology which gives purpose to random activity, and the drastic change in behavioral expression which seems out of keeping with the magnitude of the stimulus—the "I've had enough" reaction. Anthropologists often speak of the patterned qualities of culture. In studies of culture change, they point to the frequent quantumlike nature of cultural processes. Up to a point, new cultural elements and social patterns are assimilated into the value configuration. After that critical point is reached, however, it is no longer a substitution of content, but a change in overall form, in gestalt, that directs the activity.

Such critical thresholds exist along several parameters of social behavior. The cognitive-informational element is surely one. It is simply not possible to induce certain types of social changes until certain requisite levels of education, for example, are widespread throughout the society—witness the complex difficulties of national development in Africa and elsewhere.

But perhaps even more important in determining social transformation is the threshold that relates to stress, to defenses against stress, and to the levels of stress that are tolerated before the organism shifts to other courses of action to reduce the perceived threat. Such threats come in various disguises; and, indeed, the wide scope of stress affecting human behavior—real and symbolic —makes the analysis of stress in human populations a highly complex affair. There are straightforward physiological threats to survival. We in the affluent West tend to dismiss them as unimportant, but they are daily companions to much of the world. There are threats to self-esteem, to social acceptance and acceptability, to strivings for cultural success, to worldly security. All of these create continual problems for man in modern society. Indeed, given the widespread inducement of unneeded needs yet wanted wants by the power of modern advertising, the proliferation of transportation systems, and the movement of people—in short, the diffusion of images and information—it is hard to say that there is a stable environment to which human beings are adapting. For in terms of information and image the environment is now incredibly richer and more complex than it has ever before been in human history. And with such waxing information come alternative courses of action and the need for decision, for evaluation, for reconciliation of possibilities. Reconciliation may come through rejection and repression, compromise among diverse possibilities, compartmentalization, or other ego defense mechanisms. But in the background is the haunting threat of *relative deprivation* along any of several dimensions; for the groups and cultural images with which an individual may compare himself are now legion. And the means available to cope with these new goals and new crises in decisionmaking are relatively fewer. Unquestionably White's concept of "effectance motivation" and the stresses that arise from its frustration along so many fronts has much to say about the cause of behavioral disorders. In many areas of life, the condition of modern man is indeed that of being frustrated.

Stress—incipient disorganizational processes—may also arise from sheer overload of information, as Miller (1960) suggests. The multiple possibilities, the variety of commitments and role involvements, the dispersed allegiances, the irritations of incongruent demands, all add up to a rising tide of stress that threatens the viability of the psychobiological system.

Often, quite aside from overload, stress is induced by straightforward conflict in content of the images confronting a person. "Cognitive dissonance" and conflict may lead to pressures toward stabilization of the perceived environment. The Spindlers discuss the implications, for studies of psychocultural factors in social change, of some propositions of this nature developed by Osgood. Their first proposition is that "cognitive modification results from the psychological stress produced by cognitive inconsistencies." The Spindlers' comment makes understandable many of the things we see in a situation of culture change: "This postulate makes it explicit that the search for and maintenance of symmetry, or consonance, in cognitive elements can be included among the significant human drives, e.g., it is cognitively inconsistent to believe one way and behave another. Incongruity may be reduced by changing belief to the point where the psychological stress becomes tolerable" (1963, p. 546).

The second proposition is: "if cognitive elements are to interact, they must be brought into some relation with one another." Noting that the culture-change situation is one of interpersonal contacts, they remark that "acculturation brings potentially inconsistent cognitive elements together in the framework of individual experience" and that one protective device often employed in such a situation is the familiar one of psychic compartmentalization (p. 547).

The third proposition again shows the value of a notion such as "threshold," which Boulding applies in information theory or cybernetics. A small added input of stress, when added at a threshold, can effect much larger changes in the direction of behavior. The proposition is: "The magnitude of stress toward modification increases with the degree of cognitive inconsistency." The Spindlers note: "In rapid and disjunctive culture-change situations, the degree of cognitive inconsistency may become so great that the stress induced cannot be coped with and the individual stops trying to reduce inconsistency. He withdraws and becomes almost totally passive, or he escapes to a regressive reaffirmation of nonfunctional traditional cognitive consistencies. It seems probable that native-oriented groups on American Indian reservations recruit new members largely through this process" (p. 547). .

Pointing again to the influences of an organizing image, and to the need for incorporating both the level of stress and the quality of information into the research paradigm, they refer to some recent studies. "On the other hand, a point can be reached rather quickly in culture-change situations where inconsistencies become radical and stress intense, and the traditional forms of belief and behavior (the cognitive congruities stabilized in the traditional culture) are discarded in a rapid reformulation of belief and behavior, resulting in a new stabilization of cognitive congruities. It is possible to interpret what happened in the case of the Manus studied by Mead . . . and the Seneca Iroquois studied by Wallace . . . in this way" (p. 547).

There is a summarizing proposition that I have found useful elsewhere in outlining the ecological background for major social change (1960, 1965). It can easily be translated into Boulding's terms, especially those concerned with thresholds and with the influence of information, expressed as competing images. The proposition is as follows: systems of belief may be modified by a) Observation of fact and reasoned thinking, b) Contact with other systems of belief, c) All types of stress, d) New opportunities for achieving security and satisfying aspirations. In this formulation, the first two factors (*a* and *b*) relate most directly to the notion of cognitive information. Items *c* and *d*, while also referring to conflict in information or image, point to thresholds of stress.

SUMMARY COMMENTS

My main points need only a brief restatement.

1. It is shortsighted to conceive problems of social change apart from those of social nonchange, for the basic process involved in both is the same, so far as individual and environment are concerned: i.e., communicative and functional interrelations. "Individual" and "environment" are merely arbitrary points of focus in a complex series of relationships.

2. The basic problem, then, resolves itself into that of patterns of adaptation conceived conatively, not substantively; the framework for viewing any item of behavior is "What is its network of purposive relations, its role in the striving patterns of individuals?"

3. The language of adaptation takes numerous forms in various disciplines, but it seems clear that a unitary conception lies behind both the disciplines dealing with the single organism and those

dealing with the population as the unit, even though the conceptual bridges between the two approaches are sketchy.

4. An obviously useful set of concepts for dealing with unit-environmental relational processes may be found in communications and information theory, especially when culture is viewed as an information source or complex "image" for defining the course and boundary of behavioral activity.

5. Traditionally conceived ecological theory can be broadened to include relationships whereby an organism or a group of organisms influences another by means other than predation, parasitism, symbiosis, etc., in a strictly organic sense. It may include also effects of control and guidance structures in the organization and flow of energy. In this sense the cybernetic paradigm for understanding many of the complexities of human conduct becomes applicable.

6. In conditions of social change, no event—whether alteration or repetition—occurs which has not been passed through the "informational screen" of the psychological structure of individuals in the group. The fact that such psychological structures are largely formed by preexisting cultural standards does not result in cultural reductionism. Other factors, noncultural in nature, often affect the direction of the striving for adaptational security on the part of people concerned. Among them are stress, conflict in cultural images, and overload in informational or cultural input.

7. The latter dimensions suggest that some of the most critical problems facing researchers in problems in social change have to do with finding the most useful indicators of stress thresholds, so that explanations of direction in social change can be put on a predictive rather than a post hoc basis. Operationalization of stress thresholds will also make it necessary to develop operational indicators for psychological equilibrium (vital balance, security, essential psychical condition). When we have developed such measures, we can begin to apply this elusive but indispensable concept in cross-cultural comparative studies of social change. A beginning on this task has been made by some of the recent epidemiological investigations in cross-cultural psychiatry.

transcultural adjustment of peace corps volunteers

Thomas W. Maretzki

Several years ago a 19-year-old Texan began his training for a Peace Corps community development project in Thailand. He was younger than most trainees. One brief conversation with him—even a quick glance at this young man with crewcut, a ten-gallon hat, and cowboy boots—evoked all the Texas stereotypes. He had attended a military academy and had planned to join the Navy. He was sent overseas as a volunteer although selection board members had some misgivings. How would a Thai respond to his joviality, his costume, his enthusiasm to get something done? Should he not be expected to show more restraint? How would he work in a seemingly unstructured, isolated, rural Thai village?

Word soon reached the training site that this man was an outstanding volunteer. He was patient, resourceful, satisfied with his accomplishments, and accepted by the villagers. For several months he lived among rural Thai in almost total isolation from other Americans. After he completed his two years of service he felt as much at home in Texas as he did before he left. He now wears a Thai bracelet as do Thai men, and his hat and boots were missing when we met. He had matured; his change had been in the direction of growth, not confusion. Several other volunteers in his group, older, more experienced, more widely traveled, more favored by the selection board as predictable successes, returned to the United States before completion of their service. They, not the young Texan, had adjustment problems.

Transcultural adjustment implies the effective functioning in social and cultural environments for which the individual has not been prepared through primary socialization. In human development the primary social and cultural environment plays such a significant part in achieving physiological and psychological integration that one may assume that the adult organism is prepared to continue in balance only as long as the familiar environment remains relatively constant. Man, the most flexible of all animals, is psychologically channeled into a narrow life pattern that prepares him to interact efficiently only with a small segment of his own species. Ideally, during socialization in his primary group man will have developed a system of balances so that adjustment problems—if they occur—are routinely solved from within the cultural parameter of the group. At least, this would be predicted by elementary culture-and-personality theories that relate a personality to the cultural components that entered into its formation.

It is therefore not surprising that immersion into an unfamiliar cultural setting may cause adjustment problems. This is nothing new to American anthropologists who have extensively studied situations in which individuals or groups have had to make cultural transitions. It is a subject of relatively recent concern to other social scientists and, in particular, to those involved in action programs such as the Peace Corps. Within a couple of decades a large number of Americans began to experience the effects of being temporarily transplanted into new and unfamiliar places, which required changes of habits, relationships, and sources of satisfaction (GAP, 1958). The ability to make the adjustments required by situations in which people with different cultural backgrounds interact varies with individuals. Since this ability is partly a function of personality structure, it may not be idiosyncratic, but may appear as a modal personality characteristic that itself is determined by primary cultural influences.

Transcultural adaptation as described in the anthropological literature usually has as a final goal the merging of cultures and therefore the integration of individuals on a permanent basis. The term *acculturation* characterizes this process. The adaptation expected of Peace Corps volunteers is temporary. It requires cultural understanding, even cultural empathy, but not acculturation (or *transculturation*, the term suggested by A. T. Hallowell), with social and emotional alienation from one's native background. The volunteer is a sojourner in another culture, a status that is perhaps fraught with even more potential problems of adjustment than those faced by the immigrant.

The sojourner seeks contact with members of another society by taking up residence in their midst, but plans to limit the extent of his contact and to return to his own group. The sojourner is not a new phenomenon, although in the history of mankind he plays a significant role only during the most recent period. The development of trade, the rise of religious belief systems and organizations that could be exported, and lately the attempts to reduce differences in levels of technology and social conditions on a worldwide scale gave rise to the peregrinations of sojourners.

For the anthropologists the sojourner experience offers a laboratory situation for the study of integration of personality with cultural elements. The adjustment, or the lack of it, among sojourners may tell us something about the degree to which personality is anchored in primary culture, and the individual differences that account for adjustment problems.

We can think of different types of sojourners and the styles of cultural encounter that have occurred. This style itself has cultural overtones tied to values of their native society. On the one hand, there is the British colonial sojourner whose career abroad tends to involve overseas residence among the same foreign population for one or more decades. The British colonial remains sociologically and psychologically isolated from the host population. Other overseas residents such as the Dutch, while retaining white supremacy and overt social separation, tended to merge more frequently through intermarriage and personal friendships. Overseas Chinese have developed a curious pattern of relative social isolation, though with superficial merging where this was economically and socially advantageous. Among all these sojourner populations cultural understanding is present to a considerable degree, while cultural empathy seems to be lacking. On the other hand, there is the Peace Corps volunteer who follows a style that flows directly from American values, which tend to encourage cultural understanding and empathy and discourage the maintenance of social barriers.

Peace Corps volunteers serve only two years in one country. They seek close interpersonal relationships with host residents in order to encourage changes through a person-centered approach. This makes volunteers much more prone to adjustment problems than any group that retains social and psychological isolation. It is also likely to produce more changes in the personality of volunteers than occur among the British, Dutch, or Chinese sojourners, for the Peace Corps approach involves the whole person. It is the very antithesis of the defensive preservation of traditions that George Orwell describes so vividly in the small British community of Kyauktada in *Burmese Days*.

Humans have a differential capacity to incorporate during their lifetime environmental stimuli as information and symbol systems which become integrated with their individual behavior. The "replication of uniformity" concept of personality is therefore not as likely to explain transcultural adaptation of sojourners as does an approach which stresses diversity of motives, habits, and other personality potentials (Wallace, 1961). In personality development the acquisition of symbol systems determines cognitive and effective behavior patterns. Ego identity is developed through mastery of such a system as initially experienced in the interpersonal relations network of the family. But human plasticity also provides a capacity to reach beyond the primary symbol systems of effective communications in the family or primary social group. New meaningful symbols can be shared, new channels of cognition can be developed, and new affective patterns may be partially substituted for existing ones or added to them.

The ability to reach beyond a given primary cultural context, to be creative in the modification of one's own cultural environment, is inherent in the human species. In the long evolutionary history of humans, the appearance of divergent cultures that trace their origin to a common form reflects this capacity for change. From a limited, culturally shared repertory present during the transition from protohuman to human existence, to the complex cultures of the present, this capacity for change in individuals has played a crucial role. But what must have occurred, during the long history of man, in small tribal groups over several generations, is now carried on within a short span of time, certainly within the lifetime of an individual. The changes that in their most drastic forms move an individual from a preliterate society into the complex cultures of modern society shift the adjustment pressures once shared by an entire society over many generations to the individual within his lifetime. How such dramatic change is possible for a whole group has been reported for the Manus of New Guinea (Mead, 1956). As Mead explains it, these changes were successful because they were not a partial modification, but a complete transition from one whole pattern to another. Mead uses the analogy of learning a second and third language to illustrate what takes place in learning another culture. "Beneath the pattern of a second language would be found the 'mother-tongue culture,' first and differently learned" (p. 365).

Anthropologists are interested in the degree to which a culture is open or closed to outside influences. Such distinctions have not been well developed so far for comparative purposes (Fuchs, 1964).[1] Psychologists approach permeability through studies of individuals. Differences in authoritarianism or dogmatism can

[1] Openness of culture refers to possible free variations within a cultural pattern.

be measured independently of cultural permeability, but they have a modal, cultural base (Oliver, 1965). While it is well known that extremely rigid persons will not succeed in establishing close interpersonal relations abroad and find satisfaction in transcultural experiences, it is also likely that too flexible a personality structure will lead to adjustment problems. High permeability may be desirable for immigrants, but is not as functional for those who choose to return to their own culture.

The challenge for sojourners is to tolerate transcultural experiences, but to stop short of the crucial transition where cultural identity—and with it personal identity—become confused or totally altered. The change that is bound to occur in the sojourner results in personal growth and maturation, a capacity to function effectively without the support of primary cultural symbols. If it results in a total cultural shift, a merging into another culture, or too close a cathexis to the symbol system of another society, adjustment problems are likely to be as great as in the case of avoidance of any transcultural involvement. The Peace Corps volunteer must be able to tolerate permeability without threat to his basic personality structure. He must be selective in his cultural experience without being rejecting to the detriment of his primary task.

This is perhaps one of the most difficult demands made on modern man in his interaction with his fellowmen. It requires the continuous expansion and sharing of a communication system. Unless one subscribes to a theory of increasing cultural homogeneity in the world, analogous to genetic panmixia, the continued existence of basic cultural differences of individual societies must be assumed and respected. Peace Corps volunteers are fortunate that their organization has provided them with the currently available knowledge of psychiatry and social science.

It is desired of Peace Corps volunteers that the integration of new symbol systems in different cultural contexts occur as part of a general developmental sequence following primary socialization without threat to ego identity. The psychiatric view toward capacity for such development is contained in Caplan's crisis theory as outlined for Peace Corps purposes in the *Manual for Psychiatrists Participating in the Peace Corps Program*. The key phrase here is that "a person usually behaves in a fairly consistent and predictable manner. He has emotional ups and downs, but, on the whole, his psychological functioning maintains a steady state of equilibrium. This equilibrium is influenced by the fact that during his growth and development he has acquired a repertoire of coping and problem-solving mechanisms so that in his usual life situation he knows what to expect, and so that he knows that when he is faced by a problem he can deal with it in a reasonable satisfactory manner and in a relatively short period of time" (p. 74).

If the interaction of personality system and sociocultural environmental system are seen from the point of view of a cybernetic model and in the light of the statement in the *Manual* that "the upset of a crisis appears to be precipitated by unexpected or temporarily unsurmountable problem-solving methods of the individual," the ability of a sojourner to handle unfamiliar symbol systems is crucial for effective functioning. This ability must exist in spite of continued roots in one's own symbol system. The sojourner, therefore, must be an individual who combines permeability with strong ego-identity. For volunteers this is an ego-strengthening experience—as is any past experience of positive problem-solving in an unfamiliar situation.

The *Manual* lists the "complicated system of forces" explaining alternate paths of developmental growth or breakdown by volunteers as a result of conflict in transcultural context. These forces are summarized (p. 80) as:

1. Personality—the current representation of patterns of behavior which have crystallized during the individual's past life in relation to biological, psychological, and sociocultural factors

2. Ego Strength—associated with state of fatigue or freshness, and with physical health

3. Current Meaning of a Situation in Relation to Past Experience—symbolic links with the past and the renewal of old conflicts stimulated by factors in the current situation

4. Current Psychological and Sociocultural Interaction—interaction of the individual with his social milieu; the role of relationships with significant others

To these could be added:

5. Clarity of Project Goals—enunciation of goals which are understood by sojourners and recipients, and which are internally coherent and realistic

6. Response of Recipients—expectations of host-country nationals, patterns of acceptance or rejection

The psychiatric problems of volunteers have been well summarized by W. Walter Menninger and Joseph T. English (1964). The 0.7 percent of all volunteers who had to return home before termination of service on account of psychiatric problems, and the additional 0.7 percent who returned early because of other adjustment problems, are so small a proportion of all those who serve that the Peace Corps may be proud of its record.

Nevertheless, when criteria for adjustment problems other than early returns are used, it is found that a significant number of volunteers admit to occasional stressful periods abroad. These low periods tend to produce a variety of reactions which may last only briefly, or may take several weeks to overcome. During a conference at the end of service volunteers are asked to list periods of stress or low morale on an unsigned questionnaire. Reactions they describe include anxiety, depression, irritability, and anger.

Dr. English has summarized the nature of these crises; it is recognized that regionally there are variations caused by the different nature of projects and the difference in acceptance or rejection by local populations.

1–2 months—Crisis of arrival: Marked by ititial excitement and anxieties generated by the new environment

4–6 months—Crisis of engagement: Resulting from lack of structures, often the lack of challenge

11–14 months—Crisis of acceptance: The awareness of mixed motivations, learning to accept more than one gives;

the recognition of superior values in another culture and ensuing questions whether there should be changes

16–21 months—Crisis of reentry: The anxiety about return; the anticipation of losing an unaccustomed freedom, unusual responsibilities, and an ability for self-expression, unchallenged by approval of one's familiar reference groups

In a recent termination conference in the Philippines most volunteers listed at least two crisis periods. Several listed three, and only two volunteers out of about 70 claimed that there had been no stress during their entire two years of service.

The Peace Corps volunteer accepts an invitation to serve in a foreign country for a limited period of time. His role, while not clearly defined, is that of a catalyst. While learning to communicate with host-country nationals on the level of close interpersonal relations, using linguistic and paralinguistic means of communication, the volunteer attempts to make a contribution as a model and stimulator in the initiation of progress or cultural change. The Peace Corps expects him to participate in the daily life of local people while attempting to remain objectively neutral to the values of his own culture and that of the people among whom he works. This is much like the task of the anthropologist, who uses a similar approach as a researcher. The difference in goals makes the volunteer's task much more demanding: he helps to make decisions affecting the host society through his intimate contacts with the local population. He is an agent of change, but one who cannot function effectively unless he has reached beyond "understanding"; in the words of Lawrence Fuchs, a former Peace Corps representative in the Philippines, "Acceptance of Filipinos as persons, including their resistance to change, had to be genuine and non-manipulative to be a precondition of effective change by them" (Fuchs, 1964). This means in effect that the volunteer must first understand what goals are acceptable to the host-country population, and then must be able to identify the cultural modifications that are necessary to attain these goals, and what elements of the culture need not be transformed. He should realize that a society which strives towards industralization, accepting an entrepreneurial system to do so, has to adopt certain essential elements, although it need not be a carbon copy of the volunteer's own society. While responsibility, individual achievement, and a proper sense of timing are required for such goals, there are cultural variations in their expression. Such insights demand maturity and understanding, which require objectivity on the part of the volunteer. For example, volunteer teachers are properly concerned about the practice of grading some students on the basis of their parents' social and political status in the community, favoring those from prominent families. Here the volunteer could be expected to educate school officials, parents, and students toward acceptance of an objective grading system. Volunteers also tend to become irritated over the fact that their direct criticisms of local teachers, no matter how mild, how well phrased, and how justified, are met with shame and withdrawal on the part of the criticized, even when the American and the local teacher had apparently shared a close personal relationship. In this case the volunteer fails to accept and respond properly to modal elements in personality which do not stand directly in the way of accepted goals. There are culturally acceptable ways of handling such a situation, though they require patience and skill on the part of the American. Volunteers are not trained as social scientists. But the majority of volunteers begin to ask the right questions after a year or more abroad, and throughout their service they try to find immediate and pragmatic answers.

The ideal volunteer may be characterized as integrated with his own subculture and the totality of North American culture of which it is a part. He is sure of his place in his home country. He is capable of developing skills; he need not become a highly specialized expert, but he must be willing to apply his skills as cultural circumstances permit or require. He remains positive and satisfied even if he sees few results. He may come from any socioeconomic background, but statistically he is more likely to come from the middle class. Whatever his background, it certainly corresponds more to the conditions of an emerging middle class among the host-country population than to that of the broad base of local residents. His job as a teacher, for example, may bring him into contact with those who understand and even seem to share some of his values. But his social efforts are expected to be directed toward the large masses of uneducated or little-educated. Even if he is a specialist, teaching new or improved methods to colleagues in his field, as a laboratory technician might do, the Peace Corps still expects the volunteer to direct additional efforts to the little-educated, the farmers or laborers, and other village residents. He should not be just a professional working among colleagues. He is expected to initiate community projects, to organize games or sports for the children or educational projects for adults. His house, if he does not live with a local family, is open to visitors at all times. His social conduct follows local customs, not those of his own society, as long as basic moral conflicts with his own value system do not demand from him an unreasonable compromise—or, if they are broadly shared American values, compromise his role as a Peace Corps volunteer. To find the proper balance in conforming to the demands of both cultures and of the volunteer role is probably the most difficult part of a volunteer's task.

Peace Corps is a service organization that requires deep commitment, the ability to adjust to different living conditions, possession of skills, and submission to a rigorous training and selection process. Many volunteers, especially when President Kennedy first announced the idea, were drawn to the Peace Corps as a way in which they could do something personally to improve interpersonal relations and to help less technologically developed (or, as it is generally thought, less fortunate) countries.

Volunteers are selected carefully. Only those who have adequately mastered previous life situations are invited to serve. Even now only about 20 percent of those applying are accepted for training. Of those in training, an average 20 percent do not go overseas as volunteers.[2] Training is as much a key to a successful operation of Peace Corps programs as is selection. Ideally,

2 Of every 100 applicants, an average of only 16 go abroad as volunteers.

these two preparatory stages are totally integrated, since the psychological goal of training is to strengthen coping mechanisms through knowledge of different cultures and, in so doing, to develop greater awareness of oneself in an unfamiliar environment (Maretzki, 1965).

Only a small number of those entering the training comprehend the realities of Peace Corps service. These realities include, for many projects, a latent job role, working in situations lacking familiar structure, or a lack of a real desire by host-country people to accept help from anyone even though their government invited the Peace Corps to send volunteers. This is not what a committed, service-oriented, conscientious, and achievement-driven young American might call optimum working conditions. It is remarkable that in the experience of the Peace Corps, the unfamiliar and often depriving physical conditions play only a minor part in adjustment problems. Young Americans learn to shift to eating rice, public bathing, and riding on local buses more easily than they do to coping with an ill-defined working situation, relating to a different hierarchy of authority, or being isolated for long periods from accustomed intellectual stimulations.

Some of the realities of Peace Corps projects are communicated to applicants and trainees through their personal contact with volunteers or former volunteers. Most facts about their prospective service are presented in training. Nevertheless, as George Guthrie has stated, "A number of thoughtful volunteers offered the observation that they did not believe a word they were told during training" (Guthrie, n.d.). Volunteers prefer to respond to a new environment through their own observations and experiences after arrival abroad. What training can and does accomplish in areas other than language and skill training probably lies largely in developing attitudes and sensitivities along with factual knowledge.

The awareness that Peace Corps itself has unclear, or even conflicting, notions about project goals and about effectiveness may come only after the volunteer reaches his destination. Gradually there also comes a recognition of obstacles raised by the recipient society. Regardless, therefore, of the suitability of the individual's own primary personality qualities, his capacity for cultural and psychological permeability, and his ability to transfer some of his past experiences into the present situation, the lack of clear project goals and the passivity of recipients are potential sources of adjustment problems.

One dimension of project-goal conflicts can be described as professionalism versus interpersonal, intercultural involvement. Success as a volunteer, or effectiveness in the eyes of the Peace Corps, depends on doing well both in a job skill and in intercultural relations. The volunteer may favor one approach or the other, depending on his talents and inclinations, but also on his ability to cope with all the demands. Emphasizing one over the other may turn into a form of withdrawal or may indicate maladjustment to the task at hand.

The Philippine Peace Corps program over the past four years has searched for a workable balance between the professional demands of an educational program that is intended to help upgrade English, science, and mathematics, and the desire to foster general contributions to local communities through initiation of various small projects involving children and adults. The first groups of volunteers in the Philippines were given an official role as "teachers' aides." This role was unfamiliar to Americans and Filipinos alike. It had no place in the existing school structure, and was in effect a compromise to accommodate native English speakers with little or no formal background in teaching in a school system that had well-trained professional local teachers in abundant supply. Many volunteers found that they could make greater contributions outside school by starting a number of projects; at least they could gain more satisfaction than they did where underutilization or other problems in the school assignment taxed their coping mechanisms beyond tolerance.

A former volunteer has tried to analyze the type of adjustment or nonadjustment that volunteers made to the educational-aide role in the rural Philippines community. Szanten (1964) distinguishes between those who accept and those who withdraw. While the more professionally oriented volunteer tended to return to a relative social isolation after his daily school duties, the "accepting" volunteer tended to immerse himself in local activities, manifestly to learn to understand the culture, latently perhaps to escape from an undesirable or unmanageable working situation. Of course, as Szanten writes, "Only few volunteers could be found at either extreme."

Szanten's criteria included in-school activities (participation in the school system and persistence in carryng out this responsibility); cross-cultural contributions (involvement in community projects, nature of personal relationships with Filipinos, ability to communicate in the local vernacular); and administrative factors (need for attention from the Peace Corps organization). The results of the study were inconclusive: "Since it has not yet been definitely established that acceptant volunteers had greater impact on their schools than those who tended to withdraw, it cannot be claimed that the experiment has supported our expectations concerning cross-cultural working relationships" (p. 43).

The range of feelings of volunteers, their reactions to the cultural confrontation, and the variety of their responses are described realistically by Szanten. On Rogerian psychological principles, he says that acceptance is required in cross-cultural technical assistance, since it is the "core of a non-directive 'helping-relationship'" (p. 41). Acceptance without loss of objectivity and perspective from one's own ego and cultural base is not discussed.

Because the adjustment problems for volunteers in the Philippines were considerable in the early years, the role of educational aide was changed to coteacher, with the collaboration of the Philippines Bureau of Public Schools. This change invited greater professionalism, since it raised the requirements for educational backgrounds and experience. Volunteers now needed at least a B.A. degree. They receive intensive training in teaching English, mathematics, or science by modern methods, and must be qualified to teach before being sent overseas. This took pressure off those volunteers who could not reach far into the new culture, even though they were able to make seemingly significant—though as yet unmeasured—contributions in the educational field. Such modifications in the program, and other changes related to early experiences, increased the volunteers' chances for adequate adjustment.

Questions of the proper and workable level of interpersonal relations are still being debated by volunteers and Peace Corps staff. But the conflict is no longer played out in the barrios or left entirely to volunteers to resolve. This is a reevaluation of Peace Corps goals, and more so of the sojourner's role. Given the motivational, cognitive, and coping abilities of young Americans who are most likely to volunteer for Peace Corps service, the original ideal may have been too demanding. Adjustment problems, therefore, may be partly resolved at the expense of an ideal that may never have been quite realistic. Volunteers now tend to see more frequently that accomplishments are associated with professional satisfactions. Some even profess a disdain for the "hairshirt attitude." But a workable, realistic balance of working role and intercultural role, which still requires understanding, acceptance, and cultural involvement, seems to emerge.

There is another reason why a shift in emphasis of Peace Corps goals seems realistic. The response of host-country people has not always been properly understood by volunteers or Peace Corps officials. The early attempt to saturate the Philippines with volunteers who were spread broadly over the island schools was based on an assumption that the closer volunteers were associated with the rural people, the greater their chances for a positive catalytic effect. The accepted rule for agents of change— "people are much readier to cooperate with development agents if they are treated as partners in the change process and given opportunity to do as much as possible for themselves" (Goodenough, 1964, p. 378)—was taken too literally. Americans think of a partner as an equal, and to become partners it is desirable to eliminate any social or related barriers. It is difficult for Americans to accept the idea that a close working relationship can be maintained even though the status differences of the host society are maintained. Typically volunteers in the Philippines insisted on not being called "Sir," a natural mode of address for a Filipino to use,[3] or would address a group in the vernacular when an American might be expected to address the group in English, even though it would not be intelligable to everyone. Many societies may have found it easier to establish a relationship toward colonial administrators who maintained a cultural distance than toward the sojourner who makes every attempt to understand, to accept, and even, in his attempt to establish equality, to change psychologically in the direction of their own culture. Two psychologists recently suggested that what separates societies is not so much the modes of behavior themselves, but "the need to preserve barriers between individuals and groups" (Wagatsuma and De Vos, 1963).

People may actually feel more comfortable with a sojourner who knows their culture only superficially—unless they themselves have, through experience, education, and other special circumstances, adopted values and attitudes that favor cross-cultural relations. The less educated, less experienced, and more traditional members of most societies may become cautious, or even resentful, toward an outsider as he not only becomes conversant with their language, but begins to adopt their customs and even their ways of thinking. Differences in response to outsiders are related to self-image and preferred reference groups. They also depend on the degree to which the culture is open or closed.

People such as the Filipinos may show a pattern of response to outsiders. They may express pleasure if the outsider accepts their hospitality—above all, their food—or at least tries it with expressions of pleasure. They may appreciate attempts to speak their language and efforts to study it. As long as the outsider "tries," as long as he stumbles over some phrases or lacks vocabulary, thereby maintaining an acceptable social distance, his interest

[3] An example cited by Frank Lynch, S.J., in personal discussion.

may be accepted; he and his hosts may find mutual satisfaction in exploring each other's good will. But as the novelty wears off, as the sojourner attempts to assume a more intimate role among his hosts, adopting their food preferences, styles of dress, and way of living, latent resentment may appear.

In this area the Peace Corps has used a typically American intuitive approach that may occasionally turn enthusiasm into amateurism. Some of the questions of interpersonal interaction in intercultural context have not been well enough thought through by those who prepare volunteers for their overseas tasks. The self-image of host-country people, their relative openness, the conflicts created by the desire to please while preserving social isolation, are too easily brushed aside; unrealistic claims of "acceptance" and "understanding" are made. Volunteers who retrospectively evaluate their experiences, and local surveys by well-trained, objective native researchers, will ultimately be needed to provide the answers to these questions. Unrealistic expectations held by the Peace Corps or by well-meaning, enthusiastic volunteers may create stresses whose sources are not clear. Only those with an unusual degree of maturity and sensitivity will be able to interpret adequately the stimulus they provide their hosts and the depth of feelings and understanding they evoke.

This does not imply that volunteers do not receive satisfaction from their ability to live with the people among whom they work and to like them. Guthrie (n.d., p. 10) writes that "the most satisfied Volunteer seems to be the one who is two days from the Embassy and who gets along with fewer conveniences . . . the Volunteer in the remote community who has been led to make peace with the society." Even if Guthrie is right in assuming that the American in a remote community profits from sharing the experiences of his hosts, the volunteer is likely to escape adjustment problems only if he perceives his relationship to local populations with some detachment. As the young Texan volunteer put it after returning from Thailand, "You have to retain some sense of identity. The greatest challenge is to maintain a sense of orientation in the absence of sufficient markers."

As anthropologists we like people to be flexible, to be open to influence. We don't like people to be rigid, authoritarian (in the sense of the studies by the Berkeley psychologists), resistant to influence. But can people be too flexible? Can people be too open to change, too easily influenced, too permeable?

A high permeability may be desirable for immigrants but a drawback for Peace Corpsmen, who are to return to their own culture. A total shift in culture, in values, is not desirable in this role. The Peace Corpsman must combine permeability with a strong, firm ego identity. He must understand what goals of change are acceptable to the people of the host country; he must know how to make changes; and he must recognize what not to change. If he does these things successfully, his time in the Peace Corps, like any successful problem-solving, can be a strengthening experience, an occasion of growing and maturing.

CONCLUSION

The transcultural adjustment of Peace Corps volunteers requires unusual insights and sensitivities. Their role demands understanding and acceptance of another culture without transculturalization. The volunteer whose personality has not changed as a result of his experience abroad has probably not been totally involved in his complex work situation, and may have resorted to a form of withdrawal from the challenge of the sojourner role. The volunteer who returns with feelings of alienation from the way of life in his society may have overreacted to the cross-cultural experience. The best-adjusted volunteer is likely to return showing visible and demonstrable growth and maturity, increased sensitivity and ego-strength. His goals have come into focus, and his ability to carry them out has increased. As Szanten aptly put it, volunteers who made an accepting response to cultural confrontation "did not lose themselves in the Philippines, if anything, they tended to more fully find themselves" (1964, p. 38).

If these are, indeed, the results of the sojourner role of a Peace Corps volunteer, the next challenge to us is to help other societies understand the need for developing their transcultural experiences into a personality-building process that ultimately will help all cross-cultural communications. In man's evolutionary present, a capacity for transcultural experience and a proper adjustment to it is a necessity for all men.

social scientists and economists

Herbert W. Hargreaves

With the nearly universal dissemination of the social dictum that goods are good and extreme forms of poverty are bad, economists in increasing numbers have addressed the question: how is it possible to produce the appropriate types of change in the "deprived" regions? The studies have thus far failed to yield satisfactory answers, and their authors have become increasingly aware of the limitations of schemata that consider chiefly the relationships between commodities and resource constraints upon production. Long ago economists concluded that the growth objective required a rapid increase in productive resources, especially in countries in which high rates of population growth are conjoined with low incomes. This trite generalization, however, only prefaced the basic problem: how is the rate of investment in new kinds of physical and human capital to be increased to levels sufficient to sustain rising standards of living?

In extremis, economists have suggested that the problem of economic development in the world's impoverished "two-thirds" belongs mainly, if not wholly, to other social scientists; and David McClelland (1961) has staked out the main competing claim on behalf of social psychology. Seizing upon the inability of economists to make universally valid statements about the causes of differences in economic development, he has advanced his own generalization and prescription. Levels of income depend upon the antecedent human needs for achievement ("*n* Ach.").

Since *n* Achievement is, according to his evidence, the principal force acting upon economic growth, and its lack the chief constraint, it follows that new human aspirations are a precondition of economic development, and policymakers who seek this goal must begin with programs to change people.

I will accept his charge against the economists, but will deny that it is the important one; accept his hypothesis as part of the operational attack on poverty, but deny the usefulness of the statistical generalization; and accept his broad conclusion with reservations. The points of disagreement are important, however, only insofar as they reveal the terms upon which the disciplines can usefully be brought together. For economists and possibly other social scientists, the main sources of irritation in McClelland's work are byproducts of a common difficulty. The materials in another discipline can only be sampled, and the view, if not the sample itself, is certain to be biased. We can reduce the confusion of overstatement if we can identify the points at which views are complementary and disagreements are resolvable.

In its own terms, McClelland's complaint that economists have failed to produce generalizations is justified. Demographic explanations of poverty, market explanations of growth, and health explanations of labor productivity are unacceptable because they are falsified by cases. His own generalization, in his view, meets the criteria of science. Countries lie in order along a growth-potential spectrum ranging from zero to largest, and the approximate position of any particular country can be predicted by the results of the *n* Achievement tests. Where people reveal a high need for achievement, the subsequent growth rate is demonstrably high, and so on down the scale. Since correlations do not imply either that *A* causes *B* or vice versa, he seeks causation in the connecting links—the high achievers provide the economy's supply of entrepreneurs and are the source of economic growth. Fair enough. Universals of this sort never came from the pens of economists.

Controversies over the merits of styles of learning place unnecessary blocks in the path of fruitful communication between specialists. McClelland dismisses population studies because they have produced no generalizations. But population growth rates do affect the size of the work force, the relation between the work force and other productive factors, and the relation between consumption and output. In other words, the variables through which we relate population and growth rates, if they are to be related sensibly, yield the hypothesis that they are related. Inasmuch as this relationship has been proved in at least one case (Coale and Hoover, 1958), the hypothesis does not appear to be valueless. Since economic and social systems are a highly heterogeneous universe, the hypotheses that might conceivably yield to the all-case proof that McClelland demands are not likely to be fruitful. Generalizations about similar cases promise more illumination than statements about all of them.

The importance of diversity stands out in McClelland's own work. Differences in the need for achievement were crucial to his explanation of growth differentials, but he could not treat them as "ultimate" explanations. Unlike lands, these needs were not given to a society in fixed quantities. He therefore widened his search to include the causes of a low need for achievement, finding them in various types of cultural affiliation in which group norms were in conflict with individuation. Thus different types of religious doctrine and familial and community organization became the ultimate explanatory variables. In a sense, the histories of men were in partial control, and those histories differed from place to place. Economists would want to add that the struggle for income was also part of that history—that the methods by which men adapted themselves to economic necessity became part of the fabric of tradition. This is not to argue for economic determinism; many kinds of adaptation were possible. But it is difficult not to believe that the ways in which men perceived their economic problems affected the ways in which they organized their activities.

On the "causes" of human behavior, the conceptual gap between McClelland and the economists is wide, but the practical consequences of their arguments are not irreconcilable. His experimental method required a measure of n Achievement that would be independent of the behavior he wanted to explain. This procedure, however, did not imply psychological determinism, and he claimed only that he wanted to "see man as a *creator* [italics his] of his environment, as well as a creature of it" (p. 392). But the apparatus with which he explains the "creature," the catenalike propositions that link the past to the present, together with the dictum that the causes of behavior cannot be inferred from behavior itself, distinguishes his scientific vision from that of modern economists. Schultz's suggestion that the low output of traditional agriculture can be explained in terms of a "unique set of preferences related to work and thrift" was inferred from behavior and is therefore not science (Schultz, 1964, p. vii). Nevertheless, this "model" of behavior accommodates the causal factors which McClelland wanted to include as well as those he did not consider important but which are vital to Schultz's argument. The productive factors on the farm, including the farmer himself, were creations of the past. And while these do not fix the farmer's ability, they are restrictive enough to "cause" him to put a low value on the kinds of change he knows and understands. The differences between behavior theories of McClelland and Schultz dissolve into differences in their judgment of the efficacy of various instrumentalities of education.

Disagreements in this vital territory are, however, deeply imbedded in differing conceptions of the controls on human behavior. McClelland seems to say that man, insofar as he is a creature of his environment, owes his motives only to his social environment, and that neither his motives nor his power to act is in any way conditioned by economic facts. When he writes that people get about what they want (p. 105), he means that wants are determined by social factors but not by the technical conditions under which people produce income. Although he works hard to refute Marxian "determinism" (p. 391), at another point he argues that people are changed by new economic things, such as motors. Can it be that they were never shaped by the things that have long since become traditional parts of the economic environment? His emphasis on the importance of human development in economic growth is unexceptionable, but his total preoccupation with the creative side of man's nature has brought him joyfully to the abolition of the economic problem.

The instrument of transformation is a man, presumably synthesized by experiment, who has no special interest in personal enrichment but who, nevertheless, provides the kinds of action that lead to national enrichment. "The desire for gain, in and of itself, has done little to produce economic development. But the desire for achievement has done a great deal" (p. 391). "What had been done out of a desire to please, to make money, or to get time off from work, might now be converted into an activity in which standards of excellence were defined and pursued in their own right. Viewed in this light it would not be at all surprising to imagine that an increase in n Achievement should promote economic and cultural growth" (p. 46). Economists will surely recoil at the idea that the first three motives have nothing to do with economic growth; they may even recall Adam Smith's story of the boy who invented a labor-saving device so that he might enjoy more leisure. We can agree that Gutenberg must have been a man dedicated to ends beyond the profit motive. But how could there have been a printing industry to contribute to the national income and to learning if no one had been inspired by the profit motive to apply Gutenberg's idea to the production of cheap reading matter? The traditional craftsmanship of the Middle Ages involved the pursuit of standards of excellence, but it is not clear that the craft spirit provided much growth. Excellence for itself is often a victim of economy.

If both sides could recognize the essential features of the economic process, their disagreements would become minimal. For both McClelland and Schultz, the goal of economic development requires that people depart from tradition and acquire new purposes. But Schultz feels that the new knowledge and profit opportunities provided by appropriate forms of education and technical change would be sufficient to replace old modes of work with more productive ones. We may not know why a man crosses the street, to use McClelland's phrase (p. 38), but if we know how groups of men respond to a new set of alternatives, do we need to ask why? People behave "as if" they were working for money, and the activities that are related to that behavior, irrespective of "causes," are the sources of economic growth. Enough behavior of this sort has been observed among so-called tradition-bound people to deny the validity of contradictory statements. Abstraction from psychological and social man may be a barrier to the development of fruitful lines of inquiry on specific classes of management problems, but it still yields results in economics.

There is no controversy about the relation between entrepreneurs and economic development, but McClelland's peculiar conception of these agents of change raises a question about the alleged relationship between the high n Achievement groups and the supply of entrepreneurs. Even if we can be confident that his tests reveal that people who are most likely to accept risks in return for psychic rewards go to a doctor instead of a healer, and approve other people for their performances rather than their affiliations, can we be equally confident that they have identified the sources of the relevant types of motivation? As another reviewer pointed out, a society may offer risk-takers more acceptable opportunities in politics, arts and letters, and the professions than in business (Katona, 1962). The author's description of high achievers strengthens the supposition that these would be the preferred choices. This is not to argue that such occupational preferences are not culturally desirable, but only that other activities are more important sources of economic growth. But while McClelland's conception of the entrepreneurial function raises additional doubt about the value of his scientific generalization, he might still insist that the low n Achievers are not a promising source of change agents and that the central problem of economic development is the creation of larger numbers of highly motivated people. Can any agency do this without offering them rewards more substantial than the symbols of approval that McClelland and his coworkers attached to good performances on the *n* Achievement tests? While his science was meant to obviate the "chicken-egg" problem, it is still not obvious on his evidence that high *n* Achievement is not a consequence of economic development.

We must also question the value of the generalization from the other end of the *n* Achievement-growth relationship. McClelland is aware of the difficulties involved in the measurement of growth, and I do not need to belabor the point. But given a technique of measurement, however inadequate, aspects of the connection are puzzling. Since the existence of high *n* Achievement is taken as a precondition of high rates of economic growth, the *post hoc ergo propter hoc* complaint is easy, but not fair. There are more serious questions. If it is true that motives are stable—McClelland's treatment of their origin suggests that they are—it is also true that economic growth is not stable and not unidirectional. Shifts in rates of growth from positive to negative and through varying magnitudes of both suggest that a good deal of change is independent of the previously measured *n* Achievement, and that economists must continue to explain the variations in other ways. Period averages may diminish the difficulty for McClelland's purpose, but one is left to wonder how long the long run should be. Even if we could answer, this would not eliminate the reversal difficulty. If the human qualities that McClelland associates with high *n* Achievement are as he bills them, the high achievers ought not to have been subverted by an extravagant government (Uruguay in the 1960s), or by a conservative government (the United States in the late 1950s), or by any other set of economic factors. In short, variable and reversible growth after the measurement of *n* Achievement shifts the high *n* Achievement countries in the growth continuum and denies the validity of McClelland's thesis.

While McClelland's central scientific proposition possesses more form than substance, his general claim that human change is requisite to economic development merits emphasis, though not to the exclusion of other kinds of change. Numerous economic studies have demonstrated the futility of change in the physical inputs of production without change in the knowledge, attitudes, and perspectives of people. However, it has not been the primary mission of economists to study people as people but only as agents in processes related to the transformation of goods, including the services of people, into other goods, including the "ultimate satisfactions" of consumption. Economists recognized the capital aspect of people, but they thought of it chiefly in terms of the productivities of human effort which could be changed by the instrumentalities of education in its widest sense. But economists also thought of education as a competitor for capital; since larger amounts of other things—given a supply of human ability—would also increase production. According to this perspective, there is an economics of education, a need to value its alternative products and the alternative techniques by which those results could be produced. As in any industry, there was room for product improvement and for cost-reducing or output-increasing innovation, but the technical competence to describe, prescribe, and evaluate belonged to the educational "engineers." This is the general field in which the other social sciences might render their most valuable services in their specific relationship to economic development.

How has McClelland helped? In fairness, it should be noted that he did not intend to produce a book on educational psychology, and his ideas on the subject emerge largely as implications of the relationship between n Achievement and economic development. He was not concerned about the cost of his recommendations, and he implicitly assumed that they would be productive enough to justify the unknown cost. Economic planners need more. Specifically, they want to know what kinds of human change obtained by what means at what costs can be reconciled with the competitive claims against the resources available for all change. While McClelland cannot be blamed for not addressing himself to the economic question in these terms, he can be criticized for prescribing economic action without reference to the issues.

He argues for the development of large industry instead of

cottage industry on the ground that larger groups of labor at new kinds of work in new technical and physical environments will more effectively destroy the old traditions and substitute other-directedness. If his recommendation were taken literally it would mean that planners would choose this alternative irrespective of its cost in other things. It is true that the productivity of large industry, given an effective labor force, might meet economic criteria for investment in particular industries. But large expenditures on particular kinds of capital for the purpose of changing the labor force would raise difficult problems in the reconciliation of investment with growth objectives. Schultz argues that the farmer's traditional work methods must be destroyed, but he does not propose to accomplish that end by putting farmers into new bunches. Surely the simple changes in environment and in knowledge by which Schultz proposes to alter the outlook of farmers can also be employed to increase the productivity of small industry. And since most industry is small, plans that neglect it are not likely to yield the best possible rate of economic growth.

McClelland's insistence on the deemphasis of tradition as a precondition for a strengthened n Achievement has important implications for the control of schooling. Since children who have been removed from the dominating influence of fathers early enough in life are more likely to become high achievers, according to his case studies, the educational process ought to be separated from the family influence. And since the known occupations to which the young might be removed in the critical years (8 to 12) are, by his own admission, very limited, schooling is the obvious substitute. It is not clear, however, how the heavy-handed ideology that he openly advocates as the general carrier of education could be used to remove the schools from parental influence without a centralization of power that would be tantamount to political revolution.

Economists in their ignorance may wish to question the relevance of the "whole" constellation of traditions and cultural institutions. McClelland has argued from an anthropological standpoint that cultures work as "wholes," but at the same time he appears to deny that the obstructing "wholes" will be replaced by any unique set of social institutions. The principal desideratum appears to be the minimization of conflict between tradition and change based upon new knowledge and incentives to behave in new ways. Economists who believe that education adds new competences to the individual have assumed, perhaps unconsciously, that small changes of this type could be made effective without a direct attack upon the whole cultural organization. McClelland argues that the old structure will crumble under the impact of economic change, but, except in the case of large industries, economic change cannot be used as an instrumentality for cultural revision because the existing structures are insuperable barriers to change. Perhaps the economists have been wrong. But it is not clear that groups whose members have a high n Affiliation cannot be induced to work more effectively under new kinds of management techniques. McClelland admits as much when he says, "In producing work, one motive may substitute for another so that even though the achievement motive may be weak in some people, their output may well be the same as somebody else's because of a stronger desire to please the experimenter" (p. 41). He is, nevertheless, led to prescribe a "holistic" type of education because economic development depends upon high achievement, and "partial educational influences which might increase achievement do not appear very effective when they are unsupported by ideological conversion of the total group in which experience occurs" (p. 416).

The difficulty for economists rests in the fact that McClelland's conception of the growth process is too limited. According to the view expressed above, production may be independent of the need for achievement, but not of work. But since economic growth is rising production, it is not clear that growth cannot be obtained through the operation of the baser motives that simply lead to more work. Economists will readily admit, however, that iterative labor of the old type is not sufficient to increase output rapidly, and that the high achievers may be the major innovators. But innovations are not very productive unless they are widely copied, and it is not clear that the kind of person McClelland wishes to multiply would be an effective copier. In short, economic growth is not the kind of one-input production problem to which he has reduced it. His kind of education has a place in the process, but it is not the only productive education.

But with all these differences, which are perhaps largely matters of emphasis and balance in statement, one more feature of McClelland's industry deserves special comment. Although economic development is taking place the problem of acceleration persists, and an important part of the solution is the rapid discovery of the kinds of people who will promote the change. In developed economies, the market system in league with education effectively performs this function. Able people are not likely to remain undiscovered. The less-developed countries are not similarly endowed, and the scarcity of entrepreneurs, managers, and skilled workers may have a stronger effect upon production than other capital limitations. Where this is the case, the most urgent investment program is the identification of people on whom educational resources might be most effectively spent. It is necessary to add, however, that economists will want to know whether a random selection of prospective talent might not be nearly as efficient, and much less expensive, than McClelland's psychocultural approach.

McClelland, reversing the social scientist's procedure (p. 391), began with individuals as they revealed themselves in experiments and, by inference, created society as it was. But in order to reach his vision of the new society, he was obliged to relate the two by appealing to other experience. In beginning with a logical vision of society, economists may have repeated the methodological "error" of the social scientists, but they revised their accounts of ongoing societies to include the relevant features of McClelland's empiricism. From this base, they, too, were obliged to appeal to other experience for clues to the kinds of change that could be expected to lead to economic development. Thus both came by different routes to their own identifications of the appropriate agents of change, and both include tradition-breaking forms of education. The minds of men are, in varying degree, shaped in part by their social past. Economists, however, are obliged to include the economy, and they are not likely to believe that experiments which cannot easily influence working behavior (p. 40) have produced useful substitutes for factors that work "as if" they were influencing such behavior.

In the field of development, economists work among the disciplines in their own way, and they are perhaps less parochial in their use of facts and more strongly committed to their methods of using them, than their detractors imagine. Sermons on methodology are not obviously productive.

intercultural differences in personality

Joseph C. Finney

In this paper I shall present a general theory of personality and of personality differences; show how differences in culture are especially relevant to the understanding of personality differences; and, finally, present some quantitative evidence on personality differences across cultures.

The working model of personality is based upon the theory of control systems, servomechanisms, or feedback processes. Its specific content, however, is derived from the fields of psychology, psychiatry, and psychoanalysis (Finney, 1962b).

The human organism, like other animal organisms, consists of processes, chemical, physical, and so forth, constantly going on. Although writers sometimes say that the human organism maintains itself in equilibrium, that is not true in the accepted sense of the word *equilibrium*—as for example in the definition of chemical equilibrium. A chemical equilibrium constant defines a specific ratio of the products of the concentrations on the left side of the equation to the products of the concentrations on the right side. No matter what concentrations you start with, you rapidly approach this ratio of products with the passage of time. That means that the concentrations of each specific substance depend upon the quantities that were put into the system in the first place. The human body reaches chemical equilibrium only when it is dead. During life, the organism maintains itself so that certain specific concentrations or quantities stay at a fixed level regardless of what quantities are put into the system. That state is called equifinality (von Bertalanffy, 1952). It means that the organism maintains itself in a steady state, which is different from the equilibrium state. The organism can do so only because it is an open system, and can put its waste products out of the system as fast as other things are put in. A steady state is, in a sense, an unnatural one. The organism must constantly keep working to maintain it. The condition is one of negative entropy; although this appears to violate the second law of thermodynamics, it is possible because entropy is increasing elsewhere, so that the law holds for the organism plus its environment, though not for the organism alone.

Each organism has certain crucial variables which it works to maintain within specified constant limits. As time and evolution have gone on, the number of crucial variables has increased. Some of the crucial variables are studied in physiology. Among them are pH or acid-base balance, sodium and chloride ion concentrations, oxygen concentration, carbon dioxide concentration, glucose concentration, blood pressure, and heart rate. Each of these variables has at least one physiological mechanism to keep it within limits, to raise it when it gets low, or to lower it when it gets high. Some of these crucial variables have several control mechanisms apiece, so arranged in sequence or hierarchy that if one mechanism fails another mechanism is there to back it up. Presumably these mechanisms were developed in the course of evolution because they were adaptive—that is, increased the chances of survival.

Likewise, we have certain psychological processes that are crucial variables, and must be kept within certain limits. Among them are fear or anxiety, anger or hostility, and hedonic tone, which we call elation at one end and depression or discouragement at the other. So we have control mechanisms, usually called defense mechanisms, to keep anxiety, hostility, and hedonic tone within limits.

Freud, who brought the term *defense* into personality psychology, described a number of defenses (1936). Among the ones we shall be concerned with are repression, making oneself unaware of one's impulses; reaction formation, systematically doing the opposite of one's impulse; and projection, avoiding blame by throwing the blame onto someone else, or, as Freud put it, attributing to others the impulses that one does not want to recognize in oneself.

The control mechanisms or defense mechanisms may be compared to thermostats. Your house may have a cooling system of air conditioning controlled by a thermostat. Suppose that you have set the thermostat at 75. That means that when the temperature rises to 75, your thermostat turns the air conditioning on, working to cool the house. If there are two degrees of play, the air conditioning will turn off when the temperature gets down to 73. When the temperature of your house hits 75 again the thermostat will turn the air conditioning on again. The cycle keeps repeating.

The human organism that we are describing is much more complex than a house. We are concerned not with only one control mechanism but a whole set of different control mechanisms. The workings are highly complex because the several systems are related; the output of one may be the input of another. For example, the defense mechanism of projection, casting the blame on others, may succeed in reducing anxiety at the expense of increasing hostility, which may call for another defense mechanism. (The same is true of physiological defenses. In diabetes, one control mechanism works to lower the blood sugar but has the drawback of causing dehydration and acidosis, which need to be controlled by other servomechanisms.)

The accompanying diagram shows some of the workings of an organism. An external cue impinging upon an organism elicits a response of the autonomic nervous system either intrinsically or, most often, through classical Pavlovian conditioning; it may also send a message to higher levels, including the verbal ones. Some of the autonomic responses are reported back to the central nervous system in the form of drives, urges, or emotional reactions. The drives are among the crucial variables and demand a response to reduce them. Drives are distinguished from other crucial variables by demanding an outward response, that is, a response by skeletal muscles, a response that is visible to other people and affects them. Outward actions, in one way or another, serve to reduce the drives; when this happens, the action becomes reinforced—that is, more likely in the future to occur when the drive is aroused. An action may also turn out to reduce or satisfy drives other than the one that elicited it, and hence we get a building of various secondary drives and an appearance of functional autonomy of motives.

Two defense mechanisms are shown in Figure 1. As certain thoughts or impulses begin to enter awareness, the defense mechanism of repression[1] is called into play and prevents further entry. As certain impulses begin to enter action, the defense mechanism of reaction formation stops them. Although it is not shown in the diagram, a distress or drive is evidently evoked by the incipient entry of the impulse into awareness or action; the drive is reduced by the operation of the defense mechanism. Presumably we learn defense mechanisms by reinforcement, just as we learn outward responses by reinforcement.

At any rate, the outcome of the defense mechanisms is to

[1] It is usual to distinguish repression from dissociation, but I use the two words as synonyms. Both names describe a process in which the bringing together of two ideas is inhibited by a conditioned avoidance, because anxiety is produced whenever the joining begins to happen. So the person continues to hold inconsistent ideas, and may put them into action at different times. The inconsistent ideas do not confront each other in awareness, and so the discrepancy does not come into awareness, and the two thoughts do not become integrated. Repression is usually described as a process in which one system keeps another system out of awareness. Dissociation is usually decribed as a process in which two systems alternate in reaching awareness and control, as in Morton Prince's case of Miss B, or the *Three Faces of Eve*, or Stevenson's fictional *Dr. Jekyll and Mr. Hyde*. Extreme cases like these three are rare, but mild forms of alternation of personality are common. Since repression is not continuously successful (note "return of the repressed"), it seems clear that repression and dissociation are essentially the same thing.

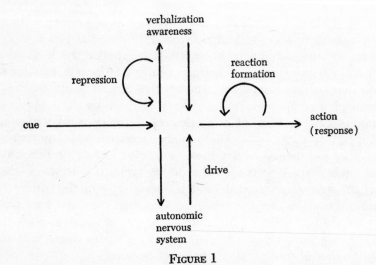

FIGURE 1

change the drives into new and more complex ones. The more important of such drives are the urges for specific kinds of ways of relating to people. Dependency, masochism, controlling, and competition are examples of such basic patterns of personal interaction (Finney, 1963a).

The word *personality* refers to all the ways in which persons differ from one another in the workings that we have described. For example, people differ in the specific situations or cues that arouse their emotions, and in the specific kinds of outward actions that they take to satisfy their emotions. These differences arise from learning and may be highly specific according to the experiences of the individual. The specific content of the outward cues or outward actions constitutes the specific content of personality and the specific content of cultures. But I want to exclude the highly specific differences of content from our definition of personality, since in a way they are superficial, and to use the word *personality* to refer to the functional relationships of the control mechanisms. This limitation does not restrict us entirely to processes quite within the organism, since it includes the urges for particular patterns of relations with other people.

To put it most bluntly, I am defining personality as the set of "thermostat" settings of a person; as the set of thresholds at which his various defense mechanisms come into operation.

Unlike physiological control mechanisms, these thresholds differ from one person to another. As far as we know, the several physiological mechanisms for controlling the concentration of oxygen in the blood have a fixed order or hierchy for all human beings. But that is not so for the defense mechanisms that control such psychological variables as anxiety. One person will use repression-dissociation as his first line of defense, his usual method of keeping anxiety down. Another person uses reaction formation. They do so because they have learned these mechanisms differently, beginning in early childhood.

We cannot put all our urges into action, and so the urges become modified by defense mechanisms. Each of us learns these defense mechanisms in early life in his own family, within the context of his own culture. Each person builds his whole way of life on the set of defense mechanisms that he has learned, and on the set of threshold levels at which the mechanisms are set to come into play.

Each of these settings for defenses, each of these thresholds, is a parameter. A parameter is a variable that may be considered as held constant while we examine other variables. It is convenient to consider the thresholds for defenses in this way, because although they vary from one person to another they are rather constant within a person. An individual's "thermostat" setting doesn't change very rapidly but is constant for long periods of time. Essentially what psychotherapy tries to do is to change some of the threshold settings for some of a person's defenses. I suspect that acculturation must also change these thresholds, though perhaps if the two cultures are like enough, a person may get by with changing only the superficial content of cues and responses and not the threshold levels.

Personality types may be described in terms of the relative settings of the "thermostats," that is, the extent to which a person uses one defense mechanism rather than another.

Freud described personality types in terms of the bodily zones at which a person's libido was supposedly fixated, as oral, anal, phallic, and mature genital. Each person is said to mature through these personality stages, beginning with the oral, the most infantile. The oral is also called the dependent personality. The anal is also called the compulsive personality. The phallic is also called the oedipal or hysterical personality. Freud said that libido is like an army of soldiers; the more that is left behind to defend at one level, the less there is to go on to another level. Although these levels define types, we must note that they are not exclusive categories. Rather, they are quantitative variables. People vary continuously in the extent to which they have oral, anal, and phallic fixations. The descriptions are not mutually exclusive; a person may have varying mixtures of fixations at different levels.

Freud later (1936) became aware that there is a tendency for specific defense mechanisms to be used for particular kinds of urges. He noted that repression (which we shall call "dissociation") was especially characteristic of hysterical personalities, or phallic or oedipal urges. The anal urges, typical of the compulsive character, are usually dealt with by the defense mechanisms of reaction formation, isolation, and undoing. The paranoid character is one who uses projection. So it appears that we can define our character types by defense mechanisms. Instead of compulsive character we can speak of the reaction-forming character. Instead of a paranoid character, we can speak of the projecting character. I think this is an improvement. Defense mechanisms are something that we can see and measure. So far nobody has devised a way of measuring libido fixation. So I prefer to define the processes we are talking about by the defenses of dissociation and reaction formation, and not by the zonal fixations, phallic and anal.

We may also note that the several kinds of character that Freud talked about can be defined in terms of the specific problems that a child must learn to solve at each stage. In the oral stage, which is not characterized by a particular defense mechanism, the question a person must solve for himself is, "How can I get people to give me the things that I want and need?"

Some people, who are stuck at the oral stage, spend their whole lives trying to work out an answer to that question, trying to get people to give to them. There are different solutions. One obvious distinction is between the passive receiver and the oral aggressive person who keeps demanding. This particular distinction may have a genetic or inherited basis; Cattell found that his factor D, which is assertiveness or oral aggression, appeared to be more hereditary than environmental. At any rate, kinds of dependency urge may also be divided according to success or failure, which is apparently learned. One person goes through life happily and successfully depending upon other people. Another person goes through life depending on other people and getting let down and disappointed by them. The latter mechanism may be described as oral masochism or dependent masochism. It generally goes with bitter feelings, feelings of being deprived (Finney, 1961a).

Note the oral symbolism in the word *bitter*. It refers to tasting, an activity of the mouth. Its symbolic use to describe a severe feeling of disappointed dependency was part of our language long before Freud. It seems that Freud's theory of the connections of certain bodily zones with certain emotional processes contains a symbolism that is natural and not arbitrary.

At the anal or compulsive or reaction-forming level, the basic problem that a person must solve is, "How can I deal with the demands that people make on me, the rules and regulations that people try to impose on me?" In working out a solution, there are at least four ways in which a person can diverge from the average: he can be stubborn, submissive, rebellious, or evasive. The first two at least represent what Freud would call anal fixations or compulsive character. Rebelliousness seems to be a carryover of assertiveness or oral aggression affecting the solution of the compulsive problem. Both Cattell and Gough, in working out personality tests, have found that demandingness, rebelliousness, and showing off tend to go together, and so we may regard all three of these as manifestations of oral aggression, of which demandingness is the central quality.

Freud (1908, reprinted 1950) described the compulsive character as showing three chief characteristics: being orderly, stingy, and stubborn. We cannot draw sharp lines around the ways in which we use words for related concepts. Orderliness includes both being systematic and being neat.

The phallic or oedipal problem that each person must solve is, "How can I deal with situations of rivalry—situations in which I want someone's affection and must compete with a third person for it?" This is the problem typically dealt with by repression or dissociation of one's urges and actions from one's awareness.

Now let us describe in a little more detail the interpersonal relations and other processes that are characteristic of each of these personality types.

First, the hysterical or dissociating type. (This is the same type that Dr. Prince calls *motoric* and that Dr. Wikler calls *ludic*.)

A person of this type is much concerned with how other people will respond to him. Indeed, most of his actions seem designed to affect other people, to get other people to respond to him in a certain way. It may be, for example, that he wants other people to respond to him by making sexual advances to him. Or it may be that he wants people to feel sorry for him and to take care of him. So he sends messages out, to get people to respond to him in those ways. But the most remarkable thing is that he is unaware that he is doing so. He is taking part in a transaction among persons, without being aware that he is playing a part in it. He is communicating, sending a message, but he does not admit it, either to other people or to himself. If you tell him that he has sent a message, he will deny doing so. The most obvious example is a flirtatious woman. Such a woman sends out subtle messages to the men around her, inviting them to make sexual advances to her, and implying that she may be receptive. It is hard to describe the form that the messages take. They may consist of facial expressions, of gestures, of slight movements of the body, and of changes in the tone of voice. Usually, she is not at all aware of sending the messages. They are part of what scholastic philosophers would call her *habitus*, her ways of doing things that she carries about with her, without any thought. The messages are subtle enough so that nobody could confront her with evidence that she sent them. Nonetheless, her messages are clear enough so that men get them and respond. They respond with sexual advances that may be equally subtle or may be quite open. The woman's next response may take various forms. She may be satisfied with having proved her attractive powers and may call a halt to the exchange; or she may occasionally proceed into a sexual relationship. If she goes into a sexual act, she is likely to be frigid and to fail to reach orgasm. She may lead on into various games of the sort described by Eric Berne.

Now what is most important to notice about this transaction is that she has denied taking the initiative and has denied responsibility for her actions. She has placed herself in a passive role. As she sees it, she is not the person who has done anything. The other person has done something. She herself has only been acted on. The other person must bear the responsibility. Of course this appearance of passivity is false. In a subtle way, she has taken the initiative, but she is not aware of it, the other person may not be aware of it, and neutral bystanders may also be unaware of it.

Early in his psychiatric career, Freud discovered that patients with conversion hysteria often told him of being the victims in early childhood of sexual attacks, while patients with compulsive psychoneurosis often told him of having taken the initiative in sexual acts in childhood. For a while Freud thought that those sexual happenings in childhood were the causes of the later development of the hysterical and the obsessive-compulsive psychoneuroses, respectively. Later he became aware that those infantile acts may not have happened at all, or, if they happened, may not have happened in the way in which they were described. The truth is that the hysterical person tends to think of himself as a passive participant, while the compulsive person thinks of himself as being in control of what he does throughout life.

Notice, then, that the most important thing about repression or dissociation is not that it makes a person unaware of his own urges, but that it makes him unaware of the connections between his urges and his actions, or what happens to him; that it makes him unaware of the messages that he is sending to other people asking for certain kinds of interaction.

Sexuality is not the only kind of interplay in which people use this hysterical or dissociating manner. People also dissociate their hostility; that is, they make themselves unaware of their hostility even while they put it into action.

In a community mental health clinic I once interviewed a young woman who impressed me as a hysterical or dissociating character. (After a little experience in clinical psychiatry, you get so that you can recognize people of this kind very quickly, by their general manner and way of speaking, even though you cannot put your finger on what it is about them that gives that impression. Since this way of dealing with people is a normal defense mechanism and not restricted to patients, a psychiatrist or clinical psychologist quickly learns to identify the chief normal defenses used by his friends and acquaintances, and you can often identify the typical defenses and life style of a stranger in a few minutes' conversation.)

Anyway, I asked the young woman to tell me about her father. She said, "My father is the most wonderful man that I have ever met! He never used to beat mother and us children. Except when he was drunk."

Now that is a classical hysterical or dissociating statement. It carries a message at one level, and a very different, even contradictory message at another. Consider this question: What was the intention of her message? What was the result of her message? Clearly, the result was to make me feel that her father was a bad man and that her father had mistreated her. That was the result, and we may take it that it was the intention, at least unconsciously. It was a hostile message. We draw the conclusion, and rightly, that she hates her father.

But suppose we tell her that we think she hates her father?

She will answer, "Oh, no! I don't hate my father. I love my father dearly. I've just told you that he's the most wonderful man that I have ever known."

So the hostility is unconscious. And her aggressive act in saying something bad about her father, making me dislike her father, was done unconsciously. As far as her conscious feelings are concerned, she has only love for her father, and would do nothing against him.

Still another need or urge is very commonly satisfied by hysterical or dissociating mechanisms. That is dependency need, the need to be taken care of. People may express this need, too, without being aware of it, by exuding a helpless air, so that other people have the urge to take care of them.

Often, too, another mechanism, conversion, works with repression to get dependency satisfied. In conversion, a person develops a symptom that resembles that of a medical disease. It may be vomiting, or smothering feelings, or headache, or backache, or pains in some other part of the body. It may even be shaking, trembling, paralysis, or blindness. Persons with these hysterical conversion reactions often have an attitude that Charcot described as "la belle indifférence." In these symptoms, which imitate medical sicknesses, a person is asking to be taken care of. He is asking for sympathy, he is asking to be relieved of the responsibility of working and of facing many of the other worries and responsibilities of life. Sickness gives a person a legitimate reason to quit working, to avoid shouldering responsibilities, and to be taken care of by other people.

Converson reactions may express not only dependency needs but also other needs, including hostility and sexuality.

The hysterical or dissociating person thinks of life not as a series of actions which he performs but as a series of things that happen to him. He thinks of himself as a passive participant, as a person to whom things happen, rather than as a person who does things and brings things about.

An interesting description of hysterics has been given by Sullivan, and another by Szasz. Both of those descriptions seem rather antagonistic. One gets the impression that both Sullivan and Szasz disliked hysterics. Another interesting description is that given by Jay Haley. Another source worth reading is Eric Berne's book *Games People Play*. For the hysteric is above all the person who can play games. He can do so freely because he need not be aware of what he is doing.

Another process that one often hears about is described in the phrase *hysterical acting-out*. Now, in psychiatric usage, *acting-out* means much the same thing that laymen means by *acting up*. The word carries a disapproving connotation. It usually means action that is harmful to other people, seems immature to the observer, and often doesn't even make much sense from the standpoint of the actor. Some people add that *acting-out* is action whose motivation is unconscious; but, if so, that makes *acting-out* the same as *hysterical acting-out*. For hysterical acting-out means acting out without awareness; it means acting out by a hysterical or dissociating person who uses the mechanisms that we have just been discussing.

Now it is by no means true that hysterical people are always people who act out to a great extent. Many hysterical or dissociating people lead quiet and rather harmless lives. What is characteristic of them is that whatever acting-out they do is unconscious. Perhaps it would be better to say that acting-out (or assertiveness) and hysteria (or dissociating character) are two orthogonal dimensions, unrelated to each other, and that when they coincide in the same person we have hysterical acting-out.

Now let us describe the compulsive or, as I prefer to call it, the reaction-forming character. This character seems to develop in childhood from the question of how to deal with authorities. But the persistent concern that the reaction-forming character has throughout his life is not so much with individual authorities as with impersonal authorities, the internalized authorities, the rules and regulations that he carries about with him, and their relationship to other impersonal rules and regulations that he encounters throughout life. His concern is with a generalized other; with an abstraction; with a principle. "It's not the money, it's the principle of the thing!"—that is a classical statement of a compulsive or reaction-forming person.

The specific behaviors or manifestations of the reaction-forming character depend on the interaction of this factor with other factors. As we found with the dissociating character, the reaction-forming character can be either compliant or assertive. At one time I advanced the hypothesis that all the various defenses tend toward compliance and away from assertiveness; but if there is a tendency in that direction the tendency is not strong enough to keep us from seeing people who combine assertion with each of the defenses. Depending on the factor of compliance versus assertion, compulsive reaction-forming characters may be either submissive or stubborn. In either case, however, they are consistent, organized, systematic, planning, self-controlled, and predictable.

Reaction-forming or compulsive characters feel an inner need to impose categories on things, to impose concepts on events, to impose a system, an abstract system, on whatever they encounter. Perhaps this is what is most basic about reaction formation. This process deals with impulses or urges not by putting them into action immediately, not by gratifying them right away, but by imposing a system on them. Any system implies the postponement of gratification to a time determined by the system. A person learns to get satisfaction from the system itself.

Freud described the triad of compulsive qualities, orderliness, thrift, and stubborness. In his discussion, orderliness included being neat as well as being systematic. Neatness is a specific kind of concrete behavior that manifests the abstract principles of orderliness. (Perhaps one may think of orderliness as an opposition to entropy or randomness; although, paradoxically, the orderly scientist may systematically follow a random sampling procedure.) Thrift also seems to be a manifestation of orderliness; it consists in systematically following a budget rather than spending at the time an impulse occurs. Thrift also involves the delay of gratification, which we have mentioned as an inevitable accompaniment of system. The third-described anal or compulsive quality, stubborness, also flows inevitably from system; it may also be described as rigidity or persistence. All these qualities, with their varying manifestations in concrete behavior, can be seen as consequences of reaction formation, the abandonment of immediate gratification of urges and impulses in favor of following an abstract system.

While Freud's description of this character type was a keen one, his connecting it with toilet training and with libidinal fixation in the anal zone have not been supported by much evidence. Several studies, including one of mine (1963a), have tried to correlate the compulsive character traits with either the age at which toilet training occurred or with its severity, only to find no correlation. Still, there is something appealing about Freud's analogy or symbolism. The issue of giving or withholding, a common form of the compliance-versus-stubbornness issue, is especially pertinent to the infant being toilet trained. Notice that either putting forth or withholding can be compliant and that either putting forth or withholding can be assertive, depending upon the demands being made. After all, what the mother demands of the infant is not that he should always withhold or that he should always expel his feces, but rather that he move his bowels when and where his mother specifies, and retain the contents at all other times and places. The defiant child may expel when he is not supposed to, and may stubbornly refuse to put out when it is demanded of him when on the toilet chair. A four-way classification is needed, to account for the four possible combinations of putting forth versus withholding, and compliance versus assertion. These considerations apply not only to infant behavior in the toilet training situation, but also to adult behavior in the more generalized way. Assertion or noncompliance by smearing people (even though in the abstract and not the literal sense) is a different sort of behavior from assertion or noncompliance by stubbornly and stingily refusing to give what people are asking.

In describing what he called "inner-directedness" David Riesman seems to have been speaking of the people whom we have called reaction-forming or compulsive—people whose behavior is guided by fixed persistent inner principles or systems. Riesman spoke of such people as being guided by an internal gyroscope, in contrast to the "other-directed" people who are guided by something analogous to radar. Notice that it is the inner-directed character, in Riesman's terms, or the compulsive and reaction-forming character, in our terms, whose behavior is directed toward the *generalized* other. McClelland misunderstood this point. McClelland said that success in building an economy depends on people's quoting the same price to strangers as to friends, that is, dealing with people in the abstract, in terms of the generalized other. He is probably right about that. But he is mistaken in applying Riesman's term *other-directed* to this quality. Careful reading of Riesman's work shows that it is Riesman's inner-directedness that is related to the generalized other. Riesman's other-directedness is related to particular other persons, not to abstract or generalized ones. Riesman's tradition-directedness is also related to particular others, though not to the same set of them.

Riesman pointed out that both his gyroscope- or inner-directed person and his radar- or other-directed person are complying with the expectations or demands of other people. The other-directed person is constantly trying to please the people who happen to be immediately around him. The inner-directed or gyroscope person, on the other hand, is trying to comply with and please the people who taught him the rules when he was a little child (and who are now present in him in the form of abstractions and generalizations).

We may ask, is the reaction-forming compulsive person more selfish or less selfish than other people? No clear answer can be given. It might seem that a person who is willing to postpone the gratification of his impulses in favor of a fixed principle is being unselfish; but perhaps he is only seeking his greater advantage in the long run. By seeking future advantage and not immediate pleasure, he is being utilitarian and not simply hedonistic, but is still self-centered, and in a colder way. In

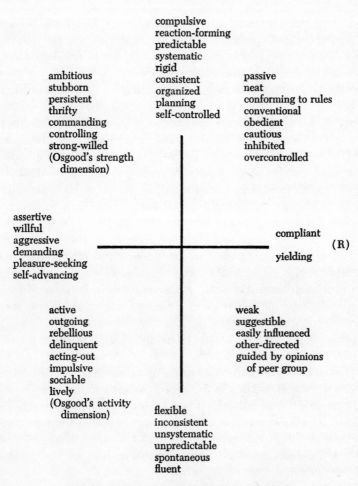

FIGURE 2. Intersections of two dimensions

following his system, the reaction-former sacrifices other people's pleasure in favor of his system, just as he sacrifices his own. Think of the rigid, compulsive, reaction-forming Puritan missionaries who destroyed the hedonistic way of life of the Hawaiians (Finney, 1962a). Systems of fixed principles may seem fixed virtues to one person, but arbitrary rules to another.

The accompanying figure (Fig. 2) shows the intersection of the compulsive or reaction-forming dimension with the factor of compliance-versus-assertion. In another study (1963a) I have reported evidence that the intersection or combination of compulsiveness with assertion is characterized by aggressive rigidity and stubbornness. Compulsiveness and assertion may, however, combine in a persistent drive for self-advancement, an urge that may be called ambition or need for achievement.

There have been a number of studies of compulsive or reaction-forming character; but almost all of them have been studies not of this character in general, but of a more intensive, less extensive group, defined by the combination or intersection of high scores on this factor with high scores on some other quality. For example, Adorno and others studied what they called *The Authoritarian Personality,* which, on examination of evidence, appears to be a very rigid reaction-forming character that is also hostile, perhaps cruel, and perhaps paranoid. After that study came a number of studies of rigidity, a quality that was always defined with an unfavorable connotation. Luchins, for example, studied a kind of rigidity that keeps people from learning. The undesirable poles of several of Gough's scales of the California Psychological Inventory seem to describe a compulsive character who is also submissive, passive, cautious, vacillating, constricted, inhibited, conventional, awkward, dull, pedestrian, and perhaps stupid. So far all the attention of psychologists seems to have been given to the undesirable aspects of the compulsive or reaction-forming character.

Neglected have been the very real positive values of reaction formation. The same behaviors may often be described with favorable or unfavorable words, depending only on the viewpoint. If we like what a person is doing, we call him firm; if we don't like what he is doing, we call him stubborn. Or, taking a slightly different aspect, if we like what a person does we may call him consistent, while if we don't like it we may call him rigid or inflexible. The reaction-former keeps working toward the same goals for a long time. He does not give up easily—a quality that is often highly valued. He has a long memory for unfinished tasks, to mention a kind of behavior that has been investigated experimentally (the Zeigarnik quotient). One of the items scored for rigidity on the California Psychological Inventory is, "I am slow to make up my mind and slow to change it." That statement shows a difference between the reaction-former and the dissociater. The reaction-former or compulsive has great difficulty making a decision, especially to change from one allegiance to another, to change jobs, religion, or marital status. He compares and compares again, and worries about his choice. If he changes from one religion to another it is a profound decision reached after great suffering. In perceptual terms, the competing gestalts keep competing. In contrast, the dissociater makes such decisions quickly and easily, with no backward glances and no doubts about the rightness of his decision afterward. To put it in terms of experimental psychology, the reaction-former behaves as if he were always in approach-avoidance conflicts, while the dissociater behaves as if he were only having a series of approach-approach conflicts. (An exception is sexuality, in which the dissociater gives some evidence of being in approach-avoidance conflict. The only kind of worry that hysterics admit on the MMPI is sex, item 179.) When a compulsive or reaction-forming person is anxious, the anxiety takes the form of worrying; if the worrying is so persistent as to constitute a psychoneurosis, we call it the obsessive-compulsive reaction.

Many of the qualities that we commonly call virtues are reaction formations. Among them are thrift, which is a reaction formation against squandering money on immediate pleasures; self-reliance, which is a reaction formation against dependency; courage, which is a reaction formation against running away; even temper, which is a reaction formation against anger; gentleness, which is a reaction formation against aggression; helpfulness, which is a reaction formation against cruelty or sadism; and generosity, which is a reaction formation against stinginess. The last two, being reaction formations against compulsive qualites, may be considered as reaction formations against reaction formations.

Clinically we sometimes see a two-layer reaction formation in which the second reaction formation brings the person back to a state not quite the same as at the beginning. It is fairly common for a person to develop a reaction formation against dependency and to become independently aggressive; and then, reacting against that quality, to become conscientiously cautious and gentle.

The compulsive or reaction-forming character seems particularly suited for success in business, in the capitalistic economic system. In 1906 Max Weber described a certain basic personality or character type as resulting from the teachings of Protestant Christianity and as causing the rise of the capitalistic economic system. If I may summarize and enumerate what Weber described at great length, this character is systematic and methodical; frugal and unwilling to spend money, preferring to accumulate it; puritanical, unwilling to indulge himself in pleasures of any kind; unwilling to be dependent, insistent of being self-reliant, and contemptuous of those who are dependent, especially beggars; and very conscientious, with a strong sense of responsibility and adherence to duty. The more closely we examine this description, the more closely it resembles the description that Freud gave of the anal or compulsive character two years later.

Scientists also need to be highly systematic, compulsive, reaction-forming, and rigid or consistent in their concepts. But there are limits to the value of reaction-formation. A person who is too consistent, too rigid, too inflexible, too systematic, will be lacking in originality or creativity. Apparently success in science requires a personality that is more compulsive than the average person, and yet not too compulsive. Likely, the dampening of creativity is worse if reaction-formation is combined with a high degree of compliance and conformity.

Altogether, then, we see that reaction-formation, like dissociation, is a feedback process that all normal people use to a greater or lesser extent. It is characteristic of some people to use reaction-formation more than others, and we have discussed at length the advantages and disadvantages that go with it.

While we have given most attention to dissociation and to reaction-formation, we do not ignore the other defenses. Isolation and undoing seem to be secondary defenses characteristic of the compulsive or reaction-forming character, just as conversion, denial, and rationalization are secondary defenses characteristic of the repressing or dissociating character. Projection we have already mentioned. Another important defense is the formation and use of conscience, ego ideal, or superego.

Conscience has much in common with reaction-formation or compulsivity. A person who is called conscientious and responsible is likely to be high both on measures of conscience strength and on measures of compulsiveness. Still, there are differences. In psychoanalytic theory, true conscience or superego is considered to be a higher and more mature level of development than is the character formation by anality or compulsivity. The theories of Piaget say much the same thing. Piaget describes an early stage of conscience development in which rules and regulations are arbitrary and unchangeable; that description sounds like what we have called the compulsive or reaction-forming character. Piaget's description of the mature conscience implies a person who sees that rules are made by people, and that rules can be changed when a change will benefit the people involved. Another way to put it is that the rules at the compulsive or reaction-forming level are abstract and impersonal and disregard the welfare of particular individuals, while at the level of mature conscience obligations are not so much abstract and impersonal as concerned with doing the right thing for the good of real living persons.

The next question that arises is, how are these several defense mechanisms, the several feedback processes, related to each other? We have considered them as dimensions or factors, but are they orthogonal? If a person uses reaction-formation a great deal, can we predict whether he will use dissociation to a high degree or very little? Sometimes people speak of hysterical character and compulsive character (or, in our terms, dissociating character and reaction-forming character) as if they were opposites. To some extent I have tended to do so, too. Under certain circumstances that must be so. Suppose that each person is subject to the same amount of stress, so that each person needs to use his defense mechanisms to the same degree. And further suppose that there are only two defense mechanisms, dissociation and reaction-formation, so that a person always has a choice between the two. If those conditions were fulfilled, there would be a perfect negative correlation between the two; the more a person used reaction-formation, the less he would use dissociation. If we increase the number of available defenses from two to three, four, five, or more, the size of the negative correlation drops rapidly toward zero. And the use of each defense becomes almost independent of the extent to which each of the others is used. So that if we want to consider dissociation and reaction-formation, a person could be high in one and low in the other, or vice versa, or he could be high or low in both. Furthermore, let us remember that some people are subject to more stress and need to use defense mechanisms or feedbacks more than other people do. (To return to our thermostat illustration, two houses may have the thermostat set at the same threshold for turning the air conditioner on, one may run more than the other because one house is in Alaska and the other in Florida; or they may be side by side but have different insulation.) Now when we ask to what extent a person is a reaction-forming character, we may mean one of two things. We may be asking what position reaction-formation holds in his hierarchy of defenses (whether it is the first or the last to be called into action), or we may be asking what its rate of operation is. If we ask the latter question, remember that a person under stress may have to call all his defenses into play, so that the correlation between the use of the several defense mechanisms may become a positive one.

Up to this point I have discussed the defense mechanisms partly from an abstract or logical point of view, as in the feedback model, and partly in terms of the actual workings as seen in the nonquantitative evidence of clinical practice and experience. I have also referred to a few experimental studies and testing methods that tangentially concern the defense mechanisms or character types. What about direct experimental evidence, or direct measurements? Unfortunately, they have been scant.

Sears first found, in ratings given to college students by their own fraternity brothers, that the three classical compulsive qualities described by Freud correlated with each other with three coefficients almost identical to each other at +.39. This remarkable result appeared only when ratings of general goodness or desirability were removed by partial correlation. Otherwise, the fact that the students regarded orderliness as good, and stinginess and stubborness as bad, obscured the relationship and distorted the correlations.

In studying mothers and their children I made some discoveries about compulsive character and how it is transmitted from parent to child (1963a). In other work I have developed scales to measure the defense mechanisms and their character types from personality tests of the true-and-false type (1965).

In the period after World War II came a number of studies of repression or dissociation as "perceptual defense." It was shown that individuals differed in repression, at least as seen in perceptual tests. The most relevant of those studies for our purposes are those of Eriksen, dealing with hysterical character (or repressing character), in which he showed a relationship among three things: the psychiatric diagnosis of hysterical conversion reaction, an experimental test of repression in perception, and a measure from the MMPI, the difference in T scores between the Hy and the K-corrected Pt scales.

The best evidence that patients who have hysterical conversion psychoneurosis are of a particular personality type is in the list of items derived by Hathaway and McKinley to correlate with that psychiatric diagnosis. Patients with conversion reactions strongly endorse a list of naive, innocent, and idealistic statements about human nature. The statements are reminiscent of the character Pollyanna from the book of the same name.

It is a disgrace that concepts in such widespread clinical use, and of such fundamental importance, are backed by so few experiments and such inadequate measures.

What about the epidemiology of differences in the use of defense mechanisms, or what are so often called character types? There is common agreement among many psychologists and psychiatrists that these things vary from nation to nation, but the impression has not been supported by much investigation or evidence.

Two thousand years ago Virgil said, "Varium et mutabile semper femina" (a woman is always a fickle and changeable thing). Translated into modern psychiatric terms, that amounts to saying that women are more hysterical and less compulsive in character than men. Or, in the terms that we prefer, women use dissociation more and reaction-formation less than men. Psychiatrists and clinical psychologists in the United States commonly say that same thing. And it may be true in all cultures that the women tend to use the hysterical defense of dissociation more than men, while the men tend to use the compulsive defense of reaction-formation more than women.

There also appears to be a difference by social class. It is generally conceded that middle-class people postpone gratification more, are thriftier, and generally are more compulsive and reaction-forming, while lower-class people tend more to use hysterical defenses such as dissociation and conversion. Hollingshead and Redlich (1958, p. 226) showed that one psychoneurosis, conversion reaction (hysteria), is commoner in the lower classes while psychoneuroses, notably depression and obsessive-compulsive reaction, are commoner in the middle class. Phobic and anxiety reactions, generally regarded as intermediate between the hysterical group and the compulsive group of psychoneuroses, showed peak occurrence at an intermediate social class.

There is also a general impression that compulsive character is more highly developed in the northern part of the United States, explaining perhaps why the northern states have prospered more than the southern states. The stereotype of the southern belle is an extreme example of the hysterical character type. It seems, then, that within the United States, if you are looking for repressers or hysterical characters, you will be more likely to find them among lower-class women in the south; and if you are looking for reaction formers or compulsive characters, you are more likely to find them among middle-class men in the north. These are the general impressions that many of us have. But who can prove that they are valid? Who has good tests or measures of these qualities, and who has given them to large numbers of normal people in different parts of the country?

Now let us state a hypothesis: cultural groups differ in the extent to which their individuals use the several defense mechanisms. I have had occasion to investigate this matter in Hawaii.

From the common opinions that people held, and from what they told me about the different cultural groups of Hawaii, it struck me that a large part of the differences could be summed up by saying that the people of certain groups are reaction-formers, and that the people of certain other groups are dissociaters. From the descriptions it appeared that the Chinese, the Japanese, and the Koreans were reaction-formers, while the Filipinos, the Puerto Ricans, and the Portuguese of Hawaii were dissociaters (more specifically, assertive dissociaters, given to what psychiatrists call hysterical acting-out).

Furthermore, I concluded from my observations of the people in Hawaii that these group impressions had quite a bit of validity. Persons of the several ethnic groups, not only patients but also normal people going about their daily living, seemed to be using the defense mechanisms that corresponded to the popular impressions about each ethnic group. That is not surprising, since I am going on the hypothesis that normal people build their whole way of life around a particular choice of defense mechanism.

In the case of the three compulsive groups, Chinese, Japanese, and Koreans, most people said quite frankly that they felt the three groups had much in common. After all, those three peoples came from the same part of the world. I did not find anyone, however, who volunteered the opinion that the Filipinos, the Puerto Ricans, and the Portuguese were alike. My impression of the similarity of those three groups arose from consideration of the common opinions about them, which led to the conclusion that there was a common thread that could best be summarized by the term *hysterical* or *dissociating* character.

The white people who came to Hawaii from the United States mainland, and who are called haoles, appeared to me to be using both dissociation and reaction-formation to various degrees, the latter probably more than the former. In this way they were like the white people of the mainland. As for the Hawaiians, who are Polynesians, to the best of my observation they seemed neither to be systematic and compulsive reaction-formers, like the Orientals, nor dissociaters like the Filipinos, Portuguese, and Puerto Ricans. To be sure, the kapu (or taboo) system of the old Hawaiians may be described as a primitive kind of reaction-formation; but it is not internalized like the compulsiveness of the Japanese and the Europeans.

How shall we test our hypothesis? Obviously, the most effective way to test it would be to take some very good measure of dissociation, of reaction-formation, and of other defense mechanisms, and to apply those measures to large numbers of the general population of each of the several ethnic groups. Then we could see if the groups differed in the expected directions. Unfortunately, however, our measures are not very good, and it is hard to get normal population groups to sit down and take a bunch of tests.

So I used a more indirect method. I asked students at the University of Hawaii to give me their own judgments, in the form of scores, concerning each of eleven ethnic groups in Hawaii, on each of fifty qualities (1968). Those doing the ratings were themselves of many different ethnic groups; the largest group were Japanese. About half the students were women. Each of the fifty qualities was defined by a pair of words or a pair of phrases, one for each pole of the quality—for example, warm, cold. Each student was asked to give a number on a seven-point scale, from 0 to 6, to each of the eleven groups on each of the fifty qualities.

Now, you will say that I am not measuring anything about

the Chinese or the Japanese or the Filipinos, that I'm only measuring stereotypes, measuring what people think about the Chinese or the Japanese or the Filipinos. That is true. I am postulating, however, that the opinions that people have are not without some factual basis. The opinions, of course, are contaminated with people's value judgments. It is well known, for example, that the Chinese regard the Hawaiians as lazy, while the Hawaiians regard the Chinese as stingy. Both terms have a negative value judgment. But evaluation, good or bad, desirable or undesirable, is not the whole meaning of a word. If we remove the evaluative factor, there still remains a factual or objective content, which, I believe, is usually used with some validity. Often we can find a pair of terms that mean the same thing objectively but have opposite value judgments. For example, while the Hawaiians call the Chinese stingy, the Chinese call themselves thrifty. I suggest that stingy and thrifty may have the same objective meaning, when the evaluative factor is taken out. They refer to the same objective behavior. Likewise, while the Chinese call the Hawaiians lazy, the latter think of themselves as relaxed (Finney, 1962a). It may well be that the favorable term, relaxed, and the unfavorable term, lazy, have the same objective meaning and refer validly to the same behavior, when we abstract away from the desirability or undesirability of the terms used. Other pairs of terms that seem to have the same behavioral referents, but opposite evaluative factors are persistent: demanding; firm: stubborn; consistent: rigid and inflexible; flexible: unreliable and unpredictable.[2]

So I drew up a list of fifty qualities in paired phrases, making it a point to include a number of phrases to tap reaction-formation, and a number to tap repression or dissociation. I wanted the phrases to meet both of two conditions: they must be simple

[2] After this paper was prepared, I heard Margaret Mead make the same point in a paper at the 1966 meeting of the American Anthropological Association, even using some of the same pairs of terms as examples. She pointed out that New Englanders may dislike being called stingy, but like being called thrifty. She argued that anthropologists should always use the favorable terms, especially in describing nonliterate peoples, for whom the anthropologist's published description may become the authoritative history and the basis for self-characterization.

and nontechnical so that people who are not psychiatrists or psychologists could judge people validly on them; and they must be designed so that the students would pick the same group of people whom the psychiatrists or psychologists would rate high on a technical concept such as "compulsive" or "reaction-forming." Since lay people are not familiar with the processes that psychiatrists or psychologists refer to, I selected the phrases to describe not so much the process itself as the results of the process.

It was easy to think of terms well known to the lay public which correspond well with the psychiatrists' concept of the compulsive or reaction-forming character.

Pairs of phrases used for the reaction-forming character were as follows:

3.	clean, neat	dirty, disorderly
4.	self-reliant	dependent
7.	strict sex life	free sex life
10.	stingy	generous
11.	consistently firm	can't say no
12.	tense, worries	relaxed
17.	ambitious	not ambitious
20.	consistently works hard	easygoing, happy-go-lucky
21.	cautious	impulsive
23.	hides feelings	expresses feelings
27.	thrifty	spends money freely
28.	orderly, systematic	not so
29.	stubborn, rigid	flexible
30.	may be cruel or unkind	never cruel or unkind
34.	meticulous work	dislikes details
36.	money-conscious	not so
37.	values education	content to stay uneducated
40.	plans years ahead	lives in the present
43.	sullen, sulking	not so
44.	careful of duties and obligations	not so
47.	good businessmen	not so
48.	polite	not so

(Items 4, 7, 10, 21 and 23 were actually presented with the right and left sides reversed from what is shown here.)

Those adjectives came partly from my concept of the compulsive or reaction-forming character, and were partly suggested by what people said about the Japanese and other groups in Hawaii, which in turn had suggested to me that these groups were of a compulsive character. So it would not be surprising if the phrases indicated certain groups to be compulsive characters.

It was harder to think of phrases that would be understood by the lay public and still correspond with the psychiatrists' and psychologists' concept of the hysterical or dissociating character. As we have noted, this is what Dr. Prince calls motoric character. Evidently this concept is not so much rooted in commonsense trait-descriptive adjectives as is the reaction-forming character. The phrases that I came up with for the dissociating or hysterical character are as follows:

21.	impulsive	cautious
24.	naive	not so
38.	shows off (flashy if extreme)	doesn't
39.	dramatic	matter of fact
41.	acts intuitively	acts on practical logical evidence
42.	flirtatious	not so
45.	hot-tempered	slow to anger

As we look at this list, it seems to me now that it overstresses hysterical acting-out, that is, that phrases seems to describe the assertive dissociater and not the compliant dissociater. If I were doing it again, I would try to balance it by adding some phrases to describe the compliant dissociater, such as "youthful," "childlike," "idealistic," "romantic," "artistic," "impractical dreamer," and "has faith in people." Some other phrases that occurred to me later might help to describe the dissociating character are "fickle, changeable," "sexy," "seductive," "moods change quickly," and "unpredictable."

About ten years earlier, Vinacke had had the University of Hawaii students check adjectives to describe the various ethnic groups in Hawaii. Among my fifty pairs of phrases I included some adjectives chosen because Vinacke had found that they selectively described one group or another.

The following predictions were made:

1. People will describe each of the eleven groups differently.

2. The descriptions will be consistent with previously reported opinions, including those of Vinacke's study.

3. The descriptions of the Chinese, the Japanese, and the Koreans will resemble each other, and the descriptions of the Filipinos, the Portuguese, and the Puerto Ricans will resemble each other.

4. The highest scores on the reaction-forming or compulsive qualities will go to the Chinese, the Japanese, and the Koreans.

5. The highest scores on the dissociating or hysterical qualities will go to the Filipinos, the Puerto Ricans, and the Portuguese.

6. The haoles will also be rated high in compulsive qualities, but not as high as the Chinese, the Japanese, or the Koreans.

7. The Hawaiians will be scored low both in reaction-forming and in dissociating qualities.

All the predictions were confirmed, and there were also some interesting results that were not predicted.

In the results reported here, only the opinions about each ethnic group by nonmembers of that group were considered. The ratings given to Japanese by Japanese, for example, were excluded, as were the ratings given to Filipinos by Filipinos, and so forth.

Average scores were calculated for each group for each of the fifty qualities. Then, on each of the qualities, the groups were ranked in order by their scores, and a score was assigned to each, ranging from ten points for the highest group to naught for the lowest group on the same quality. The following table shows the total scores for each group.

Reaction-forming qualities		Dissociating qualities	
Chinese	203	Portuguese	60
Japanese	175	Filipinos	59
Koreans	159	Puerto Ricans	51
haoles	136	haoles	49
Negroes	105	Hawaiians	36
Hawaiian-Chinese	100	Negroes	35
Hawaiian-haoles	95	Hawaiian-haoles	35
Filipinos	83	Hawaiian-Chinese	21
Puerto Ricans	66	Chinese	15
Portuguese	63	Koreans	12
Hawaiians	25	Japanese	12

All the predictions were confirmed about reaction-forming character. The predictions were confirmed that the Portuguese, the Filipinos, and the Puerto Ricans would be scored highest in hysterical or dissociating character. I admit that I had not expected to find that the students regarded the haoles as almost as high in hysterical acting-out as the other three groups.

The ratings of the eleven groups on all fifty characteristics were correlated. As was expected, the three oriental groups, the Chinese, Japanese, and Koreans, were regarded as similar to one another, and had high intercorrelation coefficients; and the three dissociating groups were also regarded as similar. Indeed, somewhat surprisingly, the three dissociating groups seemed to be regarded as being as much like one another as were the three reaction-forming groups.

It is interesting to note that the three groups that are rated as the most reaction-forming are also rated as the least dissociating, the Chinese, Japanese, and Koreans. Likewise, the three groups that are rated as most dissociating, the Portuguese, the Filipinos, and the Puerto Ricans, are among the four groups that are rated as least compulsive. (The Hawaiian group is rated least reaction-forming and about average on dissociating. The haoles are rated higher than average on both dissociating and reaction-forming characters.)

I then proceeded to do a factor analysis. The fifty pairs of phrases were used as variables, and the ratings given to each of the eleven ethnic groups were used as occasions. Using Hotelling's principal axis method and a latent root criterion, we found five factors, of which only three were sizable. The accompanying table shows the three factors, and their loadings on thirteen phrases, selected from the fifty to give a fair idea of each factor.

The first factor was clearly one of compulsive or reaction-forming character. Every one of the twenty-two phrases that had been designated in advance as defining reaction-formation came out loaded in the appropriate direction on this factor. It seems to be largely a factor of reaction-formation considered favorably, since the favorable-sounding phrases, such as "thrifty," had higher loadings on it than the unfavorable-sounding ones, such as "stubborn."

The second principal axis factor seems best described as assertiveness. The third principal axis factor seems to combine warmth, strength, self-confidence, and leadership. How do these compare with factors found in analyzing psychological tests of personality? The first two factors from the MMPI scales are those that Welsh calls A and R. In my own work, using MMPI and other scales, I found those two, plus a third, compulsivity or reaction-formation (1961b). Our first factor from the Hawaii ratings, compulsivity or reaction-formation, corresponds well with my third factor from personality testing. The second factor of the MMPI work, which Welsh calls R, is best described as compliance versus assertiveness. It seems to correspond closely, but reversed in direction, with the second factor from the Hawaii ethnic group ratings. The A or anxiety factor from the MMPI represents at its upper pole a person who is in great distress, feeling sorry for himself, appealing for help, and also dependent, bitter, masochistic, and neurotic. With some hesitation, we may tentatively consider it to be the third factor found in the Hawaii ethnic group ratings, reversed in direction.

The factors from the psychological tests of personality, like those on the ratings of the Hawaii groups, were orthogonal factors without rotation.

PRINCIPAL AXIS: Factor 1: Compulsiveness (52.6%)

Loadings (10 highest)		Scores	
Orderly, systematic	1.00	Chinese	17.1
Careful of duties and obligations	.99	Japanese	14.8
Plans years ahead	.99	Koreans	9.1
Acts on practical logical evidence	.99	haoles	7.4
Meticulous, detailed work	.99	Hawaiian-Chinese	—0.1
Values education	.98	Hawaiian-haoles	—1.0
Clean, neat	.97	Negroes	—6.8
Ambitious	.96	Hawaiians	—9.2
Consistently works hard	.96	Puerto Ricans	—10.1
Good businessmen	.95	Filipinos	—10.3
(Some other loadings)		Portuguese	—10.6
Thrifty	.92		
Stingy	.40		
Stubborn, rigid	.39		

PRINCIPAL AXIS: Factor 2: Assertion or Boldness (25.1%)

Loadings (10 highest)		Scores	
Active, rapid, excitable	.96	haoles	21.7
Demanding	.93	Portuguese	11.5
Dramatic	.91	Chinese	4.5
Shows off (flashy if extreme)	.91	Filipinos	4.4
Deceptive	.86	Puerto Ricans	3.9
Self-centered, selfish	.80	Negroes	—2.8
May be cruel or unkind	.80	Hawaiian-haoles	—4.8
Expresses feelings, outspoken	.76	Hawaiian-Chinese	—6.6
Gambles, speculates, risks	.76	Japanese	—6.7
Luxury-loving	.74	Koreans	—10.6
		Hawaiians	—13.5

PRINCIPAL AXIS: Factor 3: Desirability (14.1%)

Loadings (10 highest)		Scores	
Warm, friendly	.81	haoles	18.5
Not sullen, not sulking	.75	Hawaiians	15.8
Generous	.69	Hawaiian-Chinese	7.5
Not clannish, does not stick to own	.69	Hawaiian-haoles	7.0
Flexible (not stubborn, not rigid)	.59	Koreans	—3.8
Athletic	.57	Japanese	—4.1
Not resentful	.57	Portuguese	—4.1
Musical	.55	Negroes	—6.9
Relaxed (not tense, not worrying)	.52	Puerto Ricans	—8.5
Flirtatious	.49	Chinese	—10.3
		Filipinos	—11.2

How do our several ethnic groups in Hawaii come out on those three factors? The accompanying table shows the factor scores of the eleven groups on the three principal axes.

On the first principal axis, reaction-formation, the three highest groups are the Chinese, the Japanese, and the Koreans, in that order, followed, at a lower level, by the haoles. The least reaction-forming groups are the Portuguese, the Filipinos, the Puerto Ricans, and the Hawaiians, in that order.

On the second principal axis, the most energetic, assertive, aggressive, pleasure-seeking group is considered to be the haoles or white people of United States origin, followed by the Portuguese and the Chinese. The most compliant or least assertive group is considered to be the Hawaiians, followed by the Koreans.

On the third principal axis, the group that is considered to be self-confident, friendly, outspoken, and not anxious is the haoles, followed by the Hawaiians. The most anxious or least self-confident group is considered to be the Filipinos, followed by the Chinese.

Notice that only one of these principal axes represents a character type as defined by defenses, namely, compulsiveness or reaction-formation. The phrases chosen to represent hysterical or dissociating character, many of which were specifically assertive dissociation or hysterical acting-out, came out with loadings on the assertive factor, and negative loadings on the compulsive factor.

What happens when the factors are rotated? A Varimax rotation was done, to find "simple structure" while keeping orthogonality. The accompanying table shows the loadings of selected phrases on the three factors.

The first factor no longer represents reaction formation as such, but it is more clearly a factor of strength. The second factor is no longer so clearly assertion, and corresponds more closely to hysterical acting-out or the assertive form of the hysterical or dissociating character. The third factor is now more clearly one of warmth. The three factors now match Osgood's "semantic" factors of strength, activity, and evaluation (goodness). Calculation shows that Osgood's factors of strength

VARIMAX: Factor 1: Strength, compulsiveness-with-assertion (44.1%)

Loadings (10 highest)		Scores	
Has strength and power (not necessarily physical)	.99	Chinese	16.3
		haoles	13.0
Sophisticated	.98	Japanese	13.0
Self-confident	.97	Koreans	6.7
Good leaders	.97	Hawaiian-Chinese	—0.4
Some of them are rich	.96	Hawaiian-haoles	—1.5
Good businessmen	.96	Negroes	—7.7
Ambitious	.93	Portuguese	—9.0
Unlikely to be very poor	.93	Hawaiians	—9.7
Values education	.93	Puerto Ricans	—10.2
A good way of life, I admire them	.92	Filipinos	—10.6

VARIMAX: Factor 2: Quickness, extroversion, assertion, oral aggression with hysteria (28.5%)

Loadings (10 highest)		Scores	
Shows off (flashy if extreme)	.98	Portuguese	15.3
Dramatic	.95	haoles	12.6
Demanding	.93	Filipinos	9.3
Flirtatious	.92	Puerto Ricans	8.9
Expresses feelings, outspoken	.91	Negroes	1.4
May make money in crime	.91	Hawaiian-haoles	—2.0
Gambles, speculates, risks	.90	Hawaiians	—3.6
Deceptive	.85	Hawaiian-Chinese	—4.2
Active, rapid, excitable	.84	Chinese	—8.5
May be cruel or unkind	.81	Koreans	—14.0
		Japanese	—15.0

VARIMAX: Factor 3: Warmth, friendliness, goodness, desirability (18.1%)

Loadings (10 highest)		Scores	
Warm, friendly	.94	Hawaiians	26.6
Generous	.82	Hawaiian-Chinese	8.9
Flexible (not stubborn, not rigid)	.81	Hawaiian-haoles	8.8
Not clannish, does not stick to own	.80	Negroes	1.8
Relaxed (not tense, not worrying)	.79	Portuguese	1.4
Not sullen, not sulking	.73	Puerto Ricans	0.8
Thinks of others (not self-centered)	.70	Filipinos	—1.4
Musical	.64	haoles	—1.6
Athletic	.63	Koreans	—6.8
Can't say no to people	.56	Japanese	—13.6
		Chinese	—25.1

and activity are 45-degree rotations, in the same plane, of compulsiveness and assertiveness. His strength factor is an equal mixture of compulsiveness and assertion, while his activity factor is an equal mixture of assertion and uncompulsiveness.

Factor scores were obtained for the eleven ethnic groups on the rotated factors, too. On the factor of strength, which still seemed to include some reaction-formation, the highest ratings were given to the Chinese, the haoles, the Japanese, and the Koreans, in that order, while the groups considered weakest were the Filipinos, the Puerto Ricans, the Hawaiians, and the Portuguese, in that order. On the second factor, which seems to represent hysterical acting-out or the assertive form of the dissociating character, the highest score went to the Portuguese, followed by the haoles, the Filipinos and the Puerto Ricans. The lowest scores went to the Japanese, the Koreans and the Chinese, in that order. On the third factor, warmth and friendliness, the Hawaiians stood out all by themselves at the top, while the Chinese stood out all by themselves at the bottom.

In comparing these two ways of organizing three factors each, one thing stands out. When the system of extracting factors requires that the factors be orthogonal or uncorrelated with each other, we cannot get both a reaction-forming (compulsive) factor and a dissociating (hysterical) factor. Those two dimensions point in somewhat opposite directions, but they are neither completely opposite each other (enough to coalesce into one factor) nor at right angles to each other (independent enough to give two separate factors). So the principal axes analysis gave us a reaction-forming factor but not a dissociating factor, while the Varimax rotation did the opposite.

In Osgood's work the same three (rotated) factors of goodness, strength, and liveliness appear in analyses of judgments of all kinds. It doesn't matter whether we judge people or things or abstractions. The language and culture of the persons making the judgment doesn't matter, either. The same three factors appear. It is natural that Osgood considered the factors to be semantic. It is natural that he considered that the factors are not dimensions of the people being judged, but are universal dimensions of the judgment process, dimensions inherent in the human perceptual apparatus.

Kant came to the same conclusion about space and time. He concluded that our perceptual processes are such that we inevitably perceive the world in the dimensions of space and time. There is no way to tell whether the physical world is truly structured in dimensions of space and time at all; we just can't help construing it along those lines. Osgood's work reaches the same conclusions about the qualitative dimensions of goodness, strength, and liveliness.

In our own work, if we had only the studies on judgments, we might make the same conclusion: that the factors are only dimensions of the universal human perceiver, and not dimensions in which there is variation among the ones being perceived. But that concept doesn't explain how we get the same three factors (especially on principal axis, without rotation) from data of an entirely different kind: psychological test scores.[3] From this striking replication, we conclude that it is highly suggestive that the three unrotated factors of compulsiveness, assertion, and neuroticism are fundamental dimensions of human personality and character.

And, after all, validity of perception has survival value. It is not surprising that in the course of evolution we have come to perceive the world in dimensions that are isomorphic (and correspond rather well) with the dimensions of the events outside us in the world: the physical dimensions of space and time, and the qualitative human dimensions of compulsiveness, assertion, and neuroticism. If there were not this isomorphism, this correspondence, we could not cope with the things and people around us, and could not survive so skillfully.

Now we have examined some of the results, and we see that

[3] One may argue that the MMPI is an elaborate self-description, and so that its factors may be perceptual ones. Conceivably so. Even though most of the MMPI scales were derived from external criteria, the scales tend to be obvious, with the overt wording agreeing with the criteria. In a few scales, notably the subtle subscales of Hy and Pa, the criteria (which determine scale names and factor names) are different from or even opposite to the manifest content, the wording of the items in which a person describes himself.

it is possible to describe cultural groups and their differences in terms of what psychiatrists and psychologists call character types or factors, dimensions based on defense mechanisms. People did describe the groups in such terms. The people who did the description were University of Hawaii students, belonging to various ethnic groups themselves, and living in an area where the people of each cultural group are familiar with the peoples of the other cultural groups.

But one may ask, are these the important differences among the groups? And one may further ask, does this really tell us anything about the groups, or does it only tell us about people's ideas about groups? I shall try to answer those questions together.

Much work has tended to show that people's descriptions of other groups are stereotypes or prejudices, that is, that they are strongly influenced by likes and dislikes. This is especially true when people are describing groups of which they don't have much personal knowledge; in those circumstances, the opinions that they express are almost entirely those of liking and disliking, based on little or no factual evidence. In Hawaii, though, racial or national prejudice or antagonism of this sort is not great. Furthermore, the people of the various groups in Hawaii know each other, and so the people make their judgments from personal experience rather than from hearsay. Hawaiians encounter Japanese in their daily life. Furthermore, it has been shown that the evaluative factor, desirability, is a strong factor in the use of adjectives, but does not determine their whole meaning, and is far from being the only influence determining how an adjective is used or to whom it is applied. When the evaluative factor is partialed out or abstracted away, there remains a core of objective nonevaluative meaning, and I propose the thought that people in general use this objective portion of the meaning with some validity. In other words, even if there were a high degree of emotion, evaluation, or prejudice in the ratings, one could partial out the evaluative factor and examine the nonevaluative residue.

As we look through the factor loadings of our fifty pairs of phrases, it may questioned whether we have found a clear-cut, evaluative factor of good-versus-bad. We find a factor of warmth, which, in some previous studies, has seemed to be the most important determinant of our liking of people; we also find the phrase "a good way of life, I admire," which is somewhat more related to a factor of strength and to compulsive or reaction-forming qualities. A more detailed analysis, which is not given here, shows that, the Hawaiians are *liked* best but are not *admired;* it is the Chinese, the Japanese, and the haoles that are admired.

Furthermore, the character types or dimensions in which each cultural group scored high corresponded closely to the psychological descriptions of the several groups given by psychiatrists in Hawaii, descriptions that were based on clinical judgment and not on quantitative evidence—that is, psychiatrists agreed in calling the Chinese and Japanese compulsive, and some of the other groups, hysterical.

A variety of other evidence, not expressed directly in psychological concepts, tends to support the general conclusions. As one minor example, the reaction-forming quality of thrift should be reflected in quantity of savings. One should predict that, on the same income level, the groups who are considered as reaction-forming characters should save more money than those who are not considered as reaction-formers. Studies of this kind have been made from time to time, and have indeed shown that at the same income levels the Chinese, Japanese, and Koreans save more than do the peoples of the other ethnic groups.

The findings are also consistent with the history of the groups. One can expect that the thrifty reaction-forming groups will get ahead financially faster than the other groups. The history of the islands indeed shows that that did happen.

There have been many other minor studies, none of them comprehensive, but each contributing one small fragment to confirm a part of the general picture that we have drawn. For example, one common form of what psychiatrists call hysterical acting-out, which we should expect to find in some of the dissociating groups, is a dramatic and unsuccessful suicide attempt. Indeed, in a study of psychiatric hospital admissions, I found one group to stand out far above the others in hospital admissions for just such episodes, and it was one of the three groups who were rated in this study as of the dissociated acting-out type (1963b).

SUMMARY AND CONCLUSIONS

In this study of personality and culture I have been concerned with process rather than with content. It seems to me a more manageable way of dealing with the data. It is easy to distinguish a limited number of basic processes and study the extent to which people in each group use those processes. Contents of thought and action are much more specific and seem to me much more difficult to group meaningfully into a manageable number of categories or variables.

Personality can be defined as the set of feedback processes or servomechanisms that people use to control certain crucial variables within them. The feedback processes that I have been concerned with are the defense mechanisms—most especially, reaction-formation and repression.

The concept of character types is valuable if: *a*) these character types are thought of not as mutually exclusive categories but as variables; *b*) they are defined as people high in the use of a particular defense process; *c*) these processes are measured; *d*) these variables are related to antecedent and consequent variables, such as child rearing; and *e*) the extent of use of these processes is compared epidemiologically in different cultural groups.

An important part of what we think of as cultural differences can be explained as a difference in the extent to which various people use the various defense mechanisms.

In Hawaii, certain cultural groups were found high in the use of reaction-formation. Those groups are the Chinese, the Japanese, the Koreans, and, to some extent, the haoles.

In Hawaii, some groups were found high in the use of dissociation, including putting impulses into action without being aware of doing so. Those groups were the Portuguese, the Puerto Ricans, the Filipinos, and also to some extent, the haoles.

In Hawaii, the Hawaiian or Polynesian group, the original inhabitants, are not high in the use of either of these mechanisms.

Ease of acculturation and economic success depend upon the extent of use of these processes. In Hawaii, the groups that use the defense of reaction-formation (compulsive character) to a high degree have succeeded and prospered under the American economic system, while certain other groups that do not characteristically use this defense mechanism have not prospered.

discussion four

This morning the group has heard one highly theoretical paper, one on the identity problems of the sojourner, and some discussion by economists on the relationship of psychological and economic forces. With this stimulation the group members bring their thoughts and feelings out and explore their agreements and differences.

For a time it looks as if the old controversy between behavioral scientists and social scientists had been revived. Drs. De Vos and Finney, like McClelland, fearing lest psychology be made an epiphenomenon of economics and sociology, keep stressing that men make circumstances. Dr. Honigmann, backed by Dr. Hargreaves's paper and, later, by Dr. Weinstein, fearing lest the social sciences (in which he includes anthropology as well as sociology and economics) be reduced to psychology, keeps stressing that economic circumstances and institutions make men. (While Dr. Hargreaves's paper makes the same point, his title uses the term *social scientist* for the psychologist and not for the economist.) Of course, nobody wants his own field of expertness reduced to something else. But more than that may be involved.

The cleavage seems anachronistic in the light of the modern systems theory of circular causation (persons make society, *and* society makes persons). Still one can ask at which phase of the cycle it is fruitful to introduce changes. The psychologists suggest that we begin by trying to change persons, while the social scientists wish to begin by trying to change institutions. The issue sounds like a peaceful one, but it arouses strong feelings.

Another issue that keeps being tangled with it is, when, if ever, have we the right to become missionaries, to spread our values and way of life to other people, and to assimilate them to our culture? Dr. Honigmann feels strongly that each local group, even Gazaway's Gulch, has its own way of life, with its unique values and its own good points. He feels that we should encourage them to keep their own unique ways as much as possible, should avoid introducing our own standards or values, and should proceed cautiously, if at all, in changing other people's ways of life. For some reason that is not yet clear, strong feelings become aroused over the issue. At one point Dr. Lewis accuses Dr. Honigmann of lack of concern for human suffering, while Dr. Honigmann accuses Dr. Finney of wanting to transform human beings to fit the society.

For a while Dr. Honigmann's paper becomes the target of critical review. Drs. Weinstein, Kiev, Wittkower, Finney, De Vos, Hughes, Margetts, and Lewis, each in turn, express reservations, some mild and some strong, about Dr. Honigmann's thesis. Dr. Wittkower, in denying that psychiatrists use middle-class values to condemn lower-class patients, makes the point that psychiatrists, like anthropologists, are specifically trained not to be judgmental.

The issue keeps coming up whether a psychiatrist's judgment that one person is in better or worse mental health than another is anything but a class-bound value judgment. Dr. De Vos, from a psychoanalytic viewpoint, maintains that some people live in ways that are more mature than others, in a developmental sequence of universal validity. Dr. Honigmann regards the concept as class-bound or culture-bound. Dr. De Vos, in turn, objects to Dr. Prince's making Christianity unique, and says that Japanese sects use the same psychological mechanisms that Christian sects do. Dr. Prince believes that the same qualities in Class V that prevent insight psychotherapy also cause school dropout; and that the situation must be handled by assimilating the Class V people into Class IV, if not higher. That first step of assimilation cannot be accomplished by middle-class doctors and teachers, and it is for that purpose that he wishes to use the religious and magical methods of fundamentalist preachers. Dr. Sanua objects that it is wrong to perpetuate such ignorance and superstition.

While Dr. Opler takes the role of peacemaker on some of the issues, he has another battle to fight. He takes exception to some of the published work of his collaborator, Dr. Srole, on the Midtown Manhattan study. Dr. Opler makes the point that primitive societies produce brief, dramatic psychoses and psychoneuroses, such as hysterical conversion reaction, hysterical acting-out, amok (which may be a hysterical psychosis), and catatonia. Some societies that are not so primitive, such as Puerto Rico and the Southern Appalachian Mountains, show hysterical features, too. Other more complex societies, such as the United States, China, and Japan, produce more deepseated, longer lasting mental illnesses, with withdrawal (i.e., chronic schizophrenia). Dr. Maretzki adds that it is the societies in which people are taught internal self-controls, China, Japan, the United States, and northwestern Europe, in which people can use insight psychotherapy; while in the societies that rely on external controls over people's behavior, the people cannot use insight therapy, and must be treated by the authoritarian, magical methods described by Drs. Kiev and Prince.

By now it has become clear that the complex problems of culture change, culture difference, mental health, and poverty are deeply intertwined.

[Dr. Fulmer read a paper about the disastrous effects of the population explosion. Then he discussed the problem informally.]

FULMER: For years I've been interested in economic growth, and hence in differences in the rate of growth not only between countries but within a country. In the United States, for instance, unemployment is thrice as high among Negroes as among whites. But that's not what I came here to talk about. I wrote this paper as a challenge to psychiatrists and psychologists. There are certain trends that are foreboding. First is the population explosion. The amount of space per person is shrinking toward naught, and the cost of land and decent housing is bound to shoot up until room can't be bought at any price. Another point is that with the advance of science and technology more and more technical skills are needed to get a job and do a job. More and more, certain groups of our population who can't keep up will be eliminated—there is no need for them. Maybe it's a monster that's been let loose on us! We're on a treadmill that's speeding up all the time.

FINNEY: You've shown us a convincing picture of the threat of overpopulation. I'm puzzled that Barbara Ward, who's one of the sharpest and most highly respected economists in the world, when she lectured at the University of Kentucky said that over-population is not a serious threat. Do you suppose she said so because she is a Catholic and doesn't want to endorse birth control? Can it be that the thinking of outstanding economists is distorted by irrational, noneconomic considerations?

At any rate, Dr. Fulmer is making a couple of points. 1) As the space per person shrinks, whatever we do in public welfare and mental health will be more than eaten up by the growth of population. 2) The accelerated growth of science makes more hardships than it solves for people, because it's harder for people to meet the requirements to do jobs. Those two points give us a discouraging view of the future.

HONIGMANN: Both points can be resolved into one question: where do we propose to attack the problem? I'm not saying we can find the solution now, but we can decide where to attack it. If I understand your comments, Dr. Finney, on Dr. Fulmer's paper and on McClelland's work, you want us to transform the human beings to fit the society. The other alternative, and the one that I find more appealing, is to transform the society to fit the human beings. This is where those two problems, and many of the other things that we've discussed in this conference so far, angle together.

FULMER: When you say "transform society," do you also mean transform science and technology to fit the individuals?

HONIGMANN: Of course. And in the course of transforming both, we give new occasions for the growth of human personality. We will transform personality also. The question is where to start. Do we begin with the people, or do we begin with the sociocultural transformation?

FINNEY: I think you've misunderstood my position on the matter. I guess I didn't make it clear. Let me try to state it better.

In terms of general systems theory, as Dr. Hughes brought out this morning, a system can be made up of units that are themselves systems. A cell is a system, and a human being, who is made up of cells, is a system at a higher level. Likewise, a society, which is made up of human beings, is a system at a still higher level. Each system has its own control mechanisms or homeostatic mechanisms, which keep the system in a steady state in certain respects. If certain things get too far out of line, the system comes to an end; that is, it loses its ability to function as a system, or in plain words, it dies. Now if the homeostatic mechanisms fail to work and the processes that were to be controlled get so far or so persistently out of line that death is threatened, we say that the system is sick. Just as a man can be sick, a society can be sick, disintegrating, decaying (Finney, 1962b, 1963c).

Now, John, I disagree with your putting "the people" on one level and "sociocultural" matters on another. I agree that people are at one level and societies at another, but I think culture resides in the people and not in the societies. It surely does by Marvin Opler's definition: "Culture is what men live by" (not what societies live by). That's why I regard cultural anthropology as a behavioral science, a science of human beings, akin to psychology and psychiatry. I don't group it among the societal sciences, economics and political science.

There is one point at which Dr. Honigmann and I disagree. He asserts that when a psychiatrist says that a patient in the condition which we call schizophrenic is "sick," the psychiatrist is only expressing a value judgment—that the patient's schizophrenic condition is unpalatable or aversive to the psychiatrist, who calls the condition a sickness because he personally, or he as a member of his social class, regards it as something that ought to be changed.

On the other hand, I assert that the schizophrenic condition can be shown to be a sickness by objective measures in terms of the individual as a system. Value can be objectively defined in terms of a system. If being sick is a negative value, it is so in terms of the composition of the individual human being himself as a system, and it is something that he cannot successfully deny or get away from.

When I say that our diagnoses are independent of personal feeling and moral judgment, I mean ideally. It isn't always done. I've heard one psychiatrist, speaking to another psychiatrist about a third psychiatrist, say, "That man is sick." No evidence of sickness was given. It was a pure value judgment. He hated the other fellow, condemned what he did, and used a term to destroy respect for him. We must guard against the polemic use of diagnostic terms.

Elsewhere I have described three objective criteria by which one can tell that a person is sick (1962b, 1963c):

1. When a person is sick, the normal defenses or feedbacks are working intensively and continuously. To give a medical example: breathing becomes panting. To give psychological examples: the normal use of reaction formation becomes rigidity; or the normal use of repression and dissociation becomes extreme naivete or unawareness of one's motivations; or the normal use of projection becomes recognizable paranoid behavior.

2. When a person is sick, emergency defenses or feedbacks are called into play. A medical example would be Cheyne-Stokes breathing; a psychological example would be delusion. It is not possible to separate emergency defenses completely from normal ones, especially since individuals differ greatly in the defenses preferred in the hierarchy, but this general separation is convenient.

3. A person is sick if, in spite of the active defenses, some variables are near their outer limits of tolerance. A medical

example occurs when the concentration of sugar or carbon dioxide in the blood is very high; psychological examples are high levels of anxiety, hostility, readiness to aggression, discouragement or bitterness, or even euphoria. Some of these variables may be high as a result of the primary trouble, and others may be secondarily raised by the defenses used against the primary trouble. For example, the paranoid defense of projection of hostility may reduce anxiety but, through a spiraling positive feedback, increase hostility and aggression.

Human beings can be sick, and societies can be sick. If a human being is psychologically sick—that is, sick in a way that involves his interpersonal relations—he is treated by a psychiatrist, or a psychoanalyst, or perhaps a clinical psychologist. If a society is sick it may be treated, too, to restore its homeostasis. Now the problems that this conference is concerning itself with may be called psychosocial problems, because the homeostatic mechanisms at both levels are out of kilter; both the individuals and the society are malfunctioning systems. Deranged behaviors of individuals, such as criminality and psychosis, are human or psychological problems, but their widespread occurrence is a psychosocial problem. Among the serious psychosocial problems of America today are the persistence of pockets of poverty amid plenty; a struggle over the abolition of a racial caste system; and a struggle of our way of life with others in far parts of the world. All three of these are social problems, societal problems, in the sense that the homeostatic mechanisms of society fail to maintain the society in a steady state. All three of them are also psychological problems, in the sense that large numbers of individual human beings suffer, are in distress and turmoil, are frustrated, are in conflict over their loyalties, ideals and goals, feel guilty, are emotionally and intellectually crippled, fail to grow to their fullest possible maturity and achievement, are lacking in psychological health. To call these things social problems is not enough. It is not only the societies that are in trouble, but also the individual human beings. The problems are psychosocial.

In the old days, before Norbert Wiener created cybernetics,

the straight-line theory of causation held. One could argue whether men make societies, or societies make men. Typically a social scientist would argue that societies make men. That makes societal events the real thing, and individual human events an epiphenomenon; it makes social science important and behavioral science trivial. It also makes for a gentle approach to individuals: each man is the product of socioeconomic forces and can't help being what he is, and so nobody should be held responsible for what he does. On the other hand, a behavioral scientist would argue that men make societies. That makes individual human events the real things, and societal events an epiphenomenon; it makes behavioral science important and social science trivial. It also makes for a sterner approach to individuals; at an extreme, one may say that people in trouble have made their own troubles and should be allowed to take the consequences. Both those points of view are made obsolete by the circular theory of causation; there is no sense arguing whether the chicken or the egg came first. But perhaps we scientists have not adjusted emotionally to the change. Dr. Honigmann seems to think of me as an old-line behavioral scientist, and I to think of him as an old-line social scientist.

Even with circular causation, one can question what phase of the cycle to attack first, and here the old controversy reasserts itself. When I suggested as a title for this symposium "Culture Change, Mental Health, and Poverty," several participants suggested changing it to "Culture Change, Poverty, and Mental Health" on the grounds that poverty is the cause and mental illness the result. That is a social-science point of view, and it has strong support. Alexander Leighton is interested mainly in that phase of the cycle, and hence I consider him more of a social scientist than a behavioral scientist. The behavioral scientist David McClelland has produced evidence that changes in human motivation happen first, and changes in societies (economic systems) follow. George De Vos has taken the behavioral-science position here in pointing out that the motivations of the individuals in Rena Gazaway's hollow are not merely the results but the causes of the social conditions. And I surely incline to the psychological point of view myself.

As applied behavioral scientists, psychiatrists, psychologists, we spend our working lives treating human individuals with malfunctioning control systems. Do we do so, as John Honigmann thinks, to transform the individuals for the sake of society? Not so. We have deep feelings for our patients, and we help them to become better integrated systems for the sake of their own health, welfare, and happiness. How about those social engineers, such as economists, who try to repair malfunctioning socioeconomic systems? Do they aim to satisfy the needs of the nation or economic system as such? Or do they aim to satisfy the needs of the individual human beings in it?

The point of view that strikes me as right and as human (and this is a pure value judgment) is to identify with other human individuals and work for their welfare. I'm glad to see that in the end John Honigmann and I agree on that. We believe in working for the welfare of human beings and not to advance the welfare of a society as a superorganism.

There are people, unfortunately, who identify themselves with a society, feel fiercely loyal to it, and put its welfare first. They are then willing to sacrifice untold numbers of human beings, to cause them suffering and death, for the sake of the society, which has become sacred. Such was the case with the church officials in the days of the Inquisition. And it is the case with the Chinese Communist officials today. Perhaps it is true of all crusaders and missionaries. In their fallacy of misplaced concreteness, they feel convinced that they do right, while they make other people suffer.

DE VOS: I guess the question is how you make something sacred, so that it can't be infringed on. It's a question of values. In Japan, trees are sacred. In China it didn't work, and the land was deforested.

LEWIS: In Dr. Honigmann's paper he made a good point about ethnocentrism of class in one's own society. I've noticed that other social scientists, sociologists, and educators are much less ethnocentric, much more relativistic when it comes to primitive societies—the anthropologist has got that part of the message across—than when they deal with different classes within their own society. When we talk about ethnocentrism we usually refer to whole societies. I've heard outstanding people talk about the culture of poverty in Mexico and then say, about our own poor, "Do they really have anything at all that we can learn? Or isn't it fundamentally a question of incorporating them into the middle class?" In fact, Dr. De Vos said something like that today.

FINNEY: I know what you mean. When tourists in Hawaii see local people, grown people, going barefoot, they say, "What a delightful Polynesian custom!" But when tourists in East Tennessee or Eastern Kentucky see grown people barefoot, they say, "Look at those poor ignorant backward people!"

LEWIS: Yes, I've read Dr. Finney's discussion of Dr. Honigmann's paper. What I'm trying to say is this. One doesn't have to idealize the culture of poverty and think that it is a satisfying way of life, as the extreme cultural relativists do, as John Honigmann does. I sharply disagree with that position. But still there are some positive aspects in that way of life. Perhaps Dr. Finney, Dr. De Vos, and Dr. Margetts go too far in the other extreme, the nonrelativist direction. I have the impression that they'd like to eradicate the culture of poverty and change the way of life of Gazaway's branch to something more like our own. They don't seem to see anything good about it as it is.

FINNEY: Actually, I agree with you, though it may have sounded as if I didn't. In considering my favorite people, the Hawaiians, I have much the same ambivalence, the same sort of mixed feelings, that Dr. Gazaway has about the people of the hollow. We admire many things about them, that we like better than what we see in our culture, and we want to preserve those things in their way of life. But there are also things that we want to change, to make them more prosperous. We may try to change some things and not change others. But that's a delicate and tricky thing to try to do. Each change that is introduced has so many ramifications, and may do things that we cannot foresee.

OPLER: In Dr. Honigmann's paper, the main evidence that he

quoted came from the Midtown Manhattan study. I was a member of that study. The point was made that American middle-class psychiatrists don't understand people of other cultures, nor even the lower classes in our own culture, and so make false judgments about them. In the Midtown study we were much interested in economics. Volume I deals only with socioeconomic factors; it doesn't get into the cultural meat; it's based on a questionnaire (Srole, 1962).

We had three psychiatrists making ratings from the questionnaire: Rennie, Michael, and Kirkpatrick. Rennie came here as a poor immigrant kid; his formative background was immigrant lower middle class at best, but when I knew him he belonged to the best clubs in New York. Michael was a Czech immigrant of lower middle-class family. Kirkpatrick was second generation but his empathies and interests were always in the slums. They are not well-heeled upper-class psychiatrists looking down at the lower class, as John Honigmann seems to think they are. I'm of poor immigrant parentage, too.

I don't like the psychosocial kick that says that economics isn't a part of culture. It is! Situations under which people live are social and psychological and economic. Let's not be so antiseptic about economic factors; they interweave with psychological and cultural ones. McClelland was wrong in explaining economics away by reducing it to psychology.

I'm glad when graduate students in psychology do carefully designed studies of achievement motivation, and I think they're good. But I've talked with many historians who find that McClelland's interpretation of history, in its broad sweep, is nonsense! If you select one set of instruments, as he did, and apply them not only cross-culturally, without knowing much about Greek and other cultures (really he didn't), but also in historical depth, you're undertaking an awful lot for one man!

My trouble is with some of the other Midtown boys who stress socioeconomic status and forget culture. Leo Srole doesn't believe in the concept of culture, of ethnicity. He tries to explain cultural differences away, to explain all differences in terms of socioeconomic class. I'll give you an instance from volume I. It's stated that we predicted that the second generation of certain immigrant groups would have better mental health than the first. Well, we didn't predict that! I would predict, from every bit of sociological knowledge we have, that Puerto Rican first generation will be noncriminal, nondelinquency-ridden; the second generation, maybe. This is true of all ethnic groups. Why fool around and concoct a new hypothesis for the Puerto Ricans?

With the Puerto Ricans culture is important. You can say that they are not strongly Hispanic in culture (as Oscar Lewis said in criticizing me last night) only by comparison with people in Brazil or Mexico. Puerto Rico has a different colonial history, and I'm glad that Oscar brought it out. But nonetheless they have a cultural base, and they're not out of Gazaway's Gulch. Their way of life has Spanish elements and other elements which differentiate them from the people of the Kentucky mountains, even though both groups share a subculture of poverty.

I'm writing the next volume of the Midtown study. Most of the criticisms of volume I have been wide of the mark. The most telling criticism is that it is based on a questionnaire. We restudied people in the sample in depth, studying, like Oscar, hundreds of families—studying the family history, the Rorschach TAT, Bender Gestalt, Draw-a-Person, and sentence completion. Those aren't in volume I. I'll let you in on a secret. When we studied the same families in depth, we got different ratings from what we had got on the questionnaire, because the same psychiatrists then knew more.

KIEV: Did the psychiatrists interview the people?

OPLER: No, we had case conferences in which the psychiatrists discussed what the interviewers found. John Honigmann says that we failed to pay attention to culture. Well, we did it, but in a volume that John hasn't read because it isn't out yet. Gruenberg's review suggested that we might have missed somebody, but we had plenty of cross-checks. Every reviewer has missed the boat by failing to realize that all of volume I is based on a questionnaire. That's the curse of it. I think it's a good questionnaire, better than Cornell Medical Index, but any questionnaire has its limitations.

KIEV: We're now trying to validate items from the questionnaire. Nobody knows whether people's answers—that they had had certain symptoms—were valid. The only validation studies I've seen, by Langner, were on the total score.

OPLER: Let me give you an example. Srole has an anomie scale. "Anomie" is a little like not-belonging, the psychological quality that Oscar was talking about last night as the prime characteristic of the culture of poverty. Srole had a series of items that across the sample looked significant mathematically, if you forgot that you were dealing with apples and oranges, Puerto Ricans and Germans. They're quite different, in Midtown or anywhere. Now here's an item: "A politician doesn't care about the average man." That means different things to Germans and to Puerto Ricans, because they've had different experiences. The Puerto Rican who says that the politician does care is crazy as a coot! [Dr. Opler told some stories to illustrate the point.] Puerto Ricans showed up badly on questionnaires. I wasn't satisfied until we did anthropological and psychological studies in depth. We found that the Puerto Ricans and the residual Hungarian community upped the rates of mental impairment. It is not a pure socioeconomic phenomenon, as Srole thought it was.

FINNEY: You're disagreeing with Leo Srole's conclusion there. I invited Leo to take part in the conference. It's too bad that he can't be here to discuss the issue with you.

OPLER: Yes, and I'm disagreeing with McClelland, too. To say with McClelland that economics is only an epiphenomenon of psychology is bad history, according to the historians I've talked to. McClelland is wrong in saying that economics is nothing, and Srole is wrong in saying that economics is everything. We need a balanced orientation. I don't think that the economist who ignores social, cultural, and psychological factors will get anywhere, in understanding Dr. Gazaway's hollow or anywhere else.

FINNEY: You're saying that McClelland is wrong in trying to

explain everything in terms of individual human motivations, and also that Srole is wrong in trying to explain everything in terms of social class.

OPLER: Yes. Srole doesn't believe in culture. He replaces it entirely with the concept of social class. I don't think people becomes aware of social class until they're beyond the early formative years; they don't make the comparisons until later, until they hit school and peer-group relationships. The prediction on the Puerto Ricans and the Hungarians, a social-science prediction that came true, was based on the fact that the Puerto Rican community hadn't stabilized, and that the Hungarian community was falling apart.

WEINSTEIN: I'm an example of what Dr. Honigmann called the middle-class psychiatrist, and I suppose I can't study any class or any culture except with the background of my own values. Now I gather, reading between the lines of your paper, that your idea is not to have lower-class psychiatrists studying a lower-class culture, but to make the middle-class psychiatrist aware of the code of structure of his own behavior and take it into consideration. One has to move in with some format, otherwise the observations will have no form or structure. The East seems exotic only to us, not to the Chinese themselves.

HONIGMANN: I don't think I said that it's a good thing to be aware of our own values, but I certainly couldn't disagree with it. Rather what I emphasized is to be sure of getting the inherent structure, the inherent patterning, the inherent reality of the group; to be sure that we are wide open as receptors.

WEINSTEIN: I don't think you can just take stimuli in, unless you have a screen, some system in which to organize and perceive. We need to be culturally relative, to get the inherent structure. But the only way we can perceive it is in terms of some sort of a screen, some set of concepts that are not relative, some set of dimensions along which we can perceive or measure all cultures. Without it we can't compare cultures or even understand them meaningfully.

HONIGMANN: I'm not denying that. You cannot get away from

a screen to organize the facts. But there are broad meshes and narrow meshes. I'm asking for a very broad-mesh screen.

KIEV: There seems to be an implication in some of the papers, especially John Honigmann's, that psychiatrists, who are mostly from the middle class, have just discovered the poor, and are making value judgments about them, saying that the kinds of illnesses they have are socially undesirable. But if you examine the history of psychiatry you find that it *began* with the treatment of people in poor-houses. It was not until Freud began working with middle-class neurotics that a new kind of illness came into the scope of psychiatry. Much of the knowledge gained by psychiatry dealt with clinical conditions and had nothing to do with value judgments about those conditions. The evaluation of the personality and character disorders, and of such behavior as acting-out, in which the psychiatrists' value judgments might make a difference, is of rather recent occurrence.

LEWIS: I think Dr. Finney put it clearly. He thought it possible to arrive at some objective criteria by which one could measure degrees of illness in terms of the social, interpersonal effects, and suggested that there is no question that psychosis is more serious than psychoneurosis; that this is not a matter of middle-class value judgments; that it was as scientific a statement as you have in social science. I'd like John Honigmann's reaction to that, because I think that John's extreme relativism is leading him to say that we can't make such distinctions.

WITTKOWER: I believe that Dr. Honigmann is mistaken in saying that psychiatrists' judgments about their patients are commonly distorted by the influence of their middle-class morality. Let me give you an example. A few months ago I was confronted with a young man who had left his wife in the third month of her pregnancy and had struck up an affair. He was sent to me by his father. Now, I could have disapproved of his affair; I could have been shocked to the core. But in fact, I had the idea that this could be incipient schizophrenia. I explored him, had him tested by the psychologist, and found that it was indeed a case of incipient schizophrenia. I feel that this is rather typical of the attitude of most psychiatrists. We do not approach our patients with middle-class prejudices, but rather we ask ourselves, why is this, what is this, and why the patient does what he does. It is a tenet of psychiatric work to do exactly this, and not to be guided by middle-class value judgments.

FINNEY: It's interesting that social scientists, especially sociologists, attack psychiatrists from both sides of the issue. The sociologist LaPiere attacks psychiatrists in general, and psychoanalysts in particular, alleging that they absolve their patients from blame, excuse them from responsibility, and release them from the obligations of morality. Now Dr. Honigmann, an anthropologist speaking from a sociological point of view, criticizes psychiatrists for just the opposite. He believes that psychiatrists apply moral or value judgments too freely.

HONIGMANN: I can speak confidently when dealing with ethnographic method, but a great deal less confidently when speaking about psychiatric judgments. For what it's worth, as an outsider looking at psychiatric process, this is the way in which it looks to me. Where's the guy who said we could diagnose psychosis?

KIEV: I'm the one. The psychotic illnesses are much more severe in their social costs, they lean more readily to homicide, to complete withdrawal from civilization. People can't carry out their work role, their social roles, in extreme psychotic pathology, whereas they can do so pretty damn well in the neuroses.

HONIGMANN: There's no question in my mind that this is a value judgment. I do not think that a psychiatrist is overstepping his bounds in making a value judgment, as you've quoted me saying here; I said that a psychiatrist is overstepping his therapeutic functions—going beyond them, extending, doing something in addition. This is perfectly proper. To say that something is dangerous or maladaptive (Dr. De Vos's term) is making a value judgment. What else is it? There's nothing wrong in making value judgments.

KIEV: But we're talking about something else. We're talking about whether it is mental illness. That is something that everybody should be able to agree on, irrespective of class. The question was whether the statement that a psychosis is worse than a neurosis is based on a middle-class value judgment.

HONIGMANN: I think that it is a subjective statement. It's by your decision that you see him worse.

FINNEY: I agree with John that a physician often makes decisions based on his own values, and that it's a good idea to recognize when he does so. I've pointed that out in print. But the judgment that a cybernetic system is malfunctioning—or, specifically, that a person is sick—can be made in terms of the values inherent in the system itself, without regard to the observer's values. The neurotic or psychotic person does things that violate his own values. In Freud's terms, there is conflict between his superego and his id. And it is part of the psychiatrist's value system to refrain from imposing his own values on the patient. What the psychiatrist does is to help the patient to meet the patient's own values; that is, to reconcile the inconsistent parts of himself into a smoothly working integrated system. The only value that the doctor assumes is that health is preferable to sickness, that is, that an integrated system is preferable to a disintegrated one. And the degree of integration of a system, of health of a person, is something that can be measured objectively. The same thing that a psychiatrist does with a patient, an anthropologist does with a so-called primitive society. Can't you judge how well integrated a society is, John, in terms of how well it meets the needs of its members, without judging it in terms of the morality of our own society?

DE VOS: Can we take an extreme case, John? Tell me if this is a value judgment. Say that a woman has a post partum psychosis. She abandons her child, and the child dies. Would you say that this woman's condition is objectively unhealthy, or is it a value judgment?

HONIGMANN: By the standards of our society, how can you say anything else? Of course it is unhealthy.

DE VOS: By the standards of any society?

HONIGMANN: I don't know. It's probably universal.

HUGHES: But there is a difference in kinds of judgments. Judgments of what is sick or pathological are judgments in terms of the values of science. But you've not quite said that. You've said that it is a parochial, middle-class value judgment about other people's behavior. And this is the argument. There is a difference. We are speaking here of what the sciences of psychiatry and psychology define as normal human functioning, and what they define as correctable. This isn't a parochial human value judgment.

HONIGMANN: I don't know what you mean by a parochial value judgment. These are subjective judgments that we make as members of society. Whether they are scientific or parochial is to put them into subsets within a larger set.

DE VOS: John, do you know any society or any individual that can live without value judgments?

HONIGMANN: I do not.

DE VOS: Then this is an innate characteristic of man . . .

HONIGMANN: Indeed it is.

DE VOS: . . . that he has to live by a set of values. Then what are we arguing about? I think we're all resisting your use of the words *value judgment* as a value judgment against us.

[Laughter and several people talking at once.]

MARGETTS: I don't think that value judgments alone can add up to a diagnosis.

[Dr. Sanua reminded the group that epidemiologists have found schizophrenia nine times as frequent in the lowest class as in the upper class. He asked whether Dr. Honigmann regarded that finding as a value judgment.]

DE VOS: A statistic is not a value judgment. A statistic is based on an assessment of structural components of psychological function and has nothing to do with values.

FINNEY: The question whether schizophrenia is a worse sickness than psychoneurosis doesn't seem important to me. One reason I've called it such is the empirical observation that most people use neurotic defenses first, and only lapse into psychotic defenses as a last resort, after the neurotic defenses have failed to keep anxiety from soaring. I think that people too often raise the question whether something is normal or abnormal, healthy or sick. It tends to raise artificial barriers between psychiatrists and social scientists. If we know that we want to produce a certain change, the cause-effect relationships are all that matter, and the question of unhealthiness doesn't matter. The time when the question becomes relevant is when we raise the ethical issue, whether we are justified in intervening, trying to produce a change. Most of us feel that when an individual or a society is sick, our duty is to intervene, to try to restore it to health. At the same time, most of us are pluralists, cultural relativists: we feel that in the absence of sickness our duty is to leave the other fellow alone, to let him live his life in his own way, and not to convert him to our way. There is a tension between these two values.

Tom Maretzki, in talking about the Peace Corps, described the American culture as tolerant and pluralistic. Well, it surely has an element of that. But there is also another element, a crusading or missionary spirit, which can be highly intolerant. Remember that the U. S. government persecuted the Mormons until they gave up polygamy. In our self-righteousness we claim also the right to convert the heathen and to force other people to give up practices that we (in our culture) consider bad, sinful, unjust, or immoral. Nobody can be crueler than a missionary or a crusader. Those people can do cruel things with a clear conscience because, in their self-righteousness, they believe they are doing good, upholding justice and morality. Nowadays some of us have restrained ourselves to the point that we refrain from changing other people's way of life unless it is an unhealthy one. That's an improvement, because at least theoretically (as I have shown) we can define health objectively, while sin and injustice are pure culture-bound value judgments. I say "theoretically," because some people do let their moral values influence their judgments of what is healthy.

OPLER: I think George De Vos has been saying the right thing, and John Honigmann has formulated it correctly in his reexplanation. All judgments about human beings, dispositions, states, are judgments in the field of values. Granted what Ari said, that the psychiatrist is a little more humanistic than some other people. As a matter of fact psychiatry has been looked at askance by surgery for that reason. I find that my friends among doctors tend to come from psychiatry. Granted all that, the question is, doesn't the psychiatrist, excluding someone like Joe Finney, who's an anthropologist, too . . .

DE VOS: Psychologists claim him.

OPLER: He has a Ph.D. in that, but I want to put in a claim for anthropology. The question is whether other kinds of psychiatrists, with limited social perspectives, need information about patients from sociology to support their judgments. I think they do, that the only kind of psychiatry that can move out among people is social psychiatry. Recently it's been called community psychiatry .

FINNEY: We're discussing it on an abstract level. To make it concrete, isn't this what we're arguing about? Do we have a right to say to the people in Dr. Gazaway's hollow or to the Puerto Ricans, "We don't like you the way you are; we want to change you and make you more like us"? Or should we say to them, "Well, okay, you live your life, and we'll live ours and leave you alone"? Isn't that what we're arguing about?

DE VOS: There's a third theme here, and that concerns psychiatry as a science as well as a therapy. Psychiatrists and psychologists can classify the behavior of individuals, how they're functioning, by measurements that have nothing to do with our own values. We can find that a person's thinking processes go this way or that. We can define it objectively without considering treatment.

HONIGMANN: That's right, George, but there is also in many labels an explicit notion of how sad this is! You're right. Psychiatrists do make those classifications. But in the back there is a little click that sees some as better than others.

DE VOS: But that's a separate question. That is defined in a concept of maturation, that mental functioning grows and develops and matures. Some functioning takes place on an early, immature level, and some takes place on a more advanced, more mature level. This is the criterion that a psychiatrist or psychologist uses in making his judgments. Some behavior is more mature than other behavior.

HONIGMANN: That's where I have my fear: that the standard of maturity is a class-bound standard, or a culture-bound standard. We don't know enough about the possibilities of maturation.

DE VOS: That's where I absolutely disagree with you. I think there is an absolute standard of maturation, which can be defined. It has been discussed thoroughly in the publications of child psychologists, child psychiatrists, and psychoanalysts (Erikson, 1950). Some adult people are emotionally immature, and others live their lives in more mature ways.

FINNEY: Oscar, you're making faces. Do you care to comment aloud?

LEWIS: It seems to me that John puts himself in a very difficult box, a sort of an ivory tower. These subcultures of poverty are part of an ongoing social system. These people frequently call for help. It's not a question of our going out and forcing them to change. As soon as they become aware (and it's difficult for them not to become aware) that there are agencies that offer services, in spite of all the class barriers and so on, a lot of those people seek help. And when they seek help, what are we to do? It seems to me unrealistic to sit back and say, "Wait a minute now, I'm middle-class, you know, and any help I give them will be culture-bound; I'd better not touch these people." The result would be not doing anything about human suffering. As a matter of fact, the whole concept of concern for human suffering seems to bother John. He seems to have the idea that it's not a legitimate area of concern for anthropologists to be sensitive to human suffering.

HONIGMANN: Did you read my paper? Did you listen when I read it?

OPLER: Let me help John by drawing . . .

DE VOS: Don't be middle class. Don't help him when he's down. [Laughter.]

HONIGMANN: A great part of my paper is concerned with human suffering.

OPLER: Here's what I think is realistically involved. Any psychiatrist knows that you don't change people by exhortation. That's an anthropological principle, too. Take the Indian Service in the Collier regime. They sealed off these many and different cultures and said, "The Indian way of life is sacrosanct; let's respect it. And, Indians, please, won't you go Indian! Express your spiritual values!" Well, that was empty exhortation, too. Can't we function in a different way, by combinations of knowledge that are psychological and social? For instance, social psychiatry short-circuits a lot of problems of transference and countertransference by setting up milieu situations, or emphasizing patient self-government, or having community clubs. One of the best papers in our journal [*The International Journal of Social Psychiatry*] was written by a social worker, Ray Lerner, who got in with a group of psychotics and worked with them intimately, much as the people who work with delinquent gangs. These are effective ways to work with the situation. We anthropologists need to go in and bring our skills to bear. We need to work from knowledge of where the people are now.

MARETZKI: Dr. Prince made the point that certain societies or groups of people are able to act independently and therefore to accept therapy that draws on their insights, while others cannot. It seems a crucial difference to me.

LANTIS: I would like to come to John Honigmann's defense. We have considered the problem only synchronically and not diachronically. The anthropologist, of all people, should be able to say something about the adaptive value of mental health: what is decided through time. That is what we have completely missed. I think that what John had in mind was something like this. It may be that a psychosis, a short-term one such as we see in some of the nonliterate societies, which removes the person temporarily from the society, is adaptive in the long run, and is far better for the society than the psychoneurosis that keeps him functioning poorly in the society. In the long run the neurosis may do more harm to the individual and to the society than the psychosis. I'm not saying this is true, but it may be; we haven't looked at it. It may be more damaging to the health of the society, in its organization, in its interpersonal relations, in the development of new values, or whatever criteria you take, in the course of three, four, or five generations. This is what I think Dr. Honigmann was driving at. Somehow we have missed the point, what is the function of mental disease for society? Of one type versus another type? Not just for the individual, but for the society.

HONIGMANN: I can't take credit for having had that idea. That was not in my mind, but I think it's excellent. Newman has published an article on amok, in which he shows that it is a short-term breakdown that enables a man to get out of responsibilities that he feels uncomfortable with. And society apparently understands. In the amok episode, the man destroys a great deal of property, but afterward he is relieved of certain responsibilities and the thing is forgotten. There is—I don't know—some kind of indemnity, perhaps, that's due.

FINNEY: He may also be dead. Gregory Bateson's definition of amok is, a form of suicide in which a person runs around attacking other people until he forces them to kill him.

PRINCE: You assume, John, that psychosis appears out of a normal personality. In our culture, at least, that is usually not so. These people are inhibited and withdrawn before they develop a psychosis—afterward, even more. I don't think you can say that a person who has a psychosis doesn't do as much damage as a neurotic; he probably does more.

DE VOS: May I make an analogy? You can say that the boys with amok got it out of their system, and everything went back to normal. Amok has a useful function in that society; it discharges a great deal of aggression. There may be another analogy in the social function of the blind in Japanese society: they were masseurs and musicians; so it was very nice to have them around. Of course, you can find a function for anything. Even disease! And you can find a useful function for any disease. It slows people down; it kills some off, which lowers the population. But that doesn't really make sickness a good thing.

OPLER: I want to repeat Dr. Prince's point and add something to it. [Dr. Opler told of seeing an episode of running amok in Hell's Half Acre in Honolulu. He arrived right after the episode and saw a lot of blood and gore, just as is usual in Malaysia.] It's very destructive, even though it is short. It's an episodic catathymic outburst such as we used to have in European peasant societies, more often than now, and it seems to be based on a hysteriform conversion acting-out. Their mental illnesses were episodic, and often had spontaneous remission. In my book *Culture and Mental Health,* Mel Spiro reported a complete mental-health survey of Ifaluk, which has some 200 to 250 people. The rates of mental illness were beautifully low compared to New York City.

FINNEY: That's an important point. You're not the only one who believes that amok is no psychosis at all, but what we'd call a dissociation reaction, a psychoneurotic reaction akin both to hysterical acting-out and to conversion reaction (or conversion hysteria).

OPLER: Yes. The point that Margaret Lantis could well make is that primitive societies seem not to produce the defenses in depth, the deep-seated illnesses. It's different in the more complex societies, such as the Chinese and Japanese. Take *koro,* a delusion that the penis is shrinking in. We have a case of a Chinese man in our county hospital. It's a depth illness, long-lasting, delusional, paranoid, touched, and so on. The patients are unlike catatonics, amokers, and so on, who have short dramatic episodes.

HONIGMANN: The illnesses get more complex as culture gets more complex.

OPLER: Right.

KIEV: That point can be disputed. Do you know Yap's study of 19 cases of *koro* that he followed for 16 years? Sixteen were considered to be abnormal personalities, one was schizophrenic, and two were heroin withdrawal. They all showed the *koro* syndrome, but superimposed on some other more basic psycho-pathology that conformed to our conventional system of classification.

OPLER: I find that very unconvincing. In our hospital experience, addiction and alcoholism are not mental illnesses; you usually find schizophrenia with this overlay. I don't know what they say at the Lexington USPHS narcotic hospital; they're probably full of schizophrenics.

ENZER: We have some, but most of our addicts are passive-aggressive personalities. It depends on the subculture: white, Negro, North, South.

OPLER: Probably a lot of neurotics would develop the *koro* syndrome, because it is such a culturally advertised channel for the sick role. I want to know more about Yap's cases.

FINNEY: What's the argument about? You're all agreeing that in the complex societies of China and Japan people have psychological sicknesses that resemble those of Europe and the U. S. and Canada, and don't resemble those of the so-called primitive peoples. And you're all agreeing, moreover, that a syndrome such as *koro*, which cannot be compared cross-culturally because its content is highly specific to one culture, (and perhaps even such syndromes as alcoholism and addiction) may be a mask or surface trait covering some more fundamental entity such as schizophrenia or passive-aggressive oral personality, whose prevalence can be compared cross-culturally.

Before we move too far off it, I want to correct one impression. I seem to have been cast in the role of opposition to John Honigmann and his cultural relativism. True, I disagree with him sharply at certain points, but I strongly endorse what seems to me the main point of his message.

I especially liked your point, John, that changes should be self-directed. Like you, I feel strongly that we need to "increase the range of cultural tolerances, in order to accommodate in society the greatest possible number of temperaments, eccentricities, and unusual types." I endorse John Stuart Mill's principle that people should be allowed to live their own lives in their own way, so long as they don't attack other people. I deplore the trend toward worldwide uniformity. Diversity is a richness, an asset, a storehouse of treasures. The world will be poorer when everyone is assimilated into one way of life.

In fact, I'm more tolerant, more relativistic than you are, John, because I favor tolerance of the way of life in Mississippi and Alabama. True, I don't want to live in that society. It's one characterized by politeness, hospitality, faith, and chivalry. Those ideals are rooted in the hysterical or dissociating personality, which keeps itself unaware of its motives, especially hostility and sexuality. People of that kind seem naive. To one who doesn't know them, they seem insincere. But their lack of frankness is not truly deceptive; it rests on self-deception. Personally, I prefer to deal with people who are blunt and open and not so polite. I've often wondered whether it is the racial caste system that requires the polite naive southern personality type, at least in the United States. To hold the American creed that all men are equal, and at the same time to maintain a racial caste system, requires mental gymnastics; specifically, it requires the defense mechanism called dissociation, which prevents two opposing thoughts from entering consciousness at the same time.

Having said all that, I believe that they have the right to maintain their traditional culture. I believe that people from Michigan or New York who go to Mississippi as crusaders, in freedom marches, are being intolerant of the other fellow's right to keep his own way of life. They justify themselves in the manner that missionaries and crusaders have always justified themselves: by saying that the other fellow's way of life is morally wrong and deserves to be destroyed. That's what the Congregational missionaries said as they destroyed the Polynesian culture of the Hawaiians. That culture also included a caste system, but their main objection to it was its sexual permissiveness. Personally, I think that the sexual freedom of the Hawaiians was a more sensible way of life than the prudishness and Puritanism of the missionaries.

Last summer in Montreal I discussed social problems with a

French-Canadian psychiatrist. He felt strongly that French Canada should be allowed to maintain its separate way of life and resist assimilation to the national majority culture. I remarked that in the United States, too, one section, the South, is facing forcible assimilation to the way of life of the rest of the nation. He said, "That's entirely different. The ways of the South are morally wrong. They should be forced to change."

Now it seems clear to me that if we say that we'll tolerate diverse cultures, diverse ways of life, only so long as they are not morally wrong, that's no tolerance at all. It's tolerance only of trivial differences. For people's ideas of what is morally wrong are culturally determined, and differ from one culture to another. If two cultures truly differ, in any important way, their ideas of right and wrong must differ. Each culture will regard some features of the other culture as morally wrong. If our claim to tolerance means anything at all, we must be willing to let the people of another state or territory live in their own way, even though their way may seem immoral or unjust to us.

I regard homosexuality as a sick way of life, but I don't think it should be punished by law. For the same reason I believe that the laws that most states have passed forbidding firecrackers are needlessly intolerant. People should be allowed to take their own risks, if they like. I'd vote against curfew laws, and I might vote to legalize the use of marijuana. I have strong feelings about the rights of individuals and of communities to keep their own separate ways of life and not to knuckle under to some bigger group. Even when a person or a group has a way of life that is clearly sick, I favor encouraging a self-directed change, in which people make their own decisions; not forcing a change on unwilling people.

On the other hand, let me say this. When we find a group of people with a sick way of life, one that is failing not just by our standards but by their own, failing to meet their needs, I feel that we should offer to help them change, if they agree that they'd like to do so. I think that Dr. Gazaway's Branch is a situation of that kind. And probably every group that falls under

Dr. Lewis's definition of the culture of poverty is a situation of that kind.

WEINSTEIN: I'd like to ask a question of Dr. Prince. Ray, in your paper you talked about Christianity and giving up the entire personality, and you related it to willingness to accept the kind of treatment that is popular in the United States. Can you explain that point further?

PRINCE: My point was that if a group of people is unable to develop insight, they can use the other type of therapy that is often used in other parts of the world, the authoritarian religio-magical system. In other cultures, to get inside the cone of authority you have to sacrifice something, follow certain tabus; however, the restriction on behavior is not great. But in the Christian evangelical tradition, like this snake-handling cult, you don't just make a sacrifice of an animal: you have to change your whole personality. You have to abide by the rules that govern marital relations and even whether you go to shows. It imposes a pattern on your whole personality. So the Christian cults are more effective in changing personality than the other cults.

DE VOS: I question the difference. It's very interesting to watch new religions in Japan. They're going into the healing business, and that's their appeal. Some of them are extremely sophisticated; they hire social psychologists to set up group therapy sessions for their constituents. They have consulting psychologists and sociologists. They even made a study of line-and-staff organization, because they kept having cleavages, and they wanted to cure the organization of the cleavages. They found out that if certain individuals became subleaders, there's a danger of their creating a splinter group and going off. Some groups are now very well structured. One of them had a research team come in and study their social organization, to set it up scientifically to prevent cleavage. They have one consultant who has a dual role: he's an official of the Japanese ministry of religion.

PRINCE: That's not primitive.

DE VOS: Well, it deals with faith-healing.

PRINCE: It's more like our Christian cults.

DE VOS: Yes. Functionally it's the same. What Christianity asks is certain tabus. You give certain things up.

PRINCE: Christianity deals more with your relationship with other people. The primitive non-Christian cults don't ask for that kind of behavioral change: they only require you to do certain things, like give up certain foods, but you can be as bad a husband as ever.

DE VOS: I'd look at the evangelical Christian cults to see if there isn't a certain amount of that. In the conversion of British homosexuals to Catholicism, of which you see a great deal in intellectual circles, I don't think they change their behavior one whit, but they change the feeling of security about it, by getting inside the Catholic church.

PRINCE: I don't know. That needs to be studied.

OPLER: Dr. Prince, instead of limiting the term to magical-religious, why don't you call it supportive therapy? I've been writing about the curing cults in Nigeria, and I call it their form of group therapy.

PRINCE: The essential difference is that it isn't aimed at insight. In our outpatient treatment of chronic patients, when we don't try to produce insight we say, "This isn't really psychotherapy we're doing, it's something social." So we try to put them into a Golden Age club, or some kind of a social group. But that isn't high-powered enough. They don't stick there. They want something magical as well. We don't have it. The Nigerians do. They can put their patients off into high-powered social groups that do magic.

OPLER: I'm worried about your dichotomy. The distinction isn't that sharp. It's only a different degree of emphasis. It's only in the most orthodox classical psychoanalytic literature that you find the magical insight, the marvelous cure. I helped set up the Los Angeles Institute of Psychoanalysis and got my training there, and I'll be damned if the psychoanalysts in that crew, who were split into a Horney group and an orthodox group, practiced insight therapy 100 percent. Nonsense! When Ralph Greenson loses Marilyn Monroe, by suicide, after she was in Payne-

Whitney clinic, I think you have some evidence that he didn't produce much insight.

WEINSTEIN: The whole concept of insight is ethnocentric. Residents present cases of patients with schizophrenia, and say, "He has no insight." I say, "What do you mean?" They say, "He doesn't know what caused it." I say, "Do *you* know what the cause of schizophrenia is?" [Laughter.] I think it's a cliche.

FINNEY: I agree that mental hospital psychiatrists often misuse the term *insight*. When they say that a patient has no insight they may only be complaining that the patient doesn't humble himself, doesn't admit that something is wrong with him. But I think that Dr. Prince and Dr. Opler use the word *insight* with a precise meaning. Animals have no insight. Their actions such as hunting food or seeking a mate are purposeful and goal seeking, but they have no awareness of their goals. A bird, while building a nest, doesn't know why he builds it; he doesn't know that a baby bird will be born in it. We human beings have some capability of insight. We can fantasy the future and mull over the past. When we do something we are often able to recognize what urges are behind it and what goals or future satisfactions it is aimed at. This awareness of goals, this ability to put our motives into words and reflect on them, is what we mean by insight. The capacity for insight, for reflective self-awareness, is a recent acquisition in the phylogenetic evolution, and we hold it precariously. Not one of us has full insight; we don't need it. Some people have more of it than others. When one uses the word *insight* precisely, and Dr. Prince and Dr. Opler do, it is not ethnocentric.

Thomas Hardy wrote, "The purposive unmotived dominant Thing / That sways in brooding dark our wayfaring." *Purposive* and *unmotived* are contradictory terms. Hardy meant that the cosmic spirit, like some tiger that devours us, has no insight into its motives and cannot be reasoned with. It's a God that is blind, deaf, and merciless—a stark religion without comfort.

DE VOS: I think Dr. Prince has a legitimate dichotomy, but I object to excepting Christianity from what we say about other religious groups.

FINNEY: Among religions, nobody has mentioned Communism. A number of studies have been published about the intensive indoctrination methods used to convert people to that religion, especially in China. It seems to me that that's a religion which demands even more total commitment than Christianity—twentieth-century Christianity, anyway. Perhaps earlier Christianity demanded a heavier commitment.

DE VOS: They [the Communists] don't have insight therapy.

FINNEY: The Communist religion is not one that stresses the healing of physical symptoms as one of the side benefits; perhaps that's why it wasn't mentioned.

WEINSTEIN: Healing of mental illness, though. It is claimed that mental illness comes from bourgeois wrong habits of living.

FINNEY: Their methods of education and political indoctrination are psychotherapeutic in a broad sense. They depend strongly on arousal of guilt, and then on identifying the evil parts of oneself with certain "bad" agencies and the good parts with the Communist regime; projecting the evil, and then attaining a great sense of relief by identification with the government. It's a real form of psychotherapy. Perhaps they haven't put as much stress on relief of physical symptoms because conversion reactions are not so widespread in Communist China as they may be in some other cultures.

MARETZKI: The distinction between external controls and internal controls is significant. Are societies differentiated in symptoms of schizophrenia according to emphasis on those lines? I think of Japan, where insight therapy is practiced, perhaps because the people have internal controls, in contrast to Okinawa, which is Japanese in culture but somewhat different, where insight therapy is not possible. Those two societies illustrate the distinction between people who are brought up with internal controls and those in which external controls are stressed. I think it makes a difference in the symptoms of schizophrenia, and in the therapy that can be applied. Insight therapy is widely used in Japan.

DE VOS: There are class differences in new religions in Japan. The dancing religion, the more motoric groups, are lower class; whereas in Seicho-no-iya, discontented middle-class housewives get together in groups and talk about how husbands are really like babies—how they have to coddle them. So there are psychological differences between classes, which go with Dr. Prince's distinction between the motoric and the internal verbalizing. The lower classes use hysterical, motoric mechanisms, while the middle classes are more compulsive and work for insight, to become aware of their motives and label them with words. The psychological differences between classes is the same in Japan as it is in the U. S. and Canada.

PRINCE: The amok that we've been talking about is characteristic of the more primitive groups. The withdrawn kind of psychosis with loss of affect that we see over here so much is found in Japan and China as well as in northwestern Europe and the United States and Canada. I've studied some fifteen healing clinics or shrines in Nigeria. There were a good number of withdrawn, flattened persons, and they're regarded as sick. I think that such people would be regarded as sick in any culture. I don't believe that even in Gazaway's Gulch they are unaware of what mental illness is.

SANUA: What we seem to be saying is that since we are not able to approach the lower-class individuals through insight therapy, we have to use any kind of method that enables us to approach them; we can even sell our souls to the devil, which in this particular case is God. [Laughter.] In this way we seem to perpetuate something I don't think we should perpetuate, that is, ignorance and superstition. That's one reservation I have about your suggestion, Dr. Prince. My second reservation is, who is to do the job? Many psychiatrists would not be willing to become preachers. This is a practical question I'm raising. Entirely apart from the moral issue involved in perpetuating an ignorant, superstitious way of life.

FINNEY: In Dr. Kiev's book *Magic, Faith, and Healing,* there is a chapter by Dr. Prince on indigenous Yoruba psychiatry, in which he advocates that native healing practices not be abandoned, but be integrated with western medicine. He refers to Dr. Margetts as a "dissenting voice," and he quotes Dr. Margetts as follows:

> One hears something of the usefulness of so-called traditional therapy in the treatment of African mental patients. This refers to tribal methods of treatment by medicine men or religious healers, who may define mental illness by concepts of magic, superstition and religion, in addition to or in place of primitive medicine and surgery. . . . There is no doubt that in the very remote areas the native healers do some good (usually on the basis of strong positive suggestion based on fear and faith), but they often do harm too, though perhaps irresponsibly. There is probably no more reason to fit traditional healing into a mental health program in this day and age in Africa than in any other country in the world.

Dr. Prince goes on to say:

> It seems clear that there is no good reason to encourage indigenous healing practices for physical illness in any culture. Western diagnosis technique and Western pharmacological and surgical knowledge far outstrip every other known system of medicine. In addition, Western practices are universally acceptable: they are not culture-bound.
>
> Psychological medicine is different, however, in a number of ways. Western psychiatric techniques are not in my opinion demonstrably superior to many indigenous Yoruba practices. I feel confident that investigation of the indigenous psychiatry of other groups will lead to the same conclusion. Psychotherapeutic techniques fit with the cultures in which they have developed and cannot cross cultural boundaries so successfully as can physical therapies.

May we have some comments on that?

PRINCE: Dr. Margetts and I certainly do disagree. My own position can be stated as follows: 1) My observations in Nigeria suggest that indigenous methods of handling psychiatric disorder are efficacious. This was as true of the treatment of psychoses as it was of neuroses. Although there are very few studies of this sort, there are many impressionistic accounts indicating that indigenous healing techniques are effective in other cultures. 2) Western medical facilities and personnel are grossly inadequate in most developing countries. Furthermore, the resources that are available are utilized for the more deadly medical problems such as the infectious diseases and malnutrition rather than for psychiatric disorders. 3) The indigenous healers who treat mental disorder are often highly regarded by the local populace.

Dr. Margetts seems to hold that indigenous healers should be suppressed for the following reasons: 1) Many of these healers are quacks who exploit the gullible; 2) They tend to perpetuate the erroneous religious and magical world view of the populace; 3) Some of their treatment techniques are damaging (for example, physical beating of the psychotic); 4) Their treatment centers are unsanitary.

It seems to me that these developing societies are not the only places where quacks are to be found. I think, too, that the indigenous peoples themselves know who are the quacks and who are the respectable healers who come from families of healers and are well trained in their lore. I believe that the way to dispel the religiomagical world view is not by suppression nor by fiat, but by a gradual educational process. As someone has said of our western culture, "No one ever disproved the existence of witches; the belief in witches was simply outgrown."

It also seems to me that the way to diminish maltreatment of the mentally ill (where such occurs) is neither to ignore the indigenous healers nor to drive them underground. Rather, some sort of working arrangement should be developed so that a western psychiatric center could link up with a network of indigenous treatment centers. The result could be the development of mutual respect, perhaps the facilitation of referrals, and also the provision of some degree of control if undesirable treatment practices are employed. It seems to me that the indigenous healers will be around for a long time in most areas. They will gradually disappear as a more western world view becomes pervasive. Theirs is a valuable rearguard action, in my view.

MARGETTS: I have every respect for Dr. Ray Prince. I think that Dr. Prince's comments on African psychology and traditional medicine are well worth considering. But, Ray, it seems to me that you are inclined to be something of a mystic. Why should we encourage uneducated native African healers any more than faith healers, chiropractors, hypnotists, and other quacks in our own culture? I don't think "magical methods" of healing are of practical importance. I myself am very much interested in them. In fact, that is one of my chief areas of research interest, as you know. But I don't recommend them for use nowadays in Africa or anywhere else.

PRINCE: Oh, I don't mean to restrict our collaboration with faith healers to Africa. It can also work in North America. Let me show you what I mean. To go back to Dr. Sanua's first question: the Class V people in the U.S. and Canada have a lot of broken families. The women have a series of husbands. To my way of thinking, an unstable family that neglects the children, and so on, cannot produce children who are capable of insight, or even of entering our school system satisfactorily. Those two outcomes are linked; I think the same factors that keep them from using insight psychotherapy make them school dropouts. So we have many bad things going on. Now, how do we get the Class V up to the Class IV? There at least we'd have a stable working-class family, albeit an authoritarian one. Now psychiatry has no role here: we can't do it. Maybe the religious groups can. The first step out of the poverty way of life is a religious or magical maneuver, bringing the Class V by a cone of authority up to Class IV. The offspring of a Class IV person has a much better chance, being at least part of a stable family, and can more easily go up the scale, into the middle class.

FINNEY: Dr. Honigmann, can we have your reaction to that?

HONIGMANN: The second question hasn't been answered yet: how can we do this?

FINNEY: I suspect that Dr. Prince's proposal to assimilate the lowest class, Class V, into the next class, and then possibly on up into the middle class, is objectionable to Dr. Honigmann, who feels that an attempt to assimilate them is ethnocentric. But there are some aspects of Dr. Prince's approach that Dr. Honigmann must approve of: starting with people where they are, with methods fitting their own indigenous culture.

PRINCE: I'll try to answer Dr. Honigmann. Of course, as I said in my paper, the middle-class psychiatrist—or any psychiatrist—can't do this. It's completely alien to him to go onto street corners and preach and convince people of sin. We must leave it to the people who can do it. I suggest that we pay more heed to these things, have a look at them, see what's happening there, see how effective that kind of religious or magical maneuver is, in changing personality and in stabilizing families.

DE VOS: There are examples of this in lower-caste groups, but it's political. It's perhaps magico-religious, but in a political sense—the Black Muslims among the Negroes, for instance, the Japanese outcastes, and certainly the Communist movement. The belief system, in each case, integrates the individual, gives him a sense of purpose, and a kind of an orientation, of effectiveness, and he latches onto it. It takes him out of the culture of poverty, as Oscar Lewis would say.

FINNEY: Can we ethically endorse those political movements? German Nazism gave a sense of integration to its members, as Erich Fromm pointed out, but it did a lot of harm to other people, who were its victims. Communism does the same.

DE VOS: Well, you get the same thing in lower-class France. If you look at the people around Paris, they're integrated. My experience was that the lower-class French did not have the unorganized neighborhoods we have in America. Though they were poor, they did not have a culture of poverty, by Oscar's definition. In their case it's a political allegiance rather than a church allegiance that does it.

KIEV: That or any kind. Remember Dr. Gazaway's pictures of the snake-handling cult. In that kind of institution there may be some therapeutic resources for those people. I think that's where Dr. Prince's paper dovetails with Dr. Honigmann's. If we were to go in to help these people, we wouldn't look askance at the snake cult, but we would try to integrate our activity in some way with its leaders, because those leaders are aware of who's most disturbed.

HOCHSTRASSER: I'm confused with your suggestion that the cult leaders don't have any insight of their own, but have insight into other people.

FINNEY: Don't let that surprise you. It happens all the time. Each of us is blindest about himself.

KIEV: What I'm suggesting is the kind of thing that Dr. Lambo has shown to work in Abeokuta, where patients come in to the village hospital during the day for conventional western psychiatric treatment, and on the weekends have their native sacrifices, led by native witch doctors. And Dr. Lambo isn't sure which of the two forms of treatment works best for those people. I think that in that sort of situation, where the people have some of those resources, their own healers have no knowledge of Freudian psychodynamics but have an intuitive skill in helping certain people recover.

FINNEY: Yes. Let's not take too literally the comment that a faith healer is a great psychologist. That's like calling Babe Ruth a great physicist. A physicist is aware that force equals mass times acceleration, and can express that law in words and in mathematical formulas. Babe Ruth couldn't do that, but he had an intuitive grasp of how to use that principle to accelerate a baseball. The skills of the magical healer are not what we usually call insight. They are like Babe Ruth's, not like the physicist's.

But how do we feel about Dr. Prince's suggestion that the lower classes should be assimilated into the middle class? Is that ethnocentric?

DE VOS: Yes, and it's still something that has to be done. The lower class is a residual structure. It no longer serves a useful purpose. It is reproducing a nonfunctioning structure nowadays. [Babel of voices.]

LEWIS: But when all is said and done, people in the culture of poverty are less lonely and less alienated than the modern middle-class man is.

LANTIS: I'd like to make a suggestion that I think goes beyond that. If you look at the sets of relationships of a group of people, you find relationships with the material world, relationships with people, and relationships with the supernatural, which is a symbolization or projection of the interpersonal ones. We've talked a lot about the lower class, the people in poverty, as being especially concerned with the material, the physical, doing heavy labor, and expressing their anxieties by physical means, motoric and other bodily symptoms. I believe that we see the beginnings of a fundamental change in the lower class in our own society, at least: the interpersonal relations, which were already very skillful and have been used for their advantage, are becoming much more important, and the material, much less important. When people get their sole income from social agencies or from the church, they are manipulating people and institutions to maintain themselves; they are not manipulating the physical environment. It has been characteristic of the middle class to live by manipulating people, and by manipulating words, and other symbols, mathematical and so forth. Now it's coming down into the lower class, so that we have more in common with them than we think we have, or have had in the past. There is no longer a need for physical labor. They won't be working with bricks, or be hod-carriers; they will live by manipulating people. And the ones who are getting along are the ones who are manipulating people successfully. So I suspect that there will be less difference between the classes as time goes on; not because the lower-class people will learn such skills as turning valves on in automated factories—few will do that—but because they will do things the way middle-class people do. And they're already good at it, even in this famous "branch" or "gulch" or "hollow" of Dr. Gazaway's that we've been talking about. Yesterday we were concerned about two views of these people: they are very friendly, but underneath there may be a lot of hostility. That is true. I've worked in Eastern Kentucky, too. The people are extremely friendly, as Mr. Ransdell said; they welcome people, because they're bored and want diversion; because they want to know what you're there for, that is very important; because they have a code of hospitality; and because they are just darned smart in handling people. People loom very large in the world of the illiterate. If they're not dealing with symbols (and they have very few symbols), their world consists of corn, a few pigs, and the mine, and people! They are extremely good at taking cues, understanding motives, and learning how to deal with people—often far better than people who are highly literate and have substituted symbols for face-to-face interpersonal relations. I have a feeling that we are whipping a dead horse.

FINNEY: I disagree with the comparison you have drawn. Cheating to get on the relief rolls, to be supported without working, is the very opposite of the traditional middle-class Puritan compulsive ethic of hard work and self-denial. And you confuse us by using the word *manipulate* equivocally. Manipulating people, especially when done intuitively, is altogether different from manipulating words and mathematical symbols by a deliberate, carefully thought-out plan. It's like the difference between Babe Ruth and the physicist. It's two altogether different ways of life.

OPLER: In our society (read Koos, 1954) lower-class urban people are going to chiropractors instead of doctors. When doctors speak the language of this kind of person, there is rapport. I think Dr. Lantis is talking not only about their stake in human relations, and their adeptness, which she put so well, but also about a kind of meaning that these people understand. For instance, in Nigeria, Lambo often stands aside and has Chief Awoldi or some other practitioners handle cases, too. That's very wise. I found a lot of cases in Nigeria which the curing cult took over from the psychiatrist because the psychiatrist didn't talk the language or didn't make a go of it. There are some analogies in American medicine. We were told yesterday about a doctor in Eastern Kentucky who gave a water injection, whereupon the patient got up and walked again. That's magic, just as in Nigeria. Jerry Frank's book *Persuasion and Healing* is full of treatments of conversion hysteria in our society. The use of a placebo in medicine is a typical example. The Puerto Rican goes to the curer and has root medicine shots; when the curer helps him, he thinks it's organic disease and not this highfalutin psychiatric stuff that hurts his pride. If and when psychiatry can make that kind of accommodation with the concepts people have of illness, I think psychiatry can function, too. I see no reason why placebo technique is any better because you're wearing a tie and a white coat. To me, it's the same no matter who does it, an American medical doctor or an African tribal magician.

PRINCE: In our western culture, when a doctor gives a man an injection of sterile water, there is a whole network besides the placebo. That's what I meant by the cone of authority. It's much more complex thing than just the doctor's saying, "I'm giving you an injection, and your symptoms will go away." They do, maybe, but they come back.

OPLER: And when a doctor gives one at Camp Cureton in New York, or in Kenneth Clark's group at Northside Clinic, and speaks Spanish, as Oscar said yesterday, there is a different reception atmosphere for the Puerto Rican. He knows what's going on inside: that the Puerto Ricans can't face psychological illness. But he can understand family counseling. He almost shrieks for it! We had a grant from the John A. Whitney Foundation to study what the Puerto Rican can tolerate, what his conceptions of illness were and weren't. Until those things are known, you can't treat conversion hysteria anywhere.

FINNEY: Dr. Hughes, Dr. Honigmann quoted a passage from your book *People of Cove and Woodlot* and said it showed signs of culture shock. Do you care to comment about that?

HUGHES: I certainly do. I'll continue to disagree with Dr.

Honigmann. There was very little, if any, projection on my part onto the social and cultural life of the people in the depressed areas I was studying. In terms of vast reams of observational and verbal data, I think the only valid assessment that can be made on the condition of these people was that they were unhappy. Now it may well be that what John is objecting to is the use of the terms *happy* and *unhappy*. I would not necessarily quarrel with that, for certainly *happiness* is an extremely complex term. But without question the denizens of the depressed areas we studied were people who left acute frustration, disappointment, anxiety, and hostility about their total life situation. Does this not make them "unhappy"?

This is not to deny that they, like people anywhere, experienced momentary pleasure and had ways of diverting themselves to help ease the burden of existence. They laughed, they drank, they went out hunting, they played tricks on their neighbors, and so forth. But I think it was the experience of all fieldworkers that even the gratification-giving devices had a tinge of negativism and masochism about them. These were simply not healthful places to live in—and it certainly seemed to all the fieldworkers that people responded in a compound manner that we, for want of a shorter term, labeled "unhappiness."

Further on this point, I recognize the fact that I might well have been having "cultural shock." I recognized it keenly at the time and carried on an intensive dialogue with myself as to how much of what I saw was me, and how much was in the phenomena that I was investigating. I, myself, was professionally naive at that point, since I was a junior graduate student doing the fieldwork. But there were others, far more experienced and better trained than I, who came to similar conclusions. So I do not think that it was simply a question of my professional naivete or my overloading my observations with internal tensions of my own. I feel that John Honigmann is attempting to seek for some ultimate "blessedness" in every human situation—which, indeed, I do think is there. But it is not there at the level at which our data were cast, and the sum effect of our observations and studies of many different kinds was that these people are in a pretty miserable situation, and that they know it.

FINNEY: I asked because I suspected that John Honigmann's remark might have hurt Charles Hughes's feelings, and it turned out to be so. I wonder, John, if you will clarify what you meant when you spoke of Charley's description as showing culture shock. How bad is that? Is culture shock something that happens to every anthropologist when he enters a culture new to him? Or does it happen only to the immature and inexperienced? And does culture shock distort an anthropologist's perception so that we cannot put faith in his reported findings? Or can the anthropologist recognize his culture shock, take it into account, and give us valid conclusions in spite of it?

HONIGMANN: You ask what culture shock implies and whether it is frequently experienced by field-going anthropologists. I think the forms of culture shock will vary from an outraged sense of propriety to wonder and deep pity. Culture shock to me implies a heightened emotional awareness of the sociocultural environment. The rational and conceptual approach of the fieldworker, when he can manage it, begins to dim the emotion of culture shock, though it may never wholly disappear, especially in really exotic places like Southeast Asia. I don't know if anthropologists *always* get culture shock in a new environment; I only know that I have experienced it in varying degrees a number of times. What can we know of its real or potential consequences—dangerous or otherwise—when it has been poorly studied among anthropologists? I know the Peace Corps gave a contract to someone to research it, but I have seen nothing come of the work. Lambert (1966) touches on it from another point of view and is more concerned with international relations than with ethnography. I have a hunch that preoccupation with highly technical problems (kinship, etc.) will insulate its dynamics, much more than problems connected with poverty, child health, etc. will, but that's a hunch. It needs research.

FINNEY: I don't want to let this session end without challenging very strongly the proposition advanced by Dr. Hargreaves: that people act as if they were moved by economic motives. Nobody can deny that economic rewards interest us. We'd all like to get more money. But it's only one factor in people's choices—it's by no means the one overriding motive. People may reject the course of action that is to their economic advantage if it violates their religious or moral principles, or the customs of their cultural and social group; if it arouses their fear, superstitious or otherwise; if it creates a conflict of loyalties; if it means loss of self-respect or self-esteem; if it means breaking their ties with friends and family; or for other reasons that may be important to them.

Unfortunately, U. S. efforts in the underdeveloped countries have been based on economic determinism. We have concentrated on economic development and ignored the psychological needs for identity and a sense of purpose. We have often offered people a course of action that would benefit them economically and been surprised when they rejected it and took sides against us.

Seeing people make decisions against their own financial interests might surprise a social scientist, specifically an economist, but it doesn't surprise a behavioral scientist: it doesn't surprise a psychologist, a psychiatrist, or a cultural anthropologist. As behavioral scientists we know that people are not influenced only by their economic welfare.

Our government has assumed that people do things because of economic interest or because they are required to. So we have relied on two things: economic aid and military aid. The result is that people see us as bribing them or as forcing them. We have forgotten that people also do things because they believe in them. When people have a real sense of purpose they will work hard for an ideal, for a movement that they believe in, and often at great personal sacrifice. The Communists know that and have been swift to exploit idealism where they find it.

It is ironic that the Communists, despite their materialistic philosophy, have mobilized people's idealism successfully, while the Americans, with a long tradition of idealism, have based their foreign policy on the mistaken and materialistic philosophy of economic determinism.

The same mistakes that our government has made in Asia are now being made in the rural and urban slums, in Dr. Gazaway's Branch and in Harlem, with the white and Negro people who live in a culture of poverty.

references

Adorno, Theodor; Frenkel-Brunswik, Else; Levinson, Daniel J.; and Sanford, R. Nevitt
The Authoritarian Personality. New York: Harper, 1950.

Arensberg, Conrad M., and Niehoff, Arthur H.
Technical Cooperation and Cultural Reality. Washington: Agency for International Development, 1963.

Aron, Raymond
Introduction to the Philosophy of History. Boston: Beacon Press, 1961.

Balikci, Asen
Vunta Kutchin Social Change. Ottawa: Northern Coordination and Research Center Publication NCRC-63-3, 1963.

Barbu, Zevedei
Problems of Historical Psychology. New York: Grove Press, 1960.

Barker, Roger G.
Ecology and motivation. In *Nebraska Symposium on Motivation, 1960*. Lincoln: University of Nebraska Press, 1960.

Bateson, Gregory
Naven. Stanford, Calif.: Stanford University Press, 1958.

Belo, Jane
Trance in Bali. New York: Columbia University Press, 1960.

Berelson, Bernard, and Steiner, Gary A.
Human Behavior: An Inventory of Scientific Findings. New York: Harcourt, Brace and World, 1964.

Berndt, Charles
The role of native doctors in aboriginal Australia. In Ari Kiev, *Magic, Faith, and Healing*. New York: Free Press, 1965, pp. 264-82.

Berne, Eric
The cultural problem: psychopathology in Tahiti. *American Journal of Psychiatry*, 116:1076-81 (1960).

——————— *Games People Play: The Psychology of Human Relationships*. New York: Grove Press, 1964.

Bernstein, B.
Social class, speech systems and psychotherapy. In Frank Riessman and others, *Mental Health of the Poor*. New York: Free Press, 1964, pp. 194-204.

Boulding, Kenneth E.
The Image. Ann Arbor: University of Michigan Press, 1956.

——————— The place of the image in the dynamics of society. In George K. Zollschan and Walter Hirsch (Eds.), *Explorations in Social Change*. Boston: Houghton Mifflin, 1964.

Brill, Norman Q., and Storrow, Hugh A.
Social class and psychiatric treatment. *Archives of General Psychiatry*, 3:340-44 (1960).

Caplan, Gerald
Emotional Problems of Early Childhood. New York: Basic Books, 1955.

Caudill, Harry M.
Night Comes to the Cumberlands. Boston: Little, Brown, 1963.

Chance, Norman
Acculturation, self-identification, and personality adjustment. *American Anthropologist*, 67:372-93 (1965).

Clark, Margaret
Health in the Mexican-American Culture. Berkeley: University of California Press, 1959.

Coale, Ansley J., and Hoover, Edgar M.
Population Growth and Economic Development: A Case Study of India's Prospects. Princeton: Princeton University Press, 1958.

Cohen, Yehudi A.
Social Structure and Personality: A Casebook. New York: Holt, Rinehart and Winston, 1961.

D'Andrade, Roy G., and Romney, A. Kimball
Summary of participants' discussion. In *Transcultural Studies in Cognition*, *American Anthropologist* Special Publication 65, 3, 2, 1964.

Deutsch, Karl W.
Mechanism, organism, and society: some models in natural and social science. *Philosophy of Science*, 18:230-52 (1950).

——————— *Nationalism and Social Communication*. New York: Wiley, 1953.

De Vos, George
Conflict, dominance and exploitation in human systems of social segregation. In A.V.S. De Reuck and J. Knight (Eds.), *Conflict in Society*. London: Churchill, 1966.

——————— The psychology of purity and pollution as related to social self-identity and caste. In A.V.S. De Reuck and J. Knight (Eds.), *Caste and Race: Comparative Studies*. London: Churchill, 1967.

De Vos, George, and Wagatsuma, Hiroshi
Japan's Invisible Race. Berkeley: University of California Press, 1966.

Dewey, John, and Bentley, Arthur F.
Knowing and the Known. Boston: Beacon Press, 1960.

DuBois, Cora
   The People of Alor: A Social-Psychological Study of an East Indian Island. Cambridge: Harvard University Press, 1960.

Dubos, Rene
   Humanistic biology. *American Scientist,* 53:4-19 (1965).

Duncan, Otis D.
   Social organization and the ecosystem. In Robert E. L. Faris (Ed.), *Handbook of Modern Sociology.* Chicago: Rand-McNally, 1964.

Eaton, Joseph W., and Weil, Robert J.
   Culture and Mental Disorders: A Comparative Study of the Hutterites and Other Populations. Glencoe, Ill.: Free Press, 1955.

Eriksen, Charles
   Perceptual defense as a function of unacceptable needs. *Journal of Abnormal and Social Psychology,* 46:557-64 (1951).

——————— Some implications for TAT interpretation arising from need and perception experiments. *Journal of Personality,* 19:282-88 (1951).

Erikson, Erik H.
   Childhood and Society. New York: Norton, 1950.

Faris, Robert E. L., and Dunham, H. Warren
   Mental Disorders in Urban Areas. Chicago: University of Chicago Press, 1939.

Fenichel, Otto
   The Psychoanalytic Theory of Neurosis. New York: Norton, 1945.

Finney, Joseph C.
   Some maternal influences on children's personality and character. *Genetic Psychology Monographs,* 63:199-278 (1961).

——————— The MMPI as a measure of character structure as revealed by factor analysis. *Journal of Consulting Psychology,* 25:327-36 (1961).

——————— Attitudes of others in Hawaii toward Hawaiians. *Social Process,* 15:78-83 (1962).

——————— Prolegomena to epidemiology in mental health. *Journal of Nervous and Mental Disease,* 195:99-104 (1962).

——————— Maternal influences on anal or compulsive character in children. *Journal of Genetic Psychology,* 103:351-67 (1963).

——————— Psychiatry and multiculturality in Hawaii. *International Journal of Social Psychiatry,* 9:5-11 (1963).

——————— What is sickness? *Merrill-Palmer Quarterly,* 9:205-28 (1963).

——————— A factor analysis of mother-child influence. *Journal of General Psychology,* 70:41-49 (1964).

————— Development of a new set of MMPI scales. *Psychological Reports,* 17:707-13 (1965).

————— Culture change by brainwashing. *Corrective Psychiatry,* 13:76-87 (1966).

————— Normative data on some MMPI scales. *Psychological Reports,* 23:219-29 (1968).

Frank, Jerome
Persuasion and Healing: A Comparative Study of Psychotherapy. Baltimore: Johns Hopkins Press, 1961.

Freud, Sigmund
The Problem of Anxiety. Henry Alden Bunker, trans. *(Hemmung, Symptom und Angst).* New York: Psychoanalytic Quarterly Press and Norton, 1936.

————— Character and anal eroticism (1908). In *Collected Papers,* Vol. 2. London: Hogarth, 1950, pp. 45-50.

Fromm, Erich
Escape from Freedom. New York: Holt, 1941.

Fuchs, Lawrence H.
Acceptance and change by Peace Corps volunteers in the barrios of the Philippines. Paper prepared for the International Development Institute, East-West Center, University of Hawaii, Aug. 1964.

Fuchs, S.
Magic healing technique among the Balakis of Central India. In Ari Kiev, *Magic, Faith, and Healing.* New York: Free Press, 1965, pp. 121-38.

Gans, Herbert J.
The Urban Villagers. New York: Free Press, 1962.

Glazer, Nathan, and Moynihan, Daniel P.
Beyond the Melting Pot. Cambridge: M.I.T. Press, 1963.

Goodenough, Ward H.
Explorations in Cultural Anthropology. New York: McGraw-Hill, 1960.

————— *Cooperation in Change.* New York: Russell Sage Foundation, 1963.

Gough, Harrison R.
Manual for the California Psychological Inventory. Palo Alto: Consulting Psychologists Press, 1957.

Greenblatt, Milton; Emery, Paul E.; and Glueck, Bernard C. (Eds.)
Poverty and Mental Health. Washington: American Psychiatric Association, 1967.

Group for the Advancement of Psychiatry
Working Abroad: A Discussion of Psychological Attitudes and Adaptation to New Situations. Report No. 41, Dec. 1958.

Guthrie, George M.
Psychological preparation for service in the Philippines. To be published in a volume on Peace Corps training in Hawaii.

Haase, W.
The role of socioeconomic class in examiner bias. In Frank Riessman and others, *Mental Health of the Poor*. New York: Free Press, 1964, pp. 241-47.

Hacker, F. J.
Epidemiological observations on psychiatric disturbances and psychotherapy. Mimeographed paper, 1964.

Hagen, Everett E.
On the Theory of Social Change: How Economic Growth Begins. Homewood, Ill.: Dorsey Press, 1962.

Haggstrom, W. C.
The power of the poor. In Frank Riessman and others, *Mental Health of the Poor*. New York: Free Press, 1964, pp. 205-22.

Haley, Jay
Strategies of Psychotherapy. New York: Grune and Stratton, 1963.

Harrington, Michael
The Other America. New York: Macmillan, 1962.

Hartung, Frank E.
Manhattan madness: the social movement of mental illness. *Sociological Quarterly*, 4:261-72 (1963).

Hentoff, Nat
The treatment of patients. *New Yorker*, 32-77 (June 25, 1965).

Hes, J. P.
The changing social role of the Yemenite Mori. In Ari Kiev, *Magic, Faith, and Healing*. New York: Free Press, 1965, pp. 364-83.

Hinkle, Lawrence E.
Ecological observations of the relation of physical illness, mental illness, and the social environment. *Psychosomatic Medicine*, 23:289-97 (1961).

Hoffer, Eric
The True Believer: Thoughts on the Nature of Mass Movements. New York: Harper, 1951.

Hollingshead, August B., and Redlich, Frederick C.
Social Class and Mental Illness. New York: Wiley, 1958.

Honigmann, John Joseph
Culture and Personality. New York: Harper, 1954.

Hsu, Francis L. K. (Ed.)
Psychological Anthropology: Approaches to Culture and Personality. Homewood, Ill.: Dorsey Press, 1961.

Hughes, Charles C.
An Eskimo Village in the Modern World. Ithaca: Cornell University Press, 1960.

————— Under four flags: recent culture change among the Eskimos. Current Anthropology, 6:3-69 (1965).

Hughes, Charles C.; Tremblay, Marc-Adélard; Rapoport, Robert N.; and Leighton, Alexander H.
People of Cove and Woodlot. New York: Basic Books, 1960.

Hunt, Joseph McVicker
Personality and the Behavior Disorders: A Handbook Based on Experimental and Clinical Research. New York: Ronald Press, 1944.

Imber, Stanley D.; Nash, Earl H., Jr.; and Stone, Anthony R.
Social class and duration of psychotherapy. Journal of Clinical Psychology, 11:281 (1955).

Inkeles, Alex, and Levinson, Daniel J.
National character: the study of modal personality and sociocultural systems. In Gardner Lindzey (Ed.), Handbook of Social Psychology, Vol. 2. Reading, Mass.: Addison-Wesley, 1954, pp. 977-1020.

Inoue, Kiyoshi
Kaiho undo no rekishi ni manabu (Lessons we receive from the history of liberation movements). Buraku, 9:4-17 (1961).

Isaacs, Harold
India's Ex-Untouchables. New York: John Day, 1965.

Ishida, Shinichi
Shinro shido to koko sennyugaku mondai (Guidance and the problem of an entire class entering high school). Buraku, 9:51-55 (1961).

Jahoda, Marie
Current Concepts of Positive Mental Health. New York: Basic Books, 1958.

Kahn, Robert L.; Pollack, Moshe; and Fink, Max
Social factors in the selection of therapy in a voluntary mental hospital. J. Hillside Hospital, 6:216-28 (1957).

Kaplan, Bert E.
Studying Personality Cross-Culturally. Evanston, Ill.: Row, Peterson, 1961.

Kaplan, Bert E. and Johnson, Dale
The social meaning of Navaho psychopathology and psychotherapy. In Ari Kiev, Magic, Faith, and Healing. New York: Free Press, 1965, pp. 203-29.

Kardiner, Abram
The Psychological Frontiers of Society. New York: Columbia University Press, 1945.

Kardiner, Abram, and Linton, Ralph
The Individual and His Society: The Psychodynamics of Primitive Social Organization. New York: Columbia University Press, 1939.

Kardiner, Abram, and Ovesey, Lionel
The Mark of Oppression. New York: Meridian Books, 1962.

Katona, George
Review of *The Achieving Society* by David C. McClelland. *American Economic Review,* 52:580-83 (1962).

Kiev, Ari (Ed.)
Magic, Faith, and Healing: Studies in Primitive Psychiatry Today. New York: Free Press, 1965.

Kluckhohn, Clyde, and Murray, Henry A.
Personality in Nature, Society, and Culture. New York: Knopf, 1953.

Kobayahi, Ayako
Buraku no Joi (Woman Doctor of the Buraku). Tokyo: Iwanami, 1962.

Koos, Earl L.
Health of Regionville, New York: Columbia University Press, 1954.

————— *Sociology of the Patient.* 3d ed. New York: McGraw-Hill, 1959.

Kuhn, Alfred
The Study of Society: A Unified Approach. Homewood, Ill.: Irwin-Dorsey, 1963.

La Barre, Weston
They Shall Take Up Serpents. Minneapolis: University of Minnesota Press, 1964.

Lambert, Richard
Some minor pathologies in the American presence in India. *Annals of the American Academy of Political and Social Science,* 368:157-70 (1966).

Lambo, T. Adeoye (Ed.)
First Pan-African Psychiatric Conference. Abeokuta, Nigeria, Nov. 1961.

Langer, Susanne K.
Philosophy in a New Key. New York: Mentor, 1951.

Langner, Thomas S.
Life Stress and Mental Health. New York: Free Press, 1963.

Leighton, Alexander
My Name Is Legion: Foundations for a Theory of Man's Response to Culture. New York: Basic Books, 1959.

Leighton, Alexander, and Lambo, T. Adeoye
Psychiatric Disorder Among the Yoruba. Ithaca: Cornell University Press, 1963.

Leighton, Dorothea; Harding, John S.; Macklin, David B.; MacMillan, Allister M.; and Leighton, Alexander H.
   The Character of Danger. New York: Basic Books, 1963.

Lerner, Raymond C.
   The therapeutic social club: social rehabilitation for mental patients. *International Journal of Social Psychiatry,* 6:101-14 (1960).

Levinger, George
   Continuance in casework and other helping relationships: a review of current research. *Social Work,* 5:40-51 (1960).

Lewis, Oscar
   Five Families: Mexican Case Studies in the Culture of Poverty. New York: Basic Books, 1959.

———— Some of my best friends are peasants. *Human Organization,* 19:179-80 (1960).

———— *The Children of Sanchez.* New York: Random House, 1961.

———— *La Vida: A Puerto Rican Family in the Culture of Poverty.* New York: Random House, 1966.

Luchins, A. S.
   Mechanism in problem-solving: the effect of Einstellung. *Psychology Monographs,* 54:1-95 (1942).

McClelland, David C.
   The Achieving Society. New York: Van Nostrand, 1961.

McDermott, John F.; Harrison, Saul I.; Schrager, Jules; and Wilson, Paul
   Social class and mental illness in children: observations of blue collar families. *American Journal of Orthopsychiatry,* 35: 500-508 (1965).

Malmquist, Carl P.
   Psychiatric perspectives on the socially-disadvantaged child. *Comprehensive Psychiatry,* 6:176-83 (1965).

Mangin, William P., and Cohen, Jerome
   Cultural and psychological characteristics of mountain migrants to Lima, Peru. *Sociologus,* 14:81-88 (1964).

Manual for Psychiatrists Participation in the Peace Corps Program, Medical Program Division, Peace Corps, Washington, D.C. (unpublished, n.d.).

Maretzki, Thomas
   Transition training: a theoretical approach. *Human Organization,* 24:128-34 (1965).

Matsuda, Keiichi; Masutani, Hisashi, and Kudo, Eiichi
   Buraku Mondai to Kirisuto Kyo. Tokyo: Nihon Kirisuto Kyodan Shuppan Bu, 1963.

Mead, Margaret
   Some relationships between social anthropology and psychiatry. In

Alexander Franz and Helen Ross (Eds.), *Dynamic Psychiatry*. Chicago: University of Chicago Press, 1952.

————— *Cultural Patterns and Technical Change*. New York: UNESCO, 1953.

————— *New Lives for Old*. New York: William Morrow, 1956.

Menninger, Karl
The Vital Balance: The Life Process in Mental Health and Illness. New York: Viking, 1963.

Menninger, W. Walter F., and English, Joseph T.
Psychiatric casualties from overseas Peace Corps service. Paper 261, American Psychiatric Association, 120th annual meeting, Los Angeles, 1964.

Merton, Robert
Social Theory and Social Structure. Glencoe, Ill.: Free Press, 1959.

Meyer, Henry J.
Girls at Vocational High. New York: Russell Sage Foundation, 1965.

Miller, James G.
Information input overload and psychotherapy. *American Journal of Psychiatry*, 116:695-704 (1960).

Miller, Seymour Michael
The American lower classes: a typological approach. *Sociology and Social Research*, 48:1-22 (1964).

Minturn, Leigh, and Lambert, William W.
Mother of Six Cultures. New York: Wiley, 1964.

Mowrer, O. Hobart
The Crisis in Psychiatry and Religion. New York: Van Nostrand, 1961.

Murphy, Jane M.
Psychotherapeutic aspects of shamanism on St. Lawrence Island, Alaska. In Ari Kiev, *Magic, Faith, and Healing*. New York: Free Press, 1965, pp. 253-83.

Murray, Henry A., and Kluckhohn, Clyde
Outline of a conception of personality. In Clyde Kluckhohn and Henry A. Murray (Eds.), *Personality in Nature, Society, and Culture*. 2d ed. New York: Knopf, 1953.

Nomura, Nobukiyo
Tsukimono no shinri (Psychology of fox possession). In I. Oguchi (Ed.) *Shukyo to Shinko no Shinrigaku* (Psychological Studies of Religion and Beliefs). Tokyo: Kawade, 1956, pp. 247-57.

Oliver, Symmes C.
Individuality, freedom of choice, and cultural flexibility of the Kamba. *American Anthropologist*, 67:421-28 (1965).

Opler, Marvin Kaufmann (Ed.)
   Culture and Mental Health: Cross-Cultural Studies. New York: Macmillan, 1959.

———— *Culture, Psychiatry, and Human Values.* New York: Atherton Press, 1967.

Orwell, George
   Burmese Days. New York: New American Library, 1964.

Osgood, Charles E.
   The Measurement of Meaning. Urbana: University of Illinois Press, 1957.

———— Cognitive dynamics in human affairs. *Public Opinion Quarterly,* 24:341-65 (1960).

Overall, Betty, and Aronson, Howard
   Expectations of psychotherapy in patients of lower socio-economic class. *American Journal of Orthopsychiatry,* 33:421-30 (1963).

Parsons, Talcott
   The Social System. Glencoe, Ill.: Free Press, 1951.

Parsons, Talcott, and Shils, Edward A. (Eds.)
   Toward a General Theory of Action. Cambridge: Harvard University Press, 1951.

Piaget, Jean
   The Moral Judgment of the Child. London: Kegan Paul, Trench, Trubner, 1932.

Polanyi, Michael
   Personal Knowledge: Toward a Post-Critical Philosophy. New York: Harper, 1964.

Powdermaker, Hortense
   Life in Lesu. New York: Norton, 1933.

Preston, Richard J.
   Imposed and inherent cultural structures in the writings of Edward Sapir. Unpublished M.A. thesis, University of North Carolina, 1964.

Price, John
   A history of the Outcaste: untouchability in Japan. In De Vos and Wagatsuma, *Japan's Invisible Race.* Berkeley: University of California Press, 1966.

Prince, Raymond H.
   Western psychiatry and the Yoruba: the problem of insight psychotherapy, pp. 213-21. *Conference Proceedings.* Nigerian Institute of Social and Economic Research, March 1962.

———— Indigenous Yoruba psychiatry. In Ari Kiev, *Magic, Faith and Healing.* New York: Free Press, 1965, pp. 84-120.

Redfield, Robert E.
The Primitive World and Its Transformations. Ithaca: Cornell University Press, 1953.

Rice, Robert
Junk. *New Yorker,* 50-142 (March 27, 1965).

Riesman, David
The Lonely Crowd. New Haven: Yale University Press, 1950.

Riessman, Frank
Are the deprived non-verbal? In Frank Riessman and others, *Mental Health of the Poor.* New York: Free Press, 1964, pp. 188-93.

Riessman, Frank; Cohen, Jerome; and Pearl, Arthur
Mental Health of the Poor: New Treatment Approaches for Low-Income People. New York: Free Press, 1964.

Riessman, Frank, and Goldfarb, J.
Role playing and the poor. In Frank Riessman and others, *Mental Health of the Poor.* New York: Free Press, 1964, pp. 336-46.

Ritchie, James R.
Basic Personality in Rakau. Wellington: Victoria University of Wellington Publications in Psychology, No. 8, 1956.

Roberts, John M.
The self-management of cultures. In Ward H. Goodenough (Ed.), *Explorations in Cultural Anthropology.* New York: McGraw-Hill, 1964.

Ruesch, Jurgen, and Bateson, Gregory
Communication: The Social Matrix of Psychiatry. New York: Norton, 1951.

Schaffer, Leslie, and Myers, Jerome K.
Psychotherapy and social stratification. *Psychiatry,* 17:83-89 (1954).

Schofield, William
Psychotherapy: The Purchase of Friendship. Engelwood Cliffs, N.J.: Prentice-Hall, 1964.

Schultz, Theodore W.
Transforming Traditional Agriculture. New Haven and London: Yale University Press, 1964.

Sears, Robert R.
Survey of Objective Studies of Psychoanalytic Concepts. New York: Social Science Research Council, 1943.

Shannon, Claude E., and Weaver, Warren
The Mathematical Theory of Communication. Urbana: University of Illinois Press, 1949.

Smelser, Neil J. and William T.
Personality and Social Systems. New York: Wiley, 1963.

Spicer, Edward H. (Ed.)
Human Problems in Technological Change. New York: Wiley, 1952.

Spiegel, J. P.
Some cultural aspects of transference and counter transference. In Frank Riessman and others, *Mental Health of the Poor.* New York: Free Press, 1964, pp. 303-20.

Spindler, George and Louise
Psychology in anthropology: applications to culture change. In Sigmund Koch (Ed.), *Investigations of Man as Socius: Their Place in Psychology and the Social Sciences,* Vol. 6, *Psychology: A Study of a Science.* New York: McGraw-Hill, 1963.

Srole, Leo; Langner, Thomas S.; Michael, Stanley T.; Opler, Marvin K.; and Bennie, Thomas A. C.
Mental Health in the Metropolis: The Midtown Manhattan Study, Vol. 1. New York: McGraw-Hill, 1962.

Sullivan, Harry S.
Clinical Studies in Psychiatry. New York: Norton, 1956.

Szanten, David L.
Human problems in overseas technical assistance: a case study of Peace Corps volunteers in the Philippines. Unpublished M.A. thesis, University of Chicago, 1964.

Szasz, Thomas
The Myth of Mental Illness. New York: Harper, 1961.

Tapp, Jesse W.; Gazaway, Rena; and Deuschle, Kurt W.
Community health in a mountain neighborhood. *Archives of Environmental Health,* 8:510-17 (1964).

Tojo, Takashi
Sengo no Dowa kyoiku (Postwar Dowa education). In Buraku Mondai Kenkyujo (Research Institute for Buraku Problems) (Ed.), *Dowa Kyoiku.* Tokyo and Kyoto: San-itsu Shobo, 1960, pp. 49-98.

Totten, George O., and Wagatsuma, Hiroshi
Emancipation: growth and transformation of a political movement. In De Vos and Wagatsuma, *Japan's Invisible Race.* Berkeley: University of California Press, 1966.

Vinacke, W. Edgar
Stereotyping among racial groups in Hawaii: a study in enthnocentrism. *Journal of Social Psychology,* 30:265-91 (1949).

Von Bertalanffy, Ludwig
Problems of Life: An Evaluation of Modern Biological and Scientific Thought. New York: Harper, 1952.

Wagatsuma, Hiroshi
Postwar political militance. In De Vos and Wagatsuma, *Japan's Invisible Race.* Berkeley: University of California Press, 1966, pp. 68-87.

Wallace, Anthony
Culture and Personality. New York: Random House, 1961.

Weber, Max
The Protestant Ethic and the Spirit of Capitalism. New York: Scribner, 1948.

Weinstein, Edwin
Cultural Aspects of Delusion. New York: Free Press, 1962.

Welsh, George S.
Factor dimensions A. and R. In George S. Welsh and W. G. Dahlstrom (Eds.), *Basic Readings on the MMPI.* Minneapolis: University of Minnesota Press, 1956.

White, Robert W.
Motivation reconsidered: the concept of competence. *Psychological Review,* 66:297-333 (1959).

——————— Competence and the psychosexual stages of development. In *Nebraska Symposium on Motivation, 1960.* Lincoln: University of Nebraska Press, 1960.

Whiting, John W. M.
Becoming a Kwoma. London: Oxford University Press, 1941.

——————— Socialization process and personality. In Francis L. K. Hsu (Ed.), *Psychological Anthropology: Approaches to Culture and Personality.* Homewood, Ill.: Dorsey Press, 1961, pp. 355-81.

Wiener, Norbert
The Human Use of Human Beings. New York: Doubleday, 1954.

Willhelm, Sidney M., and Powell, Edwin, H.
Who needs the Negro? *Trans-Action,* 1, 6, 3-6 (1964).

Winkelman, N. W.
The psychiatric treatment of lower sociocultural level patients in a union medical center. Mimeographed paper.

Wittkower, Eric
Review of "Magic, Faith, and Healing." *American Journal of Psychiatry,* 121:1220 (1965).

index

Mexicans: and education, 88, 89; differences from Puerto Ricans, 156-57, 166-69; repression, 166; dissociating-hysterical-motoric personality, 169
Midtown New York Mental Health Study: stress measure, 12; Opler account, 284-88
migration, selective, 129
Minnesota Multiphasic Personality Inventory: and hysteria, 256
missionaries. *See* crusaders
Momotaro: Japanese folk tale, 143
Monroe, Marilyn: suicide despite psychoanalysis, 303-304
motoric personality. *See* dissociating-hysterical-motoric personality
motoric response: preferred over verbalization by poor, 28-29
Mowrer, O. Hobart: psychology of sin, 11
murder. *See* homicide

n Achievement. *See* achievement need
naive personality. *See* dissociating-hysterical-motoric personality
narcotic addiction. *See* addiction
Negro: compared to Japanese outcaste, 82-83, 86, 90, 95-96; and education, 88; in Appalachia, 129-30; in Hawaii, 258-274; unemployment, 277
neurosis. *See* anxiety reaction; depressive reaction; hysteria, conversion; hysteria, dissociation; obsessive-compulsive psychoneurosis; phobic reaction. *See also* psychosis, harmfulness compared with psychoneurosis
Nigerians. *See* Yoruba
nonbelonging, feeling of, xxii-xxiii, 73, 84, 89, 94-96, 149-51, 287, 312
nondirectiveness: paradox when direction is asked, 24, 217-218; frightening to poor patients, 25
nonrational motives: ignored by economists, 75-76, 138

objective measures. *See* measurement
obsessive-compulsive psychoneurosis: in compulsive personalities, 252; in middle class, 257
oedipal personality. *See* dissociating-hysterical-motoric personality

oral aggression. *See* demanding personality
oral personality. *See* dependent personality
outcastes in Japan: factors that maintain apartness, 84-85; resistance to education, 87-88; low functional intelligence, 89; identity hinders achievement, 90-91; emotional conflicts, 93; sense of martyrdom, 94

paradox, logical: of tolerance of intolerance; xix, 300-301; of nondirection in a directive culture, 24
paranoid personality: uses defense of projection, 240
parasitism: intestinal, 126. *See also* malfunctioning
passive-aggressive personality. *See* dependent personality; demanding personality
Peace Corps: unjustified, 57; study by Maretzki, 203-21; crises in volunteers, 210-11; task of volunteers, 211-14; goals unclear, 214, 217; role conflict, 214-15; Philippine project, 215-19; shift in goals needed, 217; volunteers grow and mature, 220-21, and culture shock, 316
permeability to acculturation: in outcaste, 85; in immigrants, 207-208; in sojourner, 208, 220
perpetuation of ways of life: through child rearing, xxii, of malfunction, 68; no guarantee of satisfaction, 73; of disadvantaged minority, 81; mechanism same as change, 201
phenomenological approach: as culturally relative, 15
Philippines: Peace Corps study, 210, 215-18. *See also* Filipinos in Hawaii
phobic reaction, 257
political movements: giving meaning to life, xiii, 95; radical appeal to outcastes, 93-96
politics: spoils system in poverty program, 61
population explosion: disastrous effects, 277-78
Portuguese in Hawaii, 258-74

contributors

AUTHORS

JOHN J. HONIGMANN, an anthropologist, is professor of anthropology at the University of North Carolina.

RAYMOND PRINCE, a psychiatrist, is assistant professor of psychiatry in the Medical College of McGill University and research director of the Urban Social Redevelopment Project in Montreal.

RENA GAZAWAY, a public health nurse and social scientist, is assistant professor for research and studies at the College of Nursing and Health of the University of Cincinnati.

GEORGE A. DE VOS, a psychologist and anthropologist, is associate professor in the School of Social Welfare, the Center for Japanese Studies, the Institute of Human Development, and the department of anthropology at the University of California at Berkeley.

HART RANSDELL is a psychiatric social worker.

TRESSA ROCHE, a public health nurse, is director of nursing at the Kentucky State Hospital in Danville.

ERIC BERNE, a psychiatrist and psychoanalyst, is a lecturer in group therapy at the Langley Porter Neuropsychiatric Clinic in San Francisco.

WILLIAM CARSE, an educational psychologist, is Coordinator of Measurement Services at the University of Texas.

OSCAR LEWIS, an anthropologist, is professor of anthropology at the University of Illinois.

CHARLES C. HUGHES, an anthropologist, is professor of anthropology and director of the African Studies Center at Michigan State University.

THOMAS W. MARETZKI, an anthropologist, is professor and chairman of the department of anthropology at the University of Hawaii.

HERBERT W. HARGREAVES, an economist, is professor of economics at the University of Kentucky.

JOSEPH C. FINNEY, a psychologist and psychiatrist, is professor of educational psychology at the University of Kentucky.

PARTICIPANTS IN DISCUSSIONS

ARI KIEV, a psychiatrist, is research associate in psychiatry at the College of Physicians and Surgeons, Columbia University.

EDWARD L. MARGETTS, a psychiatrist, is professor of psychiatry at the University of British Columbia.

MARVIN K. OPLER, an anthropologist, is professor of social psychiatry in the School of Medicine and professor of sociology at the State University of New York at Buffalo.

VICTOR D. SANUA, a psychologist, is associate professor of psychology at City College, City University of New York.

EDWIN A. WEINSTEIN, a psychiatrist, neurologist, and psychoanalyst, works at the Walter Reed Army Institute of Research and teaches at the William Alanson White Institute and at the Washington School of Psychiatry.

ERIC D. WITTKOWER, a psychiatrist and psychoanalyst, is professor of psychiatry at McGill University.

CHARLES H. ENZER was a physician on the narcotic addiction service of the USPHS Hospital at Lexington.

JOHN L. FULMER is professor of economics at the University of Kentucky.

DONALD L. HOCHSTRASSER, an anthropologist, is associate professor in the department of community medicine at the University of Kentucky.

MARGARET LANTIS is professor of anthropology at the University of Kentucky.

JOSEPH E. WARREN is associate professor of medicine and director of Rehabilitation Services at the University of Kentucky Medical Center.

ABRAHAM WIKLER, a psychiatrist and neurologist, is professor of psychiatry at the College of Medicine, University of Kentucky.